D0590659

THEY FOUGHT LIKE DEMONS

WOMEN SOLDIERS
IN THE AMERICAN
CIVIL WAR

They Fought Like Demons

Women Soldiers in the American Civil War

DeAnne Blanton & Lauren M. Cook

SUTTON PUBLISHING

This book was first published in 2002 by Louisiana State University Press.

This edition first published in 2005 by
Sutton Publishing Limited · Phoenix Mill
Thrupp · Stroud · Gloucestershire · GL5 2BU

British Library Cataloguing in Publication Data
A catalogue record for this book is available from the British Library.

ISBN 0 7509 3641 X

Printed and bound in Great Britain by
J.H. Haynes & Co., Ltd, Sparkford.

To all the brave women
who possessed the courage and imagination
to serve their country in time of crisis
and against all odds

Contents

ILLUSTRATIONS

Acknowledgments

In rediscovering the women soldiers of the Civil War, we received generous help from a number of individuals. Indeed, the assistance of friends, colleagues, fellow researchers, and professionals in the history, archival, and library fields was of tremendous help in the course of researching and writing this book.

DeAnne's colleagues at the National Archives were supportive as they learned of our moonlighting project to document these women. Michael Musick, who knows more about the Civil War and its sources than anyone else on earth, kindly and continually passed leads our way. We also thank David Wallace, Jo Ann Williamson, Lisa Miller, Dick Higgins, Jeff Hartley, William Dobak, David Langbart, Karen Stefanik, Michael Meier, Stuart Butler, Cynthia Fox, Mary Kay Schmidt, and Rebecca Livingston.

The following institutions provided expert reference service: the Illinois State Archives; the Illinois Veterans Home at Quincy; the Bentley Historical Library of the University of Michigan; the Virginia Historical Society; the Boston Public Library; the Butler County Historical Society of Kansas; the Library of Congress; the Tennessee State Library and Archives; the Ohio Historical Society; the North Carolina State Archives; the Delaware Public Archives; the Michigan State Archives; the University of Kentucky Library at Lexington; the Public Library of Cincinnati and Hamilton County; the Cumberland County, North Carolina, Headquarters Library; and the Martin Luther King Jr. Memorial Library in Washington, D.C.

We would especially like to thank William R. Erwin Jr. and James Tomberlin, Duke University; Louise Arnold-Friend, U.S. Army Military History Institute; Linda Grant DePauw, Minerva Center; John M. Coski, Museum of the Confederacy; Shelly H. Kelly, Rosenberg Library; Roy Hatch, Mercy Hospital Medical Library; James B. Kennedy, State Historical Society of Wisconsin; Cheryl Pence, Illinois State Historical Society; Edward Skipworth, Rutgers University Libraries; Stephen E. Towne, Indiana State Archives; John Selch, Indiana State Library; Roberta Copp, University of South Carolina; Stacy Allen, Shiloh National Military Park; Thomas Bennett, Portland, Maine, Public Library; John E. White, University of North Carolina at Chapel Hill; Stuart W. Sanders, Perryville Battlefield Association; Sharon Defibaugh, University of Virginia; Dan Knowles, Arlington County, Virginia, Central Library; Carol Kaplan, Public Library of Nashville and Davidson County; Cathy Miller, West Virginia Archives and History Library; Lewis H. Averett, Jones Memorial Library; Nettie Oliner, Filson Club; George K. Combs, Alexandria Library; Linda Barnickel and Susan K. Forbes, Kansas State Historical Society; and Dereka Smith, National Genealogical Society. These individuals are a credit to their professions and their institutions.

We received unparalleled assistance from fellow researchers: Marie and Bob Melchiori, Benedict Maryniak, Eileen Conklin, Ronald Waddell, Edwin C. Bearss, Stephen Sears, Joyce Henry, Virginia Mescher, Tom Hayes, Renée Chevalier, Martin and Pat Akers, Jim Leeke, Rhonda Purnell, Jane Schultz, Elizabeth Leonard, Steve Huddleston, Joyce Thierer, Kathleen Dietrich, Capt. Charles Todd Creekman Jr., Robert L. Hawkins III, Phillip Jackson, Patrick Brady, Beverly and Thomas Lowry, Andrew Schwab, Frank and Velma Crawford, Jeanne Christie, Mary Read, Kay Larsen, Andrew German, Melody Callahan, Elsa Lohman, Charles Earp, Sara Bartlett, Beth Gilleland, Ann Graham, Michelle Krowl, Thomas Curran, Anita Henderson, Mark Hoffman, Jack C. Davis, Ned D. Reed, William Bolgrien, Kenneth Poling, Terry Foenander, Joseph Fitzharris, Skip Churchill, Michael Unsworth, Lori Finkelstein, Juanita Leisch, Joe Jones, Kathy Hillard, Mike Donovan, Ron Maness, Charles Morrison, Meg Galante-DeAngelis, Wendy King, and Brian Pohanka. This book would be diminished without their generous contributions.

Invaluable are the direct and collateral descendants of women soldiers who enthusiastically shared family mementos and documents: William Boldt, Hazel Blalock Johnson, Lee Coutts, Aileen Conry, Jackson K. Doane, Ruth Goodier, Dick Kinney, Peggy Stewart Walker, Virginia K. Morey, and Robert C. Johnston. Our own friends and family came to our aid as well. Many thanks to Laura Sekela, David DeVito, Heidi Overfelt, Robert Burke, Ken and Kathy Blanton, Jennifer Hill, Ethyle Wolfe, and Laura Chapin. Friend Monroe Freeman passed away before the book was finished. His help and humor are greatly missed.

Many thanks go to Michael Parrish, editor of the Conflicting Worlds series, whose unwavering interest in and support of our efforts was terrific. His many valuable suggestions have made this a far better work than it otherwise would have been. We also wish to thank Sylvia Frank Rodrigue at LSU Press for her patience and persistence (since the 1997 Organization of American Historians meeting in San Francisco!).

A very special thank you is long overdue to DeAnne's husband, Marc Wolfe, who gave his formidable analytical skills to the project, and just as importantly, his enduring patience and unfailing love and encouragement. Lauren is equally grateful to her new husband Perry Wike for his amazing level of support and commitment. If we have forgotten anyone, please forgive the oversight and know that your contributions are appreciated.

THEY FOUGHT LIKE DEMONS

"ENTRENCHED IN SECRECY"

Women Soldiers of the Civil War

It is an accepted convention that the Civil War was a man's fight. To date, the study of the common soldier of the American Civil War has focused almost exclusively on the millions of men who performed their patriotic duty during the 1860s. From Bell Irvin Wiley's seminal works on the subject, which detail the various common military experiences of soldiers in the field and in camp, to more recent scholarship by Gerald Linderman, James McPherson, and Earl Hess that examines the more complex subject of soldiers' motivations for military service and combat, the story of the rank-and-file Civil War soldier has been told in distinctly masculine terms.[1]

Popular notions of women during the Civil War center on self-sacrificing nurses, romantic spies, or brave ladies maintaining the home front in the absence of their men. This conventional picture of gender roles does not tell the entire story, however. Men were not the only ones to march off to war. Women bore arms and charged into battle, too. Women lived in germ-ridden camps, languished in appalling prisons, and died miserably, but honorably, for their country and their cause just as men did.

This book is about the women who disguised themselves as men and enlisted in the armies of the Union and the Confederacy. No previous study of the Civil War soldier has meaningfully or comprehensively addressed these martial women. Our study is the result of more than ten years of research into the phenomenon of Civil War soldier women. Using military records, government documents, regimental histories, diaries and letters of soldiers, memoirs, contemporary newspapers, photographs, and the works of fellow historians, we endeavored to piece together the stories of individual soldier women, their experiences, and their motivations.

Unfortunately, most of the extant source material pertaining to women soldiers was not written by the women themselves. The relative absence of written material attributed to female combatants is striking, since the vast majority of Civil War soldiers were literate and they mailed millions of uncensored letters to the home front. Letters written home by only three women soldiers have surfaced. Only two distaff warriors published memoirs of their experiences. No diaries written by women soldiers have been found. Perhaps the missives and diaries of female soldiers have not survived, but more likely, women soldiers did not write them. Like the men with whom they served, the majority of women soldiers hailed from agrarian, working-class, or immigrant backgrounds, where no premium was placed on educational attainment for women.[2] Thus, women soldiers probably had a much lower literacy rate than their male comrades. Additionally, when they assumed male identities and joined the army, women soldiers usually severed contact with family and friends at home. Therefore, literate women soldiers were less likely than the men with whom they served to write wartime letters.

As a group, women soldiers never told their own story, so we went looking for the contemporaries who told their stories for them. In the course of looking for women soldiers, we encountered a variety of other women at the war front or disguised as men: battlefield nurses, vivandières, prostitutes, wives, spies, saboteurs, guerrillas, physicians, and even one chaplain. While these women have fascinating stories of their own, they are not included here. Our work focuses solely on women soldiers regularly enlisted or commissioned in the army. (This book does not consider or explore any female enlistments in the Union or Confederate navies.) Readers may be surprised by our inclusion of Confederate officer Loreta Janeta Velazquez, labeled a fraud by a number of respected historians.[3] Our research shows that they have been too quick to dismiss her. The story of her service as presented in her memoirs, *The Woman in Battle*, is largely corroborated by contemporary sources.

Understanding Velazquez and all the women who passed as men and served in the Union and Confederate armies requires an appreciation of the legal, social, and economic status of mid-nineteenth century women, as well as a familiarity with the cultural and historical precedents that encouraged female martial ambition. The rise of Victorian social and cultural ideals in antebellum America reinforced the existence of separate spheres of influence for men and women. Men's sphere was in worldly pursuits and providing for home and family, while women were confined to bearing and raising children and overseeing the private world of the home. The cult of true womanhood dictated that women always appear as demure, submissive, pious, and concerned only with home and family. Women who gave any appearance of stepping outside of highly restrictive female roles risked being labeled "not respectable." Although Victorian ideals of womanhood were not as important in the lives of the working and lower classes, yeoman farmers, newly arrived immigrants, or pioneering families, they nevertheless informed cultural norms for American society in general.[4]

While social notions of female propriety placed substantial restrictions on women's lifestyles, especially for those in the middle and upper classes, the legal and economic landscape formed even more daunting barriers for all women, whether or not they fell into the accepted and expected roles of wife and mother, and regardless of their place on the social ladder. The Declaration of Sentiments and Resolutions adopted at the early feminist Seneca Falls convention in 1848 provides an overview of women's status at the mid-nineteenth-century mark and outlines the many ways in which government and the male power structure deprived women of the inalienable rights that propertied, white American men had claimed for themselves during the American Revolution just a few decades before:

> He has never permitted her to exercise her inalienable right to the elective franchise.
> He has compelled her to submit to laws, in the formation of which she had no voice.
> He has withheld from her rights which are given to the most ignorant and degraded men—both natives and foreigners. . . .
> He has made her, if married, in the eye of the law, civilly dead.
> He has taken from her all right in property, even to the wages she earns. . . .
> He has so framed the laws of divorce, as to what shall be the proper causes, and in case of separation, to whom the guardianship of the children shall be given, as to be wholly regardless of the happiness of women—the law, in all cases, going upon a false supposition of the supremacy of man, and giving all power into his hands.

After depriving her of all rights as a married woman, if single, and the owner of property, he has taxed her to support a government which recognizes her only when her property can be made profitable to it.

He has monopolized nearly all the profitable employments, and from those she is permitted to follow, she receives but a scanty remuneration. He closes against her all the avenues to wealth and distinction which he considers most honorable to himself. As a teacher of theology, medicine, or law, she is not known.

He has denied her the facilities for obtaining a thorough education, all colleges being closed against her. . . .

He has created a false public sentiment by giving to the world a different code of morals for men and women, by which moral delinquencies which exclude women from society, are not only tolerated, but deemed of little account in man.

He has usurped the prerogative of Jehovah himself, claiming it as his right to assign for her a sphere of action, when that belongs to her conscience and to her God.

He has endeavored, in every way that he could, to destroy her confidence in her own powers, to lessen her self-respect, and to make her willing to lead a dependent and abject life.[5]

Clearly, society placed enormous restrictions on females. While upper-class and educated middle-class women might find a small measure of independence through employment as teachers, writers, or governesses, working- and lower-class women had few appealing options outside of marriage. Their employment prospects were usually limited to sewing, prostitution, or domestic servitude. Statistically, the majority of unmarried working-class women chose the latter. In New York City in 1860, maids received between four and seven dollars a month, "good" cooks earned seven or eight dollars a month, and laundresses might earn up to ten dollars per month. Women's work as domestics generally earned them a mere fraction—36 to 80 percent, depending on their location and skills—of what men garnered as farmhands, the other largest working-class employment category in the United States in 1860. In the Northeast and in a few places in the South, women found employment in factories, although they were often paid less than men for the same work. On the other hand, three months' service as a private in the Union army yielded a hefty sum of thirty-nine dollars in an age when most monthly salaries for men ranged from ten to twenty dollars.[6]

When viewed against the backdrop of Victorian oppression, the appeal of pretending to be male was obvious. Women who passed as men were, in large part, seeking economic privileges and social opportunities otherwise closed to them. Their transvestitism was a private rebellion against public conventions. By taking a male social identity, they secured for themselves male power and independence, as well as full status as citizens of their nation. In essence, the Civil War was an opportunity for hundreds of women to escape the confines of their sex.

There was no public recruitment of women into the army, yet significant numbers of them decided to enlist anyway, each making an independent decision to dress as a man and march off to war. How did so many women reach the same conclusion? The answer is that cross-dressing female heroines, both fictional and real, were a standard commodity in popular culture. In fact, military and sailor women were celebrated in popular novels, ballads, and poetry from the seventeenth century through the Victorian age. Inspired by and created for an audience of literate but lower- and working-class people, the woman warrior was a virtuous and heroic ideal. Dianne Dugaw labels this literary phenomenon the "Female Warrior Motif," explaining that these fictional and semifictional women and their narratives conformed "to an ideal type—a conventionalized heroine who, pulled from her beloved by 'war's alarms' or a cruel father, goes off disguised as a man to sea or to war. . . . [The] transvestite heroine, a model of beauty and pluck, is deserving in romance, able in war, and rewarded in both." The women soldiers of the Civil War may very well have been inspired by the fictional Sarah Brewer, the female marine of the War of 1812 (although this heroine dressed as a man to escape the life of a prostitute), or any number of European examples, both true and legendary, whose stories were widely available prior to the war.[7]

Distaff soldiers existed not only in popular fiction. Very real women warriors had taken the field in previous military contests. The first documented case of a woman in the Americas disguising herself as a man to pursue her fate and her fortune as a soldier occurred almost three centuries before the Civil War. Catalina de Erauso, whose adventures as a conquistador in the New World were detailed in her memoirs, escaped from a Spanish convent, dressed and lived as a man for many years, and when she revealed her true identity, became famous as the Lieutenant Nun. The American Revolution drew several women into the military in male disguise, including Deborah Samson, alias Robert Shurtleff of the 4th Massachusetts Regiment; Salley St. Clair, who died at the Battle of Savannah; and Corp. Samuel Gay of the 1st Massachusetts Regiment, who was discharged in 1777 upon discovery. The women soldiers of the Civil War were following a historical precedent, whether they realized it or not.[8]

But the bonafide distaff soldiers of the Civil War were setting their own historical precedent as well. More women took to the field during that war than in any previous military affair. This study examines them from a number of different perspectives. We present documented cases of women soldiers in combat, from First Manassas to Appomattox, as well as discussing their noncombat military duties and how well they fulfilled them. We consider the many ways women avoided detection in order to enlist and the numerous and personal reasons why they chose to do so. We also look at women soldiers' transitions from female to male personas and from civilian to military mind-sets. We examine women as prisoners of war and as casualties. We detail the stories of soldiers who were discovered to be women while in the army, and explore newspaper coverage and the widespread wartime public knowledge of women serving in the ranks. We also peruse the postwar lives of those women combatants who survived the conflict. Finally, we provide a brief historiography of female soldiers with special consideration of their disappearance from most twentieth-century historical treatments of the Civil War despite ample evidence that women shared in all of the hard service of their male comrades.

Nearly every woman soldier discussed in this book was white. Only three of the featured women were African American. We suspect that there were far more black women soldiers in the Civil War than our research indicates. After all, African American women had a powerful motive for supporting the Union war effort: the liberation of their race from slavery. Unfortunately, black troops received minimal attention from their contemporaries and were not celebrated by the media like their white compatriots. More precisely, while African American soldiers as a group were the subject of intense political and philosophical debate, as individuals they received little scrutiny. Contemporary accounts of the efforts of the U.S. Colored Troops are relatively few, and therefore, the presence of women in their ranks is probably significantly under reported.

The question most often asked about Civil War soldier women is, how many served? The answer most often given is about four hundred. This statistic was supplied by Sanitary Commission agent Mary Livermore in her 1888 memoirs. She wrote:

Some one has stated the number of women soldiers known to the service as little less than four hundred. I cannot vouch for the correctness of this estimate, but I am convinced that a larger number of women disguised themselves and enlisted in the service, for one cause or other, than was dreamed of. Entrenched in secrecy, and regarded as men, they were sometimes revealed as women, by accident or casualty. Some startling histories of these military women were current in the gossip of army life; and extravagant and unreal as were many of the narrations, one always felt that they had a foundation in fact.[9]

It should be noted that Livermore was writing only about Union women. Our research produced evidence of about 250 women soldiers in the ranks of the Union and Confederate armies. There were, undoubtedly, many more. Women soldiers pretended to be men and used male names. Unless women were discovered as such, either during or after the war, or unless they publicly confessed or privately told their tale of wartime service, the record of their military career is lost to us today. How many women answered their country's call in a time of great crisis? No one will ever really know.

Perhaps this is the reason that women soldiers remain the best-kept historical secret of the Civil War. We believe that we have rediscovered enough women soldiers that we can honestly assess their military service. Our essential conclusion is that, with the exception of their sex, female soldiers did not differ in any fundamental way from male soldiers. Readers may judge for themselves. What follows is the story of the women soldiers in the Civil War, as best we can reconstruct it. We believe the story to be a compelling one, and the telling of it is long overdue.

1

"THEY FOUGHT LIKE DEMONS"

A Military History of Women in Combat

W omen soldiers were present as combatants in numerous battles, skirmishes, and campaigns from the beginning of the Civil War to the end. Women fought for their country from the engagement at Blackburn's Ford, Virginia, on July 18, 1861, to the surrender of the last Confederate army. They served in both the eastern and western theaters throughout four years of bloody conflict. Women soldiers were wounded, maimed, and killed in action, and just like men with whom they served, they inflicted their share of pain and death. Despite the fact that they were not required to perform military service and indeed were barred from enlisting as soldiers, women nevertheless served the Union and Confederacy as armed combatants. Testimonials of their comrades leave no doubt about their effectiveness on the field of battle or their bravery under fire.

After the First Battle of Bull Run, the first major clash of armies of the Civil War, a Confederate soldier from Georgia wrote home to his wife that "there were a great many fanatic women in the Yankee Army—some of whom were killed. I was pointed to one of their graves. I knew that I could not be mistaken as to the spot for her foot was sticking out of the ground." The name of that dead woman may never be known, but the identities of other Union women present at Bull Run on July 21, 1861, are available. Louisa Hoffman fought with the 1st Ohio Infantry. A woman called Charlie, described as large, coarse featured, and stubborn, also fought for the Union. A little more than a year later, Charlie was again on the same field, fighting in the second battle that occurred near Manassas. Frances Jamieson from Kentucky entered the field at First Bull Run serving as a first lieutenant under the command of her husband, a captain.[1]

Two women destined for notoriety after the Civil War also fought that day in Virginia. Sarah Emma Edmonds, alias Pvt. Franklin Thompson, served with the 2nd Michigan Infantry. After an exhausting and terrifying day of battle, Edmonds was among the unscathed, and for days thereafter she helped care for some of the 1,124 Union wounded.[2]

On the opposing side, Loreta Janeta Velazquez, alias Lt. Harry T. Buford, stood with the Confederates. Velazquez arrived at First Manassas as an independent officer, not regularly commissioned and without a command. Given the confusion and disorganization of armies in the early months of the war, irregular soldiers were tolerated. Velazquez attached herself to Gen. Barnard Bee's command, and like Edmonds, came through the day's contest unharmed. Manassas was not her first battle, however. Coming to Virginia earlier that month, she witnessed the preliminary fight at Blackburn's Ford on July 18, after which she was temporarily placed in command of a company, all its officers having been killed or wounded during the engagement.

Later, in October 1861, Velazquez was present at the Battle of Ball's Bluff near Leesburg, Virginia. Confederate forces literally drove the Union troops into the Potomac River, with the Federals ultimately taking more than nine hundred casualties, many of whom died not from bullets but from drowning. As usual, Lieutenant Buford did not have a formal command but merely attached herself to a brigade. When ordered to take charge of a company missing its officers, Velazquez did so. She was fortunate that most of the fighting was in the woods, for she was still too inexperienced to know much about maneuvering men in battle.[3]

Like many of the other soldiers present at the bluff that day, Velazquez recalled the carnage with a shudder. However, her brief service with Confederate armies had already taught her that "such scenes . . . are inseparable from warfare, and those who take up arms must steel themselves against them." The steely Velazquez, still unable to secure a regular commission, spurned an offer to become a recruiting agent for the Confederacy and left the eastern theater for the west, spending her own money, writing her own orders, and searching for adventure. She was next engaged in a small action in the western theater near Woodsonville, Kentucky, on December 17, 1861.[4]

Other women soldiers also served in the western theater in 1861. A female corporal who enlisted in the 1st Kansas Infantry under the alias Alfred J. Luther was among the 873 Union soldiers wounded on August 10, 1861, at the Battle of Wilson's Creek, the only major battle fought in Missouri. Luther's comrades later vowed that the corporal was a brave and strong soldier, with an excellent reputation as a fighter.[5]

Women's participation in the western theater of operations increased in 1862. Of the approximately four thousand Union troops at the Battle of Mill Springs, Kentucky, on January 19, at least two were women. One of these was an unnamed woman of Scottish descent, serving in a Kentucky regiment. The other was a woman serving under the alias Frank Deming in the 17th Ohio Infantry.[6]

A little less than a month later, at least two women soldiers were engaged in the Battle of Fort Donelson in Tennessee. The action commenced on February 13 with a Federal attack and ended on the fifteenth with the surrender of the remaining Confederates in the fort. On the Union side was Frances Louisa Clayton, who sustained a wound during the fighting. On the Confederate side was soldier of fortune Loreta Velazquez, who arrived at the fort prior to the battle. She honorably performed her share of trench and picket duty and was among the lucky ones who escaped before the capitulation to Union forces. Still the adventurer, Velazquez followed the movements of the Confederate army and fought at the Battle of Shiloh, which proved to be her last battle. On the evening of April 7, 1862, after the second day's fighting, she was wounded in the arm and shoulder by flying shrapnel while on burial detail.[7]

Velazquez was not the only woman at the Battle of Shiloh. There were at least five others, four on the Union side and one Confederate. Nor was Velazquez the only woman wounded in the two days of fighting near Pittsburg Landing. Union soldier Jane Short, alias Charley Davis, was shot in the hand, but the wound was not serious. Another Union woman, fighting at the side her brother, was seriously injured in the leg and shoulder but survived. A third Union woman was not so fortunate. Killed in action during the battle, her identity will probably never be known. The fourth Union woman, Frances Hook, emerged physically unharmed but emotionally devastated. Her only brother was killed in the desperate fight. Confederate soldier Mary Ann Pitman, alias Second Lieutenant Rawley, and her company of independent cavalry from Tennessee also took to the field at Shiloh.[8]

Confederate soldier Mary Ann Clark was also in the western theater in 1862. Serving in Gen. Braxton Bragg's army at the beginning of the Confederate campaign into Tennessee and Kentucky, she was "wounded in the thigh a considerable piece above the knee" at the Battle of Richmond, Kentucky, on August 30, 1862. One of 451 Confederate casualties, Clark fell into Union hands and became a prisoner of war. She survived her wound, survived her incarceration, and was ultimately paroled.[9]

Two more Confederate women saw action in the west. The Battle of Perryville, Kentucky, on October 8, 1862, was a Union victory that ended Confederate Gen. Braxton Bragg's invasion of Kentucky. On the morning after the battle, a woman wounded in the left side was found by a Union burial detail, having lain untended on the chilly field all night. Another Confederate woman at Perryville was unharmed in the fight and continued her service in the Army of Tennessee. A native of Louisiana, this anonymous woman later saw action at the Battle of Murfreesboro from December 31, 1862, through January 2, 1863.[10]

Three other women combatants fought at Murfreesboro, all for the Federals, who referred to the battle as Stones River. A young woman serving under the alias of Frank Martin received a wound in the shoulder. Frances Clayton, a veteran of Fort Donelson, witnessed her husband's death just a few feet in front of her. Nevertheless, she did not falter in battle. When the call came to fix bayonets, Clayton stepped over his body and charged. The third Union woman combatant at Stones River, a sergeant, was also a veteran, having served approximately sixteen months in the Army of the Cumberland. Nearly four months later, a comrade remarked, "It seems very strange that a woman could endure the hardships of a soldier." Not only did the sergeant endure the deprivations of a soldier's life on campaign, but she did so with an additional burden that no male soldier was ever required to carry. During the Battle of Stones River, the sergeant fought while in the fifth month of pregnancy.[11]

As in the western theater, in 1862 the number of women combatants on record increased in the eastern theater. Marian McKenzie, a light-complexioned, blue-eyed soldier who stood only five feet two inches tall, served through the Shenandoah Valley campaign. Under the alias Henry Fitzallen, McKenzie took the field in this campaign that commenced on March 5, 1862, and lasted until nearly the end of the year. The operations in the valley resulted in a dozen skirmishes and battles. McKenzie survived them all.[12]

Shortly after the Shenandoah Valley campaign began, the ill-fated Peninsula campaign was launched, beginning on March 17, 1862, when Union forces under the command of Gen. George McClellan embarked from Alexandria, Virginia. The plan called for Union troops to invade the peninsula between the York and James Rivers. The bluecoats were to move up the peninsula to take Richmond, capital of the Confederacy. Peninsular operations lasted until August 20, 1862, when McClellan's defeated army completed its evacuation of the peninsula. The armies involved were engaged in a total of eighteen skirmishes, actions, and battles over the five months of the campaign. Martha Lindley, alias Pvt. Jim Smith of the 6th U.S. Cavalry, fought with her regiment on the peninsula until June, when she was detailed to hospital duty acting as orderly for the regimental surgeon.[13]

Sarah Edmonds witnessed the entire Peninsula campaign, from the hopeful start at Alexandria to the bloody disasters of the Seven Days to the sullen retreat to Fortress Monroe. As the campaign moved into full swing in April 1862, Private Thompson (Edmonds) was detailed as regimental postmaster and mail carrier, a job she retained for more than four months. During the siege of Yorktown from April 5 to May 4, Edmonds was almost constantly in the saddle, carrying mail and dispatches between the front and Fortress Monroe. On May 5, after a partial day of carrying battle orders, she ceased her courier duty just long enough to pick up her musket and fight in the Battle of Williamsburg. At the Battle of Seven Pines on May 31 and June 1, the exhausted private was given hospital duty, a task that included burying the dead.[14]

The Union Army of the Potomac fought its way to Richmond, struggling to the outskirts of the city by June 4. While the army camped, Private Thompson resumed mail carrier duty until the Seven Days' Battles, when she again picked up her gun and fell into the ranks of her regiment. The Seven Days' Battles began Wednesday, June 25, with a small affair at Oak Grove. Thursday witnessed the Battle of Mechanicsville, with Gaines' Mill the next day. There was maneuvering by both armies on Saturday, followed by the Battle of Savage's Station on June 29 and Frayser's Farm the following day. The bloody Seven Days ended on Tuesday, July 1, when the Federals were soundly repulsed at Malvern Hill. Gen. Robert E. Lee's

Confederates had defeated McClellan, forcing the Union army to retreat from Richmond.[15]

Edmonds was not the only woman who fought in the Seven Days' Battles. An anonymous woman soldier served with her husband in the 1st New York Cavalry. At Savage's Station, the wife saved her husband's life by carrying him off the field when he was wounded. She received a flesh wound in the process. She dressed his wounds in a field hospital, and when the Confederates forced a Union retreat, the hospital was captured and both she and her husband became prisoners of war. An unnamed woman in a New Jersey regiment also took part in the Seven Days battles. On the Confederate side, Lucy Matilda Thompson Gauss fought in the 18th North Carolina Infantry. Both the New Jersey woman and Gauss were fairly new to life in the army, and the Seven Days' Battles were their baptism of fire. The New Jersey woman had another baptism in her future. During the Seven Days she was in the first trimester of pregnancy.[16]

As the Peninsula campaign drew to a close in August 1862, another Union army, this one under John Pope, began forming in northern Virginia. Even before he was sure that McClellan was leaving the peninsula, Confederate Gen. Robert E. Lee sent troops to oppose Pope. Fighting began in early August. On the twenty-second, Confederate cavalry under command of J. E. B. Stuart led a raid on Catlett's Station, Virginia, and captured Pope's entire baggage train. One of the Union soldiers guarding the train and captured in the raid "proved to be a woman in disguise."[17]

A week later, the Second Battle of Bull Run began and raged for several violent days at the end of August 1862. The Union again suffered defeat, with more than one thousand soldiers killed. According to an army doctor, among the dead was a soldier known only as Margaret. She suffered minor wounds early in the battle but refused to leave the field to seek medical attention. Later that day she was mortally wounded. Sarah Edmonds also fought at Second Manassas. Along with other elements of McClellan's army, her regiment had come to the aid of Pope.[18]

Edmonds next saw action at the Battle of Antietam, this time without her regiment. Still acting as a mail carrier, Private Thompson was dispatched from Washington, D.C., with mail, orders, and other documents for McClellan's army, now operating in Maryland against the Confederates, who had crossed the Potomac River early in September 1862. On the morning of September 17 the Confederate Army of Northern Virginia, posted in defensive positions around Sharpsburg, was attacked by the

Army of the Potomac. Thus began the Battle of Antietam, the bloodiest single day of combat in American history, with casualties close to twenty-five thousand. Edmonds stayed throughout the battle to tend to the wounded. When the gunfire finally subsided, she walked the fields with other soldiers looking for wounded among the bodies. One of the soldiers she assisted was a woman whose wounds proved fatal.[19]

Including Edmonds and the unknown soldier she discovered, eight women combatants are known to have been involved in the Battle of Antietam. Seven were Union, one was Confederate, and five numbered among the casualties. Catherine Davidson fought with the 28th Ohio Infantry. She was wounded so badly in the right arm that surgeons amputated it at the midpoint between the shoulder and elbow. Mary Galloway was shot in the neck in the morning's fighting. She rolled into a ravine, where she lay for thirty-six hours unable to move and in great pain until she was found by friendly troops and taken to a field hospital. Both Davidson and Galloway survived their injuries. The fourth female casualty at Antietam was a soldier from New Jersey, the same woman who had fought at the Seven Days' Battles while pregnant. She was in her second trimester when she and her regiment arrived at Antietam, yet she did not shirk her duty. She recovered from her wound and returned to her regiment. The anonymous Confederate woman was not so fortunate. She was killed in action during the fierce and sanguinary first phase of the battle, in what became known as The Cornfield.[20]

Rebecca Peterman, known as Georgianna in the press, served in the 7th Wisconsin Infantry at Antietam, and she, too, fought in the Cornfield, but came through the battle unharmed. So did Union soldier Ida Remington. Antietam was a second battle for her; she had fought at South Mountain just three days earlier.[21]

Two of the women combatants at Antietam, Sarah Edmonds and the unidentified New Jersey woman, were present at Fredericksburg, the final battle of 1862 in the eastern theater. A third female, teenaged Lizzie Compton, was also there, and also fighting on the side of the Union. Compton was among the 9,600 Union casualties inflicted by Confederates during the December 13, 1862, battle, in which Federal troops were ordered to make charge after suicidal charge uphill against a well-entrenched enemy. Compton lived to fight another day. Edmonds had reunited with her regiment prior to Fredericksburg, yet she did not fight with them during the battle. By her own request, Private Thompson acted as orderly to

Gen. Orlando M. Poe, who commanded her regiment's brigade. She spent most of the battle riding back and forth between the various headquarters and the front, delivering and receiving orders and reports. She spent at least twelve uninterrupted hours in the saddle, often under the fire of the enemy. The battle disheartened Edmonds. She viewed the slaughter of her comrades with dismay and offered a prayer for the salvation of the Union cause: "May God bless the old Army of the Potomac, and save it from total annihilation."[22]

The unidentified woman from New Jersey was promoted to corporal prior to Fredericksburg. She was, apparently, a very good soldier. One of her comrades stated that not only was she "a young and good looking corporal," but her "courtesy and military bearing . . . struck the officers very favorably." Furthermore, he proclaimed her to be "a real soldierly, thoroughly military fellow." She was also a valiant soldier. Although in the final trimester of pregnancy, she performed her duty at Fredericksburg, and she performed it well. On January 19, 1863, a shocked colonel with the Army of the Potomac wrote home that "a corporal was promoted to sergeant for gallant conduct at the battle of Fredericksburg—since which time the sergeant has become the mother of a child." Tongue-in-cheek he added, "What use have we for women, if soldiers in the army can give birth to children?" Indeed, when she delivered her baby boy, she became the subject of much gossip among the Army of the Potomac. Yet in all that was written home about her by enlisted men and officers, neither her true nor her enlisted identity were ever mentioned. Her name, the alias under which she served, and her regimental affiliation remain unknown.[23]

It was rather symbolic that a child was born in the Union army in January 1863, for that year brought a rebirth to the Army of the Potomac. After a string of defeats at the hands of the Army of Northern Virginia, the Federals finally triumphed at Gettysburg in July. But before Gettysburg, there was Chancellorsville, four days of fighting in the dense forests near Fredericksburg that began April 30, 1863, and resulted in a Union defeat. At least two Confederate women took part in the fight, one of whom was an orderly sergeant in the cavalry. She was captured and later sent to Baltimore as a prisoner of war.[24]

Five women are known to have fought at Gettysburg, two Union and three Confederate. Defending northern soil near the Pennsylvania town was Mary Siezgle of New York and an unidentified teenaged girl who was lightly wounded in the fray. The contest at Gettysburg was horrifying.

During the three days of fighting that began on July 1, approximately 7,000 soldiers were killed in action, and more than 33,000 were wounded. While the Union women at Gettysburg emerged from the carnage relatively intact, the Confederate women, like the army in which they served, fared badly. One of the Confederate soldiers was shot in the leg and captured. She was removed to the U.S. Military Hospital in Chester, Pennsylvania, where surgeons amputated her leg in order to save her life.[25]

The two other Confederate women were casualties of Pickett's Charge on July 3. One historian called the charge "the most renowned infantry assault of Anglo-Saxon history." Nine brigades of Confederate soldiers attacked the center of the Union line, mistakenly believing it weakened after two hours of artillery bombardment. The southern troops marched half a mile over an open field to attack the enemy. Mowed down by Federal artillery, the southerners repeatedly closed up ranks and stepped over fallen comrades to continue their charge. As they drew closer to the lines in blue, the Confederates were raked by musket fire at nearly point-blank range. Deadly hand-to-hand combat ensued for those who made it to the Union defenses. After horrible punishment, the remnants of the gray brigades retreated. Both armies then gazed at the heaps of the dead and wounded strewn across the Pennsylvania field and Emmitsburg Road.[26]

The two women who marched across the field in the glorious but doomed Pickett's Charge did not return. One of them was severely wounded, unable to move herself from the pasture. That evening, a Union private from New Jersey who was detailed to guard Emmitsburg Road listened to her screams of agony. He later wrote that it was the most awful sound he had ever heard. The other woman was killed in the charge, her body later found by a Union burial detail.[27]

While the Battle of Gettysburg was raging in the east, the Siege of Vicksburg in the west was rapidly drawing to a close. It began May 18, 1863, when Federal forces under Gen. U.S. Grant moved across the Big Black River, took the heights outside of the Mississippi River city, and laid siege. Confederate forces under Gen. John C. Pemberton refused to evacuate the well-fortified city of Vicksburg. The Union army shelled the city for six weeks and assaulted it twice. Jennie Hodgers, alias Pvt. Albert D. J. Cashier of the 95th Illinois Infantry, was among the Union troops laying siege. She was captured at a Confederate outpost during a reconnaissance around the city but managed to escape by seizing a gun from one of her guards, knocking him down, and outrunning the others. Comrades also recalled Private Cashier climbing to the top of their fieldworks to taunt the enemy into showing themselves. On July 4, 1863, the Confederates, who were running out of food and had little hope of outside help, surrendered Vicksburg to Grant's army. One of the southern troops who marched out of the city that day was Ellen Levasay, a private in the 3rd Missouri Cavalry.[28]

Two days before the surrender of Vicksburg, Confederate John Hunt Morgan and his cavalry began their famous raid into Kentucky and points north. On July 4, the same day that Pemberton surrendered, Morgan and his force were repulsed at the affair of Green River, Kentucky, also called Tebb's Bend. Lizzie Compton, earlier wounded at Fredericksburg and subsequently mustered out of the United States service, had gone west and rejoined the army. She allied with the 25th Michigan Infantry as a battlefield replacement and was shot in the shoulder at Green River. This engagement did not halt Morgan's Raid, which finally ended on July 26 with the capture of the Confederate cavalry commander.[29]

Women soldiers participated in other campaigns and battles throughout 1863. From September 19 to September 21, the Union Army of the Cumberland fought the Confederate Army of Tennessee along Chickamauga Creek in northwestern Georgia, where casualty rates totaled 28 percent for both sides. An unnamed Ohio woman fought in the battle by the side of her father, and she survived the Union defeat. On the Louisiana Gulf Coast the following month, Union Gen. Nathaniel Banks began the Bayou Teche campaign. His goal was to reach Texas and establish a foothold there, but his maneuvers ended in failure in November 1863 after a month of effort. An anonymous woman soldier in the 14th Maine Infantry served throughout the difficult campaign.[30]

On Tuesday, November 24, the day before Banks's campaign ended, three Union divisions under Gen. Joseph Hooker climbed up Lookout Mountain in hopes of dislodging Confederate defenders from the heights above Chattanooga, Tennessee. The Union assault was successful, driving the Confederates off of Lookout Mountain and Missionary Ridge. The Union divisions fielded at least two women. One was Mary Ellen Wise of Indiana. She was shot in the shoulder but lived to tell about it. The second woman soldier was not so lucky. Identified only as Emily, she served with a Michigan regiment. She was shot in the side during the advance up the mountain, and her wound proved fatal.[31]

In Virginia, Union cavalry mounted an expedition to Charles City

Courthouse on December 12, 1863, and successfully raided it the following day. An assistant surgeon in one of the regiments later wrote to his father, "We captured every officer and man. . . . Among the prisoners was a female soldier, a woman of about 20 years. She had male attire, and used her rifle against us, as well as the rest. She has been in several engagements."[32]

Participation of women soldiers on the fields of battle continued unabated in 1864. They served in the Red River, Atlanta, and Nashville campaigns. The fourth year of the conflict also saw distaff soldiers taking part in most of the fighting in Virginia—at Bermuda Hundred, in the Shenandoah Valley, and as members of Lee's and Grant's grand armies, who were engaged almost constantly throughout the year from the Wilderness to the outskirts of Petersburg.

In Louisiana, Pvt. Albert D. J. Cashier fought with her regiment throughout the Red River campaign. In March 1864 Union forces under General Banks marched through the heart of Louisiana and up the Red River in a massive but ill-fated Union effort. Cashier fought in more than a dozen battles and skirmishes during the campaign, and like all the other Union soldiers who survived it, marched for hundreds of miles, often in desperate circumstances, as Union troops retreated back down the Red River to the Mississippi. The disastrous campaign concluded on May 21.[33]

Sarah Rosetta Wakeman, alias Pvt. Lyons Wakeman of the 153rd New York Infantry, was engaged in two Red River battles, Pleasant Hill on April 9, and Monett's Ferry on April 23. More than a year before the campaign, and prior to her first taste of combat, Wakeman wrote to her father, "I don't fear the rebel bullets nor I don't fear the cannon." Once the campaign was underway in earnest, Wakeman did not lose her fearlessness. In a letter home she bragged about her stamina and bravery. Fifteen days into the campaign, she informed her parents, "I have marched two hundred miles. We was ten days on the road amarching." Wakeman emerged unscathed from the engagement at Pleasant Hill, where her regiment was in the front lines. Afterwards, she wrote to her family to let them know she was alive, and she described the battle for them: "The firing took place about eight o'Clock in the morning. There was a heavy Cannonading all day and a Sharp firing of infantry. . . . I had to face the enemy bullets with my regiment. I was under fire about four hours and laid on the field of battle all night."[34]

Wakeman wrote this letter while her army was entrenched and her generals were deciding the fate of the campaign. The decision was made to flee the Louisiana high country. On the evening of April 21, the army began a seventy-mile forced retreat. By midnight of April 22, they had covered thirty-five miles in fourteen hours. At sunrise on the twenty-third, the army reached Monett's Bluff, where they found the Confederates holding the opposite high bank and blocking the Federal's advance. The Union army forced a crossing and the battle began. That afternoon, Wakeman and the 1st Brigade charged the Confederate force in a frontal attack, and their army finally defeated the Confederates and resumed the retreat. Wakeman survived the bold charge at Monett's Ferry, but she did not survive the war.[35]

As the Red River campaign drew to a close, the Union advance on Atlanta began in northern Georgia. On Saturday, May 7, three armies under the command of Gen. William T. Sherman started their moves against a smaller Confederate force led by Gen. Joseph E. Johnston. The bluecoats' goal was the capture of the city of Atlanta, the attainment of which consumed the next four months. Sherman's forces finally took the city on September 2. The four-month campaign saw more than a dozen battles, skirmishes, and raids. Women soldiers fought in at least four of the engagements.[36]

The first major battle took place May 13 to 15 at Resaca, Georgia. An unidentified Union woman soldier was killed in action there, shot in the head. Later that month, in a fight near Dallas, Georgia, several Confederate women, one of whom was a flag bearer, fell in a fierce final assault on Union lines. Sgt. Robert Ardry of the 111th Illinois Infantry wrote to his father, "They fought like demons, and we cut them down like dogs. . . . I saw 3 or 4 rebel women soldiers in the heap of bodies."[37]

July 20, 1864, witnessed the Battle of Peachtree Creek, wherein Confederate soldiers under command of Gen. John B. Hood bravely but fruitlessly attacked a steadfast Union force for two hours. Of the 4,796 casualties inflicted on the Confederates that afternoon, at least four were women. Union soldier James L. Dunn later reported that "among the reble wounded we found several women in mens clothes also among the killed." Another Union soldier was more specific: "I've picked up a great many wounded rebs & took them to our hospital among these were found a female dressed in mens clothes & a cartridge box on her side when we picked her up. She was shot in the breast & through the thy & was still alive & as gritty as any reb I ever saw. I hope our women will never be so foolish as to go to war or get to fighting."[38]

The engagement at Allatoona on October 5 was the last of the battles near Atlanta known to involve women combatants. Three of the 443 Confederates wounded there were women, but their identities are a mystery. One of them served in the Missouri Brigade, and a Union soldier who helped tend the wounded of Allatoona told her story after the battle: "A tanned and freckled young rebel, hands and face grimy with dirt and powder, lay resting on an elbow, smoking a corn-cob pipe. The doctor inquired, 'How do you feel?' and the answer was 'Pretty well, but my leg hurts like the devil.'"[39]

Women soldiers were engaged in one more battle in the west before the close of 1864. After losing Atlanta, Confederate forces under Hood moved into Tennessee in an attempt to draw Sherman out of Georgia. After fighting and losing at Franklin, Hood brought his army to Nashville. Pvt. Albert Cashier was with the Army of the Cumberland on December 15 when it emerged from its works at Nashville and attacked the Confederates. Throughout the day's fighting, the northerners beat the southerners back a full mile. Realignments were made in the lines during the night, and the next day, after a morning of artillery bombardment and despite rain and snow, Union soldiers assaulted the Confederates again. The lines of the Army of Tennessee finally broke, and the Confederates fled. For eight more days, Union soldiers pursued retreating Confederates.[40]

Cashier emerged from it all uninjured. Indeed, Cashier emerged from the entire war without ever becoming a casualty. She served a full enlistment, and long after the war, her fellow veterans remembered the diminutive private with the Irish brogue as a good and brave soldier, and expressed a great deal of admiration for her heroic fighting. Her compatriots marveled that despite her willingness to take on dangerous assignments, she was never injured or wounded. One of her fellow soldiers affirmed that Cashier was known throughout the regiment for bravery in combat. Another veteran remembered Cashier's exposing herself to sniper fire by climbing a tall tree to attach the Union flag after it was shot down by the enemy.[41]

After Nashville, Private Cashier served through one final campaign, a move to capture Mobile, Alabama. Union forces surrounded the city on March 17, 1865. They laid siege on the twenty-sixth, and the city surrendered April 12, 1865. Cashier's regiment occupied Mobile thereafter, having been among the first troops to enter the defeated city. The occupation of Mobile was the last military assignment in this brave soldier's army career.[42]

In the eastern theater, the war raged in Virginia throughout 1864, and women were there. Hardly a day of the fourth year of the war passed without some form of military maneuver in the state, the scene of virtually nonstop campaigning between forces arrayed from the Shenandoah Valley to the Atlantic Coast. On May 5, 1864, Union Gen. Ben Butler landed at City Point and Bermuda Hundred with the intention of marching up the peninsula and taking Richmond. Among his troops was the anonymous woman soldier of the 14th Maine Infantry, whose regiment had been transferred from the Deep South. Butler's command made it as far as Drewry's Bluff, where they were driven back. They retreated to Bermuda Hundred and remained bottled up on the peninsula by Confederate forces under Gen. P. G. T. Beauregard. Part of Butler's command was then deployed to the Shenandoah Valley, leaving via the James River.[43]

The 14th Maine Infantry was among the regiments sent, and the anonymous woman soldier of that regiment served in the 1864 Shenandoah Valley campaign until it ended on December 19. She was mustered out of the Federal service with the rest of her regiment on January 13, 1865. The 1864 Valley campaign was long, fierce, and bloody for soldiers of both sides. Union troops under Gen. David Hunter, who was succeeded by Gen. Philip Sheridan, faced Confederate troops under Gen. Jubal Early. The two forces fought up and down the Valley for more than six months, clashing more than fifteen times in raids, skirmishes, and full-fledged battles. On the Confederate side of the Valley campaign, Mary and Mollie Bell, alias Bob Martin and Tom Parker, fought until October, when they were sent to Richmond. The Bells were veteran soldiers, having served for about two years prior to the campaign.[44]

Elsewhere in Virginia in 1864, the great contest between Ulysses S. Grant and Robert E. Lee raged from near Fredericksburg to Petersburg. It began May 4, when Union soldiers marched southward from their positions on the north banks of the Rapidan River. From that point forward the Army of the Potomac steadily and relentlessly pushed forward, never retreating as in the past. Grant's aim was to capture Richmond, destroy Lee's army, and end the war. Achieving these goals took nearly a year.[45]

During the overland campaign, from May to June 1864, Grant's Army of the Potomac and Lee's Army of Northern Virginia fought nine major battles and a number of skirmishes and engagements in almost constant combat. Five women, two Union and three Confederate, are known to have served during this campaign. The Battle of the Wilderness on May 5 and 6 was the first of the great matches. Fought in a dense forest that was set on fire by musketry and that burned many of the dead as well as those too severely wounded to move, the Wilderness resulted in astonishing casualties. On the northern side alone, 2,246 soldiers were killed, and 12,037 were wounded. One of these was a female lieutenant who was shot in the shoulder. She was sent to a general hospital, where "the boys who were brought in with her said that no one in the company showed more bravery than she."[46]

The Battle of the North Anna River was fought on a Monday through Thursday, May 23 through 26. Lee's army had retreated from the carnage at Spotsylvania Court House and took up strong positions along the river. There they lay in wait for Grant's army on the banks of the North Anna and attacked as the vulnerable Union forces made the crossing. Most of the heavy fighting occurred the first two days. On the last day, the Union troops withdrew back across the river to attempt a maneuver around Lee's flank. It was on that final day that "a female dressed in Rebel uniform was taken." A member of the Confederate cavalry, she was captured while on reconnaissance, sent out to ascertain the position of the enemy. The very next day, Sarah Jane Ann Perkins, serving with a Confederate artillery regiment from Virginia, was captured during fighting at Hanover Junction. Perkins was a veteran soldier, having served since the beginning of the war.[47]

By May 31, the two armies reached the crossroads of Cold Harbor, near Richmond. The ensuing battle, fought June 1 through 3, was Lee's last triumph, and a terrible loss for Grant and his army. On the third day of fighting, seven thousand Union soldiers fell in less than one hour in a series of futile frontal assaults against a well-entrenched foe. Even though the Army of the Potomac lost Cold Harbor, they still managed to capture some of their Confederate adversaries, including one woman who was a noncommissioned officer. A Union soldier later informed his fiancée, "We did capture a full-fledged artillery woman who was working regularly at the piece, she was very independent and saucy as most Southern ladies are." A Union nurse wrote in her diary that among the captured prisoners arriving at White House Landing four days after the battle was "a rebel woman, sergeant of artillery."[48]

Unable to capture Richmond with a frontal assault, Grant moved his army south across the James River in an effort to capture Petersburg, only a few miles south of the Confederate capital. With reinforcements from Bermuda Hundred, the Federals attacked on June 15. Though heavily outnumbering the Confederate defenders, they could not take the city, and so the siege of Petersburg began on the eighteenth. Both armies dug entrenchments and settled in for a war of attrition. On June 25, Federal engineers began digging a tunnel toward the Confederate lines, hoping to blow up the earthworks and capitalize on the break in the enemy's defenses to end the stalemate. Before dawn on July 30, the blast went off, blowing a hole 170 feet long, 80 feet wide, and 30 feet deep in the Confederate line and killing more than 200 southern defenders. Part of the Union Ninth Corps charged into the hole and became disorganized and bogged down in what would later be known as the Crater. The Confederates soon rallied and fired down into the confused and halted foe. About four thousand Federals were casualties of the assault, including one woman soldier, shot through the head.[49]

The siege of Petersburg lasted well into 1865, marked by a constant reinforcing of the lines, intermittent sniper fire, occasional Union prodding of Confederate defenses, some skirmishes, and three more battles. On the Union side there were at least two women who endured the siege, one of whom was Mary A. Brown of the 31st Maine Infantry. She arrived on the Petersburg front with the rest of her regiment in January. The second Union woman served with the 29th Connecticut Infantry (Colored). Her regiment filed into the trenches in August 1864 and stayed until the siege ended.[50]

During the relentless siege of Petersburg, the Carolinas campaign commenced. With the goal of combining with Grant's forces in Virginia, General Sherman's command marched out of Savannah, Georgia, on the first day of February 1865. They advanced northward through South Carolina and into North Carolina. On March 16, Sherman's army fought an opening battle of the campaign at Averasboro against elements of Gen. Joseph E. Johnston's army. The Battle of Bentonville, the last significant effort to stop Sherman's advance and the last major offensive by Confederate forces undertaken in the war, was fought March 19 through 21. There was at least one southern woman at the Battle of Bentonville, a veteran horse soldier from Alabama who had served since 1862. On the last day of the battle she saw her husband fall after an artillery barrage and, "braving the fire of

Federal sharpshooters, rode forward . . . helped lift him in the saddle, and
. . . brought him back" to the rear. A Confederate veteran later remarked
that she showed "the most profound resoluteness" under fire.[51]

While General Sherman's command was engaged with General Johnston's forces in North Carolina, Lee and his army finally left the Petersburg entrenchments on April 2, and fled toward Johnston's in North
Carolina, with Grant's army pursuing on a parallel route. On April 6 the
armies confronted each other at Saylor's Creek, and the following day they
clashed at Farmville. The southerners crossed the Appomattox River later
that day and were closely pursued by Northern forces. They skirmished
on the eighth near Appomattox Station, but further Confederate resistance was futile. On Palm Sunday, April 9, 1865, General Lee signed the
formal terms for surrender of the Army of Northern Virginia at Appomattox Court House. After the surrender, a Union soldier scribbled in his
journal that "the remains of a woman in Confederate uniform were found
between the lines near the Appomattox river."[52] She was killed just one
day before her comrades laid down their arms. How long and how faithfully this woman served before losing her life will probably never be
known. How many more women died in combat, their bodies hastily buried, their sex never recognized?

The foregoing summary of the battlefield exploits of Civil War women
warriors is surely incomplete, encompassing only those women who were
witnessed on the field of battle or who wrote about their experiences in
combat. Indeed, the historical record shows that numerous other women
served in the armies of the Union and Confederacy. Unfortunately, the
full extent of women's participation as armed combatants in America's
bloodiest and most costly conflict will never be known with certainty, because the Civil War women soldiers fought for the most part in secrecy,
disguised as men and using male aliases. Those whose stories are known,
however, show that Civil War soldier women were capable fighters, willing to die for their cause, their comrades, and their country.

2

---◆‑◇‑◆---

"To Dress and Go as a Soldier"
Means and Motivations

With so many women fighting and dying on the field of battle, obvious questions arise about how women were able to pass into the army and why they would want to serve. One fundamental reason that they would want to put themselves in harm's way is that the Civil War whipped up martial passions in women as well as men. For every demoiselle who donned a soldier's uniform and went off to war, many more expressed the desire to do so and lamented their fate as women, who by virtue of their sex were prohibited from engaging in the business end of the military. "It seems so hard that we who have the wills of men should be denied from engaging in this great struggle for liberty just because we are ladies," lamented southerner Cordelia Scales. "I wish that women could fight," confessed young Lucy Breckinridge to her journal, asserting, "I would gladly shoulder my pistol and shoot some Yankees if it were allowable." Breckinridge claimed that "if some few Southern women were in the ranks they would set the men an example they would not blush to follow." Similarly, Sarah Morgan of Louisiana lamented, "O! If I was only a man! Then I could . . . slay them with a will."[1]

Some women did more than lament their female status. They actually sought permission to join the conflict. "Perceiving the reluctance of the men of this city in coming forward in the hour of need and danger," wrote Anne M. Bond to General Lee, "I am now ready with my wheelbarrow to go on the entrenchments—and I am confident there are many women ready to join me." A group of more than twenty women in the Shenandoah Valley wrote to the Confederate secretary of war stating that they had organized "a volunteer regiment for purposes of local defence" because "the latest conscription bill takes every 'lord of creation' from sixteen to sixty." They wanted to take to the field, but the secretary of war politely declined the offer.[2]

Northern women were no less patriotic, bloodthirsty, or willing to encourage male recruits by their example. Mrs. Black of Boston, mistakenly placed on the draft rolls of the Union army, showed up as ordered and stated that she "wished no substitute" and was ready to wear the uniform "and take position in line." In Richland, Ohio, there was a shortage of young men signed up for army service, which prompted an angry response from the township's women. Seven young ladies "stepped forward and requested to have their names enrolled as volunteers in defense of their country and their rights, and said, as soon as they could be furnished with uniforms, they would leave their clothing to the young men, who lacked the manliness to defend the flag of their country when it was assailed." An Illinois schoolteacher, Mary Hancock, and three of her friends not only signed the muster roll of the volunteers of North Plato, but outfitted themselves in demiuniforms and marched with the company for several months in order to provoke young men in the area to do their patriotic duty. Despite waning public sentiment for the war in the North prior to the 1864 election, an Ohio woman wrote to President Lincoln in September, "I could get up a Regt. in one day of young Ladies of high rank."[3]

Of course, the majority of women who expressed such sentiments never acted upon them, or if they did, confined their war contributions to activities more closely associated with the realm of female influence in Victorian America. Thousands of women aided their country's war effort by contributing clothing and supplies from the home front or, more directly, by going to the war front as nurses, laundresses, and cooks. Some of the more daring served as local scouts and spies attached to the military. But for other women, these occupations proved too limiting for their ambitions or desires. For these women, nothing less than becoming full-fledged soldiers would do. Mary Siezgle, for example, originally went to the front and served as a nurse but decided to stay with her husband in a New York regiment. The only way for her to do so was to put on male clothes and do "her share of actual fighting."[4]

Of course, women soldiering as men was not a new idea in world history or even American history. The American Civil War, however, is notable for the large numbers of women who shrouded themselves in male identities for the purpose of becoming soldiers, since the military was barred to them as females. Hundreds of women enlisted under male aliases in the Union and Confederate armies and served as soldiers for long periods of time. Enlisting was quite easy. All a woman needed to do was cut her hair short, don male clothing, pick an alias, and find the nearest recruiter, regiment, or army camp. In the mid-nineteenth century individuals did not carry personal identification. Indeed, most people did not even have a birth certificate. Both men and women were free to become anyone they wished to be by simply moving to a place where no one knew them and creating a new persona. Army recruiters in the North and South usually accepted whatever information the recruit provided as to name, age, and former occupation.

In theory, all recruits were subjected to a physical examination prior to being mustered into the service of either the United States or the Confederacy. In truth, the Civil War surgeon's exam was frequently circumvented by sickly men and underage boys, as well as by women inductees. This vexed army officials, particularly those of the Union, and prompted War Department orders dictating how physical exams should be conducted. These orders were ignored far more often than they were obeyed. The pressure to quickly fill regimental ranks militated against finding reasons to deny a person's proffered enlistment. With the exception of the opening months of the war, when the enthusiasm to enlist ran higher than demand for troops in both the North and the South, states found it increasingly difficult to raise the many regiments of citizen soldiers called for by two nations in need of hundreds of thousands of combatants. Despite U.S. War Department dictates that each recruit be stripped and thoroughly checked for signs of illness and disability, physical exams by regimental surgeons tended to be cursory, at best. For the most part, recruiters and surgeons only looked for reasonable height, at least a partial set of teeth with which to tear open powder cartridges, and the presence of a trigger finger. All but the obviously deaf, blind, and lame were accepted into the service. If a boy looked big enough to carry a gun and if he wanted to fight, he was usually accepted with few questions, as Pvt. Franklin Thompson of the 2nd Michigan Infantry recalled after the war.[5]

In Thompson's case, the examiner simply took the recruit's hand and asked, "Well, what sort of a living has this hand earned?" to which Thompson replied that it had been primarily engaged in getting an education. The examiner passed the small private into the army on May 25, 1861, not knowing that the recruit's true identity was Sarah Emma Edmonds, aged nineteen. Pvt. Albert D. J. Cashier and "his" comrades were all examined on the same day, were not stripped, and, testified one, "All that we showed was our hands and feet." Another claimed that "a woman would not have had any trouble in passing the examination." Thus, nineteen-year-old Jennie Hodgers slipped into the ranks of the 95th Illinois Infantry on August 3, 1862, serving an entire three-year enlistment as Private Cashier and mustering out with her regiment on August 17, 1865. Another Union soldier recalled his entrance examination, saying that "the muster-in . . . was . . . a farce; no medical or physical examination; the mustering officer hastily passed along the line, taking a look at each individual as he passed, and without other ceremony, mustered the regiment into the . . . service." It is no wonder, then, that hundreds of women found the army physical exam no barrier to joining the cavalry, artillery, or infantry.[6]

Women also found ways to avoid the medical examination requirement altogether. Sometimes, a surgeon or an officer helped them. Hattie Martin, a young Pennsylvania newlywed who wanted to join her husband in the ranks, "made known her sex to the examining surgeon, and at her earnest solicitation he accepted her as a recruit" despite the fact that this was a fraudulent enlistment according to army regulations. In the summer of 1862, Marian Green decided to follow her fiancé to war and, in collusion with the surgeon, joined a detachment of soldiers headed for the front to serve in the 1st Michigan Engineers and Mechanics. When Harriet Merrill arrived at the camp of the 59th New York Infantry in November 1861 in the company of three other recruits, she was given the standard quartermaster issue of clothing, enlisted in Company G, and was not required to submit to a physical exam. In Merrill's case, the captain of the regiment knew her true identity and assisted her in joining the regiment. Likewise, the surgeon of the 12th Indiana Cavalry arranged for his own wife to serve as his assistant.[7]

Not all surgeons or other officers ignored examination standards. Nevertheless, a resourceful woman could find her way into a regiment despite the most conscientious efforts of military surgeons and recruitment officers. A "bright, black-eyed boy" showed up at Camp Curtin and offered his services directly to the captain of the 141st Pennsylvania Infantry, thus bypassing the recruitment process altogether. Another way to avoid the surgeon was falling in with a regiment while it was actively campaigning. With ranks thinned by battle and illness during campaign season, a regimental commander might hastily accept any willing volunteer. Mary Galloway obtained a uniform and caught up with the rear of the Army of the Potomac shortly before the opening of Antietam. In the excitement of the impending fight she was able to attach herself to the ambulance train, presumably without many questions.[8]

This ploy was not always successful. In November 1863, in the vicinity of Giles County, Tennessee, a woman disguised as a man briefly joined Company F of the 64th Illinois Infantry while it was on the march. Henry Schelling, a soldier in that regiment, reported to a friend, "We enlisted a new recruit on the way at Eastport. The boys all took a notion to him." On examination, however, the recruit proved to be a woman, who was immediately discharged. "I was sorry for it, for I wanted him for a Bedfellow," lamented Schelling.[9]

Earlier that spring, a boy riding a fine horse arrived at the advanced picket outposts of the Army of the Potomac on the Rappahannock River and asked to be passed through to cavalry headquarters. The boy was wearing a coat buttoned to the chin, and a gray hat pulled down over the eyes. The private on duty, John Brooks of the 8th Pennsylvania Cavalry, grew suspicious and checked under the boy's coat for weapons, then carefully studied the boy's face. Private Brooks summoned the lieutenant, shared his suspicions about the potential recruit's sex, and the would-be soldier was sent to headquarters under guard. Private Brooks never learned what became of her.[10]

Some other aspiring women soldiers encountered numerous frustrations in trying to enlist. "Miss Martin" from Cincinnati was rejected by Union recruiters five times. Her first four attempts ended in failure not because she was a woman but because she was too short. Only on her fifth try did a surgeon ask her to strip. Martin was perplexed at her inability to get into the ranks. As a Cincinnati newspaper reported, "She says other girls have got into the Army and she could not see why she did not."[11]

Indeed, many other girls and women did get into the army, by whatever means necessary. Every single woman in the ranks was a willing volunteer. Their nations neither expected nor desired their military service. To understand why so many women, independently of each other, were moti-

vated to abandon their female identities and to enlist as soldiers, one has
to look no farther than to the reasons men were initially inspired to sign
up. In addition to succumbing to the pervading war fever of the early years
of the conflict, women joined the Civil War military for the very same
reasons as their male counterparts: to be with loved ones, to get away from
home, for the bounties and the pay, for the perceived adventure and romance of war, and because they were patriotic. Unlike male soldiers, however, some women saw disguise as a man and enlistment in the military as
a way to escape the oppressive social restrictions placed on women in that
day and age. Another difference between male and female soldiers was that
the women were under no social or cultural obligation to defend their
country. Men faced public ridicule if they failed to volunteer for military
service, while women risked social disapproval when they did enlist.[12]

A large number of women soldiers joined the army with a husband,
brother, sweetheart, or father, much like some male soldiers whose primary inducement to sign up was a friend or relative. During the Atlanta
campaign, Maj. William Ludlow encountered a wounded Confederate
who explained to her doctor that "she belonged to the Missouri Brigade
. . . had a husband and one or two brothers in one of the regiments, and
followed them to war." All of her relations were killed, and, "having no
home but the regiment," she "took a musket and served in the ranks."[13]

When Mrs. Phillips learned that her husband was very ill at Camp Convalescent in Alexandria, Virginia, she went there to care for him. When it
was time for him to join his regiment, the 140th Pennsylvania Infantry,
she dressed in a uniform and tried to join him at the front, determined to
stay with him for the rest of the war. When John Finnern returned home
from his three-month stint in the 15th Ohio Infantry and decided to reenlist in the 81st Ohio Infantry, his wife Elizabeth decided that he was not
leaving her again, so she signed up with him on September 23, 1861. Similarly, Ivory Brown served in the 1st Maine Infantry for three months in
1861. In 1864, at the age of forty-four, he decided to go back to the army,
and his twenty-six-year-old wife Mary joined him. They enlisted together
in Bangor in the 31st Maine Infantry on October 18, 1864.[14]

Martha Parks Lindley was another woman who did not wish to be left
behind. She followed her husband William to war, serving in the 6th U.S.
Cavalry, Company D, under the unimaginative alias of Jim Smith. Two
days after her husband enlisted, Martha arrived in Pittsburgh wearing his
clothes and was mustered into the regiment on August 12, 1861. She was

described on the muster roll as twenty-seven years old, five feet eight inches tall, with brown eyes, black hair, and a dark complexion. She told the recruiter that her former occupation was soldier. In truth, she was a wife and mother who left her two children in the care of her sister and, despite her husband's pleas, would not return home to them. In a postwar newspaper interview, Martha Lindley expressed her feelings about joining a Union cavalry regiment. "I was frightened half to death," she said, "but I was so anxious to be with my husband that I resolved to see the thing through if it killed me." It did not kill her, and apparently those with whom she served did not detect her fear. Rather, her "comrades . . . never knew that the . . . chap, whom everybody liked so well, was not a handsome boy, but a brave and determined woman who loved her husband so well that she refused to be separated from him." Their fellow soldiers thought that Jim Smith and William Lindley were "chums."[15]

Lucy Thompson Gauss went to war with her husband, Bryant, serving in the 18th North Carolina Infantry from August 1861 until December 1862, when she went home because she was in the advanced stages of pregnancy. At about the same time as Bryant Gauss died of wounds received at the Battle of Fredericksburg, his wife the former soldier gave birth to their daughter. She then returned to the Confederate army to retrieve her husband's body and take it home for burial. Unable to bring home his remains, Gauss went to Richmond and filed a claim for her husband's back pay and enlistment bounty.[16]

Rather than endure separation, honeymooners Martin and Elizabeth Niles enlisted together on September 2, 1862, in the 14th Vermont Infantry and served together for ten months. Mary Burns of Michigan could not bear separation from her lover, so she volunteered to serve in his regiment. An unnamed southern Unionist enlisted with her lover in the 14th Maine Infantry when that regiment was stationed in New Orleans in the summer of 1862, "and did duty until about the close of the war." The fickle Sarah Bradbury, alias Frank Morton, originally volunteered in a Union cavalry unit with her sweetheart. After he was captured, she became enamored of another soldier and stayed in the army. When she found, to her dismay, that the new boyfriend "was not a gentleman," she left the regiment, but was afraid to go home. She ultimately became an orderly in General Sheridan's escort. A woman from Iowa using the alias of Charles H. Williams enlisted because she was in love with a lieutenant. Private

Williams was described as a fine-looking soldier, in good health and with a pleasant disposition.[17]

For women who faced familial disapproval over the men they loved, escaping to the army with their intended seemed like a perfect solution. Mary Owens was still a schoolgirl in Pennsylvania when she eloped with a man her parents did not like. The newlyweds then enlisted in the cavalry. Miss Weisener of Alabama, a planter's daughter, loved E. L. Stone, a struggling lawyer of whom her father did not approve. Stone joined the Confederate army. On the pretext of delivering supplies to the troops, Weisener traveled to Tupelo, Mississippi, where he was stationed, and there the pair were secretly married. She then became a soldier in his regiment.[18]

At least two women preferred death to a long separation from their loved ones. A woman encountered by Sanitary Commission agent Mary Livermore was desperate to stay by the side of a husband. "I have only my husband in all the world," said the young wife to Livermore by way of explaining her enlistment in the 19th Illinois Infantry. The woman's pleas to be retained in the regiment after her discovery were ignored by her captain, and he ordered her escorted out of camp. That evening, she attempted suicide by jumping into the Chicago River. Another young woman, from Jersey City, left home with her lover and briefly served in the Garibaldi Guard. When she was sent home, her loneliness and frustration led her to procure a supply of arsenic. She nearly succeeded in killing herself.[19]

Occasionally a woman enlisted without the knowledge or approval of her husband or sweetheart. Annie Lillybridge joined the 21st Michigan Infantry, in which her fiancé was a lieutenant. She chose a different company from his and did not tell him of her ruse. Nellie Graves and Fannie Wilson, who had lovers in the 24th New Jersey Infantry, also chose different companies than their sweethearts and did not inform them when they enlisted. Mary Galloway joined the Army of the Potomac so she could find the lieutenant she loved. All of the men in her family as well as her beloved were at war, so she thought she might as well join them. Nancy Corbin of Tennessee felt she had little choice but to find her sweetheart in the army, as "her Father had driven her from home because she kept company with Union soldiers." Indeed, Corbin "had been previously seduced by a soldier in Woods Division. So she . . . tried to follow that soldier."[20]

In addition to husbands or lovers, some women soldiered with their brothers, and at least two went to war with their fathers. Melverina Elverina Peppercorn joined the Confederate army in December 1862 with her brother, Alexander the Great, nicknamed Lexy. Rebecca "Georgianna" Peterman went off to war in the fall of 1862 at the age of sixteen. After her discharge from the 7th Wisconsin Infantry, she was questioned about her motives for soldiering. It was reported that "she gives no reason for entering the service other than a desire to see what war was, and to be near her brother and cousin who were in the same regiment. Her cousin induced her to take the step." For two weeks, her stepbrother did not even know that Peterman was in the regiment.[21]

Frances Hook, who used the aliases Frank Miller, Frank Henderson, and Frank Fuller, enlisted in the Union army with her brother shortly after the war began. A native of Chicago, she was about twenty-two years old. Hook and her brother were orphans; their parents died when she was three. The siblings were devoted to one another, and Hook did not want the war to separate them, especially since her brother was her only living relation. Sarah Collins of Wisconsin, another orphan, was a sixteen-year-old schoolgirl when she went to war with her brother Mason. When Jane Perkins was captured by Union forces in the spring of 1864, she told the Yankee authorities that she had originally enlisted in the Confederate army with her brother.[22]

A woman from Ohio served as Pvt. Joseph Davidson and went to war with her father, who was killed at the Battle of Chickamauga. She stayed in the army following his death and served for a total of three years. Margaret Catherine Murphy enlisted with her father in the 98th Ohio Infantry.[23]

Some women not only entered the army by the side of a loved one but left it for the same reason. "This lady dressed in men's clothes, Volunteered, received bounty and . . . did all the duties of a soldier . . . but her husband being discharged, she disclosed the fact, returned the bounty, and was immediately discharged April 20, 1862," reads the service record of Sarah Malinda Blalock, who signed up with her husband Keith in the 26th North Carolina Infantry on March 20, 1862, and then left it with him a month later when he obtained a medical discharge. The twenty-year-old Malinda went into the Confederate army as Sam Blalock because Keith would not join without her. Keith did not particularly want to serve, as he was pro-Union, but volunteering seemed preferable to conscription. His original plan was to desert to Union lines, but that proved more difficult than he imagined. So he rolled around naked in poison oak and thereby received a disability discharge because the rash was so bad that the surgeon could not identify it. Malinda confessed her secret, and they both returned home to the North Carolina mountains.[24]

When Hattie Martin's husband, for whom she had joined the army, "grew unkind towards her," she left and returned home. Frances Day, alias Frank Mayne, enlisted in the 126th Pennsylvania Infantry on August 5, 1862, alongside William Fitzpatrick, whom she loved. Day, eighteen years old, was described by the company clerk as having light eyes, light complexion, and light hair. Fitzpatrick fell ill and died on August 24, just nineteen days after he enlisted. In her grief, Sgt. Frank Mayne deserted the regiment the very same day. Frances Louisa Clayton enlisted with her husband in the fall of 1861. She left the Union army shortly after Mr. Clayton was killed at the Battle of Stones River.[25]

Mary Brown left the 31st Maine Infantry not long after she joined it. Her husband suffered a bad fall on the march to Fort Davis during the Petersburg campaign in the spring of 1864. When he was sent to Harewood Hospital in Washington, D.C., Mary followed in order to nurse him. He was discharged from the hospital on June 1, 1865, and the Browns returned to Maine. Melverina Peppercorn quit the Confederate army when her twin was shot in the leg and sent to a hospital. Peppercorn went with him as his nurse. When Lexy's leg finally healed, he and his sister wanted to return to the army, but it was too late—the war was nearly over.[26]

After the Battle of Bentonville, a Confederate artilleryman recalled the bravery and subsequent discharge of a comrade: "We heard that our faithful warrior was a woman, and none other than the wife of him whose remains she had so heroically borne from the field, having volunteered, it was said, disguised as a man, in an Alabama regiment at the beginning of the second year of the war." Her husband dead and gone, this woman no longer wished to remain in the army, so "she went to the proper authorities, made known her disguise, and was honorably discharged from military service."[27]

Not all women soldiers joined the military by the side of a loved one. Molly Mooney of the 7th Iowa Infantry was a married woman who enlisted independently of her husband. He apparently stayed behind when she went marching off to war.[28] Indeed, some women soldiers joined the army because they were fleeing their families or unbearable life situations.

In the complex case of Confederate soldier Mary Ann Clark, known as

Amy, Annie, or Anna Clark to the press, a husband gone astray was the initial impetus for enlistment. Her mother told a sorrowful tale of an abusive, wayward, and irresponsible husband who left Clark and her two children to fend for themselves while he went to California and married another woman—and then wrote home to tell of it. After procuring a divorce and reassuming her maiden name of Clark, Mary Ann heard again from her former husband, who wrote to inform her that he would be returning to Kentucky with his new bride. Clark's mother wrote that "a dark gloom appeared to hang over her which seemed to thicken and grow more and more lowering. . . . She often spoke of going into the army yet strange it never occurred to me that she would really make the attempt. She left home in Oct 61 in the night and the first news we obtained of her was that she had actually joined the army, she had united with a cavalry company under the assumed name of Henry Clark."[29]

Clark's first enlistment lasted until February 1862, when she returned home and seemed to take up her old life where she had left off. Another family tragedy occurred in May, when her beloved brother-in-law, a southern sympathizer, was murdered by a pro-Union mob. "She became despondent and declared her intention of leaving the county forever," explained her mother. Clark left her daughter in a convent and her son in the custody of a priest, and her family heard nothing more from her from the night she disappeared in June 1862 until late in the year, when friends passed on a letter from soldier Clark outlining her wounding, capture, and impending prisoner exchange. For this female soldier, it appears that the army was a place of refuge from trouble and turmoil in her home life.[30]

Like Mary Ann Clark, there were other females in the military who were apparently fleeing less-than-ideal home situations. A twelve-year-old girl using the alias Charles Martin ran away from her parents to become a drummer boy. Lizzie Compton was another fugitive from some unknown domestic or life crisis. Compton was discovered in the Union army seven times during the war years, and each time gave conflicting stories about her motives for joining the army. At one point, she said she was an orphan from Tennessee, fleeing her secessionist guardians. She also claimed to be a Canadian and promised to return to her parents' home in the north. Later she told comrades that she was from Pennsylvania. Whatever Compton's true background, she clearly did not want anyone to find out.[31]

A nineteen-year-old from Brooklyn named Emily was yet another woman fleeing her family. She informed her parents that she wished to enlist, believing that she was the next Joan of Arc. Her family feared that she suffered hallucinations, so they sent her to an aunt in Michigan, hoping a change of scenery would change her mind. Instead, Emily escaped her aunt and enlisted in a Michigan regiment. In contrast, Ida Bruce only joined the army when she lost her family. A Unionist who lived in Atlanta, she joined the 7th Ohio Cavalry upon the death of her parents.[32]

A small number of women soldiers used the army as a means to escape prostitution. When the orphaned and self-educated Marian McKenzie volunteered for the 23rd Kentucky Infantry (U.S.) on October 4, 1861, she stated that she had previously been employed as a clerk, and when she was discovered to be a woman and sent to the provost marshal on December 20, 1862, she said that she had enlisted for love of adventure. What she did not reveal was that she had supported herself by working as an actress and a prostitute prior to the war. Harriet Merrill joined the 59th New York Infantry as a means of leaving the house of ill repute where she was living. She wanted to "dress and go as a soldier," and indeed she did. After two months in the regiment, she swore under oath that she "performed all the duties that the rest of the soldiers did."[33]

V. A. White is another example of a prostitute seeking redemption in the army. She left her home, "that cursed place," apparently after having a daughter out of wedlock. She made her way to Nashville and became a prostitute at 154 College Street, one of the fancier bordellos. As she later explained to a friend, "I was so downhearted that I did not care what became of me, and I know that a great many believe me to be guilty so I thought I would go where I could wear the game as well as have the name." She wore the game well, bragging, "I made money, lots of it, and lived in splendor." But the money obviously came at too high a personal cost. After four months, White decided to leave. She later wrote: "I tired and worried of that life, so I began to study how to get out of it. And at last I made up my mind to join some northern troops that was expecting to go home soon, so I pitched in as was always my way of doing. . . . I bought me a suit of blues and had my hair cut short and then made for headquarters and was sworn in as a soldier of the 1st Michigan Regiment Mechanics, Co. D you bet it felt in spots but went ahead soldiering."[34]

For poor, working-class, and farm women, bounties and pay were an important inducement to sign up. In her first letter from the army to her family in Afton, New York, Sarah Rosetta Wakeman, alias Pvt. Lyons Wakeman, boasted, "They wanted I should enlist and so I did. I got 100 and 52$ in money." Wakeman instructed her family to spend the money she forwarded on themselves; "I can get all the money I want," she wrote, referring no doubt to her handsome monthly salary of $13 plus room and board earned as a private in the Union army. At the age of nineteen, Wakeman enlisted in the 153rd New York Infantry on August 30, 1862, claiming that she was twenty-one. Recruiters described her as five feet tall with blue eyes, brown hair, and a fair complexion. She did not tell them that prior to the war, in her female identity, she had worked as a domestic.[35]

Domestic work provided some of the few respectable occupations commonly open to working class women of the time, such as cook, laundress, and chambermaid. Pay for such positions did not compare well to jobs traditionally open only to men. So it is not surprising that Wakeman and women like her found the bounties and pay offered to a soldier a compelling temptation to abandon their skirts and don uniforms. Although Charles H. Williams originally enlisted for love, she was not unconcerned about money. After she was discovered to be a woman and subsequently dismissed from the service, she was very disappointed that authorities would not let her return to her regiment long enough to draw pay for her three months of service.[36]

Although the majority of women soldiers, North and South, came from working-class, farming, immigrant, or frontier backgrounds and affluent, middle-class, and southern plantation women did not often "go for a soldier," there were exceptions, such as Confederate Mary Ann Clark. The daughter of a minister, she was college educated and her family was well-to-do. She was said to be well informed on politics and literature. On the Union side, runaway Charles Martin also possessed a fine education. The "beautiful, intelligent, accomplished, and refined" Frank Martin was educated in a convent from the age of twelve until she left to join the war at nineteen. A young woman in the 66th Indiana Infantry was from "a respectable family," and the press could not fathom why she enlisted. A Detroit newspaper noted that the parents of Mary Jane G. of Trenton, Michigan, were "estimable members of society."[37] The paper did not publish Mary Jane's surname, probably to avoid embarrassing her parents.

But Rosetta Wakeman, a yeoman farm girl with a minimum of formal education, was a far more typical Civil War soldier with regard to her socioeconomic status. Sarah Edmonds was also a hardworking farm girl, but unlike Wakeman, she had the benefit of a good public education. Twenty-

seven-year-old Miss Martin of Cincinnati was said to possess "a fair education" though she had worked as a cook and a domestic prior to the war.
Jane Perkins was obviously an educated woman, because prior to the war
she was a teacher in Virginia.[38]

Lizzie Compton, on the other hand, was unschooled and also lacking
in any religious instruction, which was unusual in the mid-nineteenth century. Melverina Peppercorn hailed from the Tennessee mountains. Hers
was a poor family of subsistence farmers, and she was probably illiterate.
Lucy Gauss was definitely illiterate, as was Elizabeth Finnern. Like many
Civil War soldiers, Finnern and her husband were immigrants, having
come to the United States from Germany. Martha Lindley and Albert
Cashier were both Irish immigrants.[39]

Regardless of their backgrounds, many women enjoyed the adventure
and the freedom that being away from home and being in the army af-
forded them. This spirit of adventure was yet another common motivation
for Civil War soldiers, both male and female. "I am as independent as a
hog on the ice," Rosetta Wakeman wrote. The young Sophia Cryder was
said to be "a girl of unblemished reputation"; however, she "did not, as
generally happens in such cases, enlist to be near the object of her af-
fections, but merely in a wild spirit of adventure," reported the Harrisburg
Patriot and Union. Jane Short, alias Charley Davis, enlisted in a Missouri
Union infantry regiment because she was "pining for the excitement of
glorious war." Rebecca "Georgianna" Peterman went to war with her relatives, but being with them was not her only motive. A country girl from
Ellenboro, Wisconsin, she was always known as an adventurous soul. Indeed, Peterman's former schoolteacher said that "plain country life was
not enough for her ambition."[40]

The passions and whims that propelled so many adventurous young
men into Civil War armies likewise motivated many women to seek the
excitement promised by the wartime military. Loreta Velazquez cited multiple reasons for joining the Confederate army, chief among them the passion to do something exciting. "I plunged into adventure for the love of
the thing," she recalled after the war. When questioned about her reasons
for enlisting in the 2nd Iowa Infantry, Nellie Williams replied that she
volunteered merely to be a soldier, adding that she liked the life. Sarah
Edmonds confessed that she was naturally adventurous, ambitious, and romantic. She said that the privations and danger of life in the army were
thrilling and stoked her spirit of adventure. Albert Cashier explained after

the war that the country needed men and she wanted excitement. As she was already living as a man, she thought she would try her luck in the army.[41]

Like Albert Cashier, a small number of women were living as men prior to the war and thus were subject to the same peer pressure felt by their male counterparts to sign up for "three years or the duration." Their motivations for enlisting might well have approximated the common concern among male inductees to prove or reaffirm their manhood by performing their masculine duty to defend and protect their country—only in the case of women passing as men, their fear of being revealed as something other than men if they did not "ante up and pitch in" was quite real. For example, Rosetta Wakeman left her job as a domestic, dressed as a man, and obtained work as a coal handler on a Chenango Canal boat. At the end of the first trip, she and her coworkers encountered Union army recruiters. Encouragement from those colleagues may have been an added incentive when Wakeman enlisted and received her handsome local and state bounties. In any event, when Wakeman told the recruiters that her peacetime occupation was boatman, she was telling the truth. Katie Hanson was another woman living as a man prior to the war. Always noted for her "predilection for masculine ways"—probably a tomboy or independent thinker in modern parlance—she left home and, disguising herself as a man, found work on a Great Lakes steamboat. Because she was "an expert rifle woman," she joined an Ohio regiment in 1861.[42]

The women who passed as men prior to the war were largely motivated to adopt male identities because of their legal, social, and economic status. Society placed so many restrictions on women that for those who found themselves to be "redundant," that is, unmarried and childless, life tended to be quite difficult. Because working- and lower-class women had few appealing options outside of marriage, these were the women who were most likely to pass as men in the antebellum period. By simply changing a set of clothes, changing a name, changing a hairstyle, and adopting a male alias, many women found that they could easily bypass all of society's barriers to creating a decent, comfortable, and independent lifestyle for themselves. Albert Cashier worked as a laborer, farmhand, and shepherd prior to enlisting in the Union army. She found that "in herding sheep it was better to have the male attire and as she was following that occupation . . . she kept that attire." Rosetta Wakeman earned more money with which to support herself and to help her indebted family while working as a boatman and serving in the army than she ever had while toiling as a domestic. Sarah Edmonds escaped an unwanted marriage and a misogynistic and domineering father by taking on a male identity and going to work as a Bible salesman prior to the war. Edmonds frankly declared that she loved her independence and hated male tyranny. She achieved the former, and fled the latter, by becoming a man in the eyes of the public.[43]

The women living as men prior to the war were seeking economic opportunities and social privileges that were otherwise unobtainable. When they took a male social identity, they also took male power and male independence. The women who had never passed as men until they joined the military soon realized that they could do many things in their male persona that were denied to them as women. One of these was voting. While in the service, Martha Lindley, as Pvt. Jim Smith, voted for Lincoln in the 1864 election.[44] No doubt other women soldiers also reveled in casting a ballot for the first time (and for many, the last).

Patriotism and devotion to country and cause were, of course, also major motivating factors for women soldiers. For southern women, patriotism meant protecting their homeland from the invading Union armies, and it meant fighting for their independence from the United States. Pvt. John Thompson showed the ultimate patriotism: She enlisted on May 28, 1861, and served in the 1st Kentucky Infantry (U.S.) for two months before arousing suspicion at Ravenswood, Virginia, where she was found to be not only a woman, but also a Confederate spy. Her commitment to the southern cause was so strong that she faced the consequences of her act with great calm, telling her captors that "she knew full well that the penalty for being a spy was death, and that she [was] ready whenever they wish[ed] to shoot her."[45]

Whatever her initial motivation for joining the Confederate army, Mary Ann Clark boasted of being "a good rebel soldier" and indeed must have been, as she was eventually promoted into the officer ranks. Loreta Velazquez said that in addition to craving adventure, she also went to war because she truly believed in the cause of southern independence. Mary Ann Pitman, alias Lieutenant Rawley, CSA, volunteered when the war broke out for the very same reason. "I thought I ought to help defend my country," she explained, adding that, since she was the "only one in the family that is living," there was no one to stop her. "I started out with the most intense feelings of prejudice against the Northern people," she flatly stated.[46]

For northern women, patriotism meant fighting to preserve the Union. Indeed, patriotism is a common theme in the army memoirs of Sarah Edmonds, who was thankful that she was "permitted in this hour of my adopted country's need to express a tithe of the gratitude which I feel toward the people of the Northern States." Even though she enlisted as much for the adventure as for her feelings of patriotism toward a country to which she had only recently emigrated, in her later years Edmonds remembered the war as "a time for entire self-sacrifice, entire self-forgetfulness" in subordination to preserving the Union. She felt that she "could best serve the interests of the Union cause in male attire."[47]

In addition to being a patriot, Mary Brown was a staunch abolitionist. She fought, she said in a postwar newspaper interview, because "slavery was an awful thing, and we were determined to fight it down." Lou Morris, who enlisted with Jane Short, said she volunteered for patriotic reasons. When they were turned out of their regiment, Morris vowed to enlist in another if she got the chance. The girl known only as Charles Norton in the 141st Pennsylvania Infantry "said she was deeply interested in the war, and desired to serve her country in some way, and was obliged to assume the disguise she adopted in order to carry out her plans."[48]

Many women soldiers claimed that the sole reason they served was either devotion to their nation's cause, or devotion to a man. They rarely admitted to a need for either excitement or money. With the ideal of domesticity reigning in American culture, women soldiers shrewdly downplayed their new independent identities as men and instead stressed their patriotism and wifely devotion as explanations for their flight from confining Victorian womanhood and rejection of home and hearth. Lizzie Cook was unusual in that she readily admitted to the *Missouri Democrat* that her "strong impulse to shoulder a musket" was due in large part to her being tired of the "monotony of a woman's life."[49]

Women soldiers did not, however, feel any need to hide their thirst for vengeance. In fact, revenge was another motive for joining Union or Confederate armies. In the summer of 1861, Charlotte Hope of Fairfax County, Virginia, disguised herself as a man and joined the 1st Virginia Cavalry (CSA) under the alias Charlie Hopper. She volunteered just a few days after her lieutenant fiancé was killed in a raid, for the sole purpose of avenging his death. Her goal was to kill twenty-one Yankees—one for every year of her dead lieutenant's life. Hope refused to be a regularly enlisted dragoon. A comrade later remembered that "he explained that if he enlisted he would be a man under pay. And he didn't want pay, he said, for the work he wanted to do."[50]

Mary Smith, who briefly served in the 41st Ohio Infantry, was "full of patriotism, pluck, and aged about twenty-two years," but her compelling reason for volunteering was the death of her only brother at the Battle of First Bull Run. Similarly, a Confederate recruit discovered in Raleigh, North Carolina, was determined to avenge the death of her brother who died in the Seven Days' Battles near Richmond. Miss Martin of Cincinnati repeatedly tried to enlist in order to avenge three of her brothers, all killed in the war.[51]

The themes of patriotism, love, and adventure may well have been planted in some women soldiers years before the Civil War. The romantic prototype of the Female Warrior Bold was introduced to Sarah Emma Edmonds as a child, when she read the fictional adventure novel *Fanny Campbell, The Female Pirate Captain: A Tale of the Revolution!* That story inspired her to dress as a man in order to escape her overbearing father and his plans to marry her off to an older man. According to Edmonds' biographer, "there was only one drawback to the . . . book in young Emma's mind: the heroine did not masquerade as a man to escape the limitations of her sex, but did so in order to rescue an imprisoned lover." Ironically, although Edmonds may not have recognized it, her wish to escape her father's authority and influence conformed to the romantic ideal of the Female Warrior motif.[52]

The flamboyant Loreta Velazquez also read about martial heroines as a child and dreamed of one day emulating the female warriors in her history books. After mentioning in her memoirs the Spanish lieutenant-nun Catalina de Erauso, Molly Pitcher of the Revolution, the Maid of Saragossa who inspired Palafox and his men to resist the French in 1808, and the Polish heroine Appolonia Jagiello, who disguised herself as a man to take part in the 1846 Cracow insurrection, Velazquez boldly settled on no less than Joan of Arc as her personal role model and inspiration, even though the high-spirited secessionist hardly patterned her wartime activities after the French saint. Velazquez reminded her postwar readers that the memory of Joan of Arc's "glorious deeds as a great-hearted patriot" remained "an example of what a woman may do if she only dares, and dares to do greatly."[53] Who knows how many other women soldiers of the Civil War were inspired to enlist by popular novels of female warriors, by folk ballads sung to them as children, or by stories of Joan of Arc and other real-life martial women?

Regardless of women's initial motivation for mustering in, once they became members of the military family that was their company or regiment, most remained in service and endured its hardships for reasons of duty to country and commitment to comrades. In this respect, women soldiers were just like the men with whom they served. Although she was prompted to sign up by the bounties and pay that would help her family emerge from debt, Rosetta Wakeman was soon anxious to take on the rebels, and she was soon complaining about the Copperheads, wishing that some of them would "Come down here and get killed. It would do me good to see it done." Indeed, throughout her army career, Wakeman showed a simple determination to perform honorably the duty required of a soldier. "I like to be a soldier very well," she wrote home.[54]

Lizzie Compton said she was not afraid to die, and she refused to wear anything but Uncle Sam's standard issue until the war was over. Frances Day, alias Sgt. Frank Mayne, deserted the 126th Pennsylvania Infantry upon the death of her sweetheart, but her sense of duty soon lured her to volunteer for service in another regiment. Sallie Curtis was anxious to "go for the war" after serving in the Federal army for about twenty months. Even though Sarah Bradbury, alias Pvt. Frank Morton, was drawn into the army by love for one man and remained for the love of another, she nevertheless felt that she was a "good and faithful" soldier, and even held hopes of earning a promotion.[55]

Indeed, women who joined with husbands, brothers, fathers, or boyfriends often soldiered on despite the death or illness of their loved one. Martha Lindley served her entire enlistment in the 6th U.S. Cavalry despite the fact that her husband was sent to Emory Hospital in Washington, D.C., in October 1862, only a year and two months into his service, after he accidentally shot himself in the ankle. He remained a convalescent in the hospital for months. Even though Martha Lindley originally joined the service to be with her husband, she nevertheless stayed with the regiment when he left and was honorably mustered out with the rest of her company in August 1864 upon the expiration of the term of enlistment. William Lindley later joined the 6th Ohio Cavalry and served in that regiment until July 1865. Martha must have had enough of war, for she did not join him in his second regiment, preferring finally to go home to their children.[56]

Confederate "Captain Billy," as her company called her, not only stayed in the service, but was promoted from lieutenant after her captain husband was killed. Mary Owens, the bride who went to war with her husband, stayed in her regiment for eighteen months despite the fact that her husband was killed by her side in their first battle. Yet another young wife, Florena Budwin of Philadelphia, was captured with her husband and sent to Andersonville Prison. She did not reveal her sex, even after her husband was killed by a prison guard, and even though such a revelation might have freed her or at least gained her improved living conditions within the camp. Instead, Budwin chose to endure the horrible conditions with her fellow prisoners of war.[57]

Frances Hook and her brother originally enlisted in a three-month regiment, during which time he was killed in action at the Battle of Shiloh. In the face of this loss, Hook reenlisted in another regiment, serving until she was captured by Confederates. The army had become her home, and she wished for no other. Rebecca "Georgianna" Peterman did have a home to go back to, but even after her stepbrother died of apoplexy in 1862, she stayed in the 7th Wisconsin Infantry for nearly two more years.[58]

Commitment to their beliefs and a desire to serve honorably at the sides of their comrades until the end of their enlistments was as strong in women soldiers as it was in the men who served the Union and the Confederacy. Sarah Edmonds eloquently summed up what many of the women soldiers must have felt: "I could only thank God that I was free and could go forward and work, and I was not obliged to stay at home and weep."[59]

3

"A FINE LOOKING SOLDIER"
Life in the Ranks

Women who wanted to be soldiers found that it was fairly easy to gain entrance into the military. Once they were assimilated into their regiments, they proved to be effective and willing combatants. Yet the notion of a woman maintaining a male persona in the army for any length of time seems incredible, if not impossible, and obvious questions arise as to how nineteenth-century women managed to pass as men for months and even years, while simultaneously performing the difficult and dangerous job of soldiering.

While there were many aspects of Victorian society and mid-nineteenth-century military life that aided their masquerade, women who wished to "go for a soldier" in the Civil War did face significant barriers. Not only did they have to make the transition from civilian to soldier, but they also had to recast themselves from female to male identities. Success as a soldier depended on adopting a radically different masculine persona, learning how to do the job, and forging crucial bonds with their fellow soldiers. If a woman could not make these transitions, then she risked failure, exposure, and most likely expulsion from her regiment.

Though many women successfully reinvented themselves not only as soldiers but as "men," others were unable to sustain their masculine fictions beyond a few days or months in camp. Living in camp was both a boon and a bane to women soldiers. Days were filled with drills, instruction, arms practice, and the business of becoming soldiers, and it was in camp that many women soldiers also learned to act like men, by observing and emulating the behaviors of the males around them. But camp life held its perils, particularly when regiments bunked in barracks rather than tents. Barracks life was more closely packed and monitored than in the more commonly found open-air tent city camps of the Civil War armies. Close quarters bred familiarity, and for those women who had yet to perfect their disguise, familiarity sometimes led to discovery and dismissal. But the fact that Civil War armies for the most part did not live in barracks, but rather in tent cities or temporary winter quarters out-of-doors, contributed to women soldiers' ability to avoid detection while they attended to the necessary sanitary matters of menstruation, urination, and bowel movements.

Most likely women sought out private areas away from camp to attend to these necessities. Latrines or company sinks were often long, open trenches only sometimes supplied with a pole or wooden planks for seats. These sinks were disgusting and filthy affairs, often located in such a way that they promoted disease and sickness in camp. Women soldiers undoubtedly answered the call of nature by heading to the woods or some other private place, and this behavior probably did not arouse suspicion because so many other soldiers avoided the sinks in the same way. For women in regiments on the march or actively engaged in combat, sanitary issues would have been much easier to cope with. Armies in the field rarely stopped to dig company sinks.[1]

Very little is known about how nineteenth-century women dealt with their monthly cycles. It was not a subject that literate women wrote about in their diaries or letters. Presumably, women used cotton rags to swath themselves and protect their clothing. Washing or disposing of this evidence may have been a problem for women soldiers. Perhaps the bloody rags were explained away as the used bindings of a minor injury. Menstruation might also have ceased to be a problem for women soldiers, particularly during the campaign season. It is entirely possible that many female soldiers became amenorrheic while in the army. Amenorrhea, or the cessation of menstruation, is caused by intense athletic training, substantive weight loss, caloric deprivation or poor nutrition, and severe psychological stress. Civil War soldiers encountered all of these, and their physical endurance was pushed to the limits. On campaign, they sometimes marched up to thirty miles a day. The poor, inadequate, and often sporadic diet of soldiers on both sides of the conflict is well known. In addition to the hardships of campaigning, the debilitating diet, and the general psychological stress of maintaining a male disguise, the horrors of battle surely produced tremendous anxiety and strain. Twice as many Civil War soldiers died from disease as from wounds received in battle. Soldiers lived under the constant threat of death or disfigurement whether or not their regiment saw combat, and chronic stress was a fact of life for the average soldier.[2]

A woman soldier who became amenorrheic simply faced one less worry in maintaining her male disguise. That left the twin problems of bathing and changing clothes. These were not daily concerns, however. Soldiers, especially those on the march, often went for months at a time without a change of clothes. They bathed just as infrequently. When three women combatants arrived in Cairo, Illinois, in January 1863, among thirty or forty other Confederate prisoners, it was noted that they were "unwashed like the others."[3]

Women soldiers who sought privacy to change clothes or bathe would not have aroused a great deal of suspicion, especially since they had already established reputations as modest men when they daily found private toilet areas. Sgt. Herman Weiss, 6th New York Heavy Artillery, explained to his wife how a woman in his regiment had maintained her male persona for close to three years: "It is no wonder at all that her tent mates did not know that she was a woman for you must know that we never undress to go to bed. [O]n the contrary we dress up, we go to bed with boots, overcoat and all on and she could find chances enough when she would be in the tent alone to change her clothes."[4]

After the war, comrades of Jennie Hodgers, alias Pvt. Albert D. J. Cashier of the 95th Illinois Infantry, stated that no one ever saw her naked. They remembered that she had a bunk mate, even though she did not particularly want one. Cashier was never discovered to be a woman while in the army, presumably in large part because soldiers spent the majority of their time outdoors with a wide latitude to seek out privacy. If Cashier's case was typical, the inherent challenges of personal hygiene would seem to have been easily met by most of the women in the ranks.[5]

A tougher challenge for women soldiers was looking like men. Cutting their hair and putting on male clothing may have ensured success at enlistment, but women came under closer scrutiny, particularly by their comrades, after they joined their regiments. Strict Victorian adherence to differences in male and female attire assisted women in their disguise, however, because so few people knew what women might look like in pants. Indeed, in the 1860s, clothing was the most potent public indication of gender. Even so, women still had to hide their feminine figures, and in this they were unintentionally aided by their armies. The uniforms issued to enlisted men, both Union and Confederate, were cut quite loose and did not fit well. As Sergeant Weiss explained to his wife, "Soldier clothes dont fit very snug to the body."[6]

Loreta Velazquez, alias Lt. Harry T. Buford, CSA, possessed the wealth and resources to have uniforms tailored just for her. She wore six wire net shields under her uniform to make her form bulkier and wider in the shoulders. Chest and shoulder straps held the shields in place under a silk undershirt. For added effect she sometimes wore a false moustache.[7] Since most of the women soldiers did not come from a monied background, they lacked the resources to go to such lengths. Some waist padding and breast binding coupled with ill-fitting army clothes was usually enough to conceal even the shapeliest of women.

Some women seemed to have an easier time passing for men than others. A woman known only as Kate, the girlfriend of one of the lieutenants in the 116th Illinois Infantry, was adept at her disguise. As a fellow private noted in a letter home, "You could hardly tell her from a man. I did not notice her till in camp . . . and then I would not [have] if some one had not showed her to me." Private Cashier was badly pock marked on her face, which rendered her appearance less soft and feminine. A woman who served in the 1st Kansas Infantry under the alias Alfred J. Luther was described posthumously as a large individual with masculine features. Confederate soldier Melverina Elverina Peppercorn was a tall, big-boned girl of sixteen. Mary W. Dennis of Minnesota was over six feet tall. Frances Louisa Clayton, who served with a Union regiment from Missouri, was described as a "very tall, masculine looking woman bronzed by exposure."[8]

Ella Reno, a niece of Brig. Gen. Jesse Reno, served in both the 5th Kentucky Cavalry (U.S.) and the 8th Michigan Infantry. Gen. Philip Sheridan described her as coarse and masculine, with large features. "She would readily have passed as a man," he recalled after the war. Capt. Daniel Reed Larned, secretary to Gen. Ambrose Burnside, said Reno was of average size, with a brown face and short, "army fashion" hair. His opinion of Reno's looks, however, was different from Sheridan's. After meeting her in May 1863, he wrote that Reno was "not a bad looking woman; how she ever passed for a man I can't see."[9]

Of course, beauty is always in the eye of the beholder. Maj. Joseph Darr, provost marshal in Wheeling, West Virginia, said that Marian McKenzie was "coarse-looking" and "very short and very thick." The Cincinnati *Daily Commercial,* on the other hand, said that the twenty-year-old McKenzie was "quite good looking, over the medium height, and [had] fine blue eyes with rich, dark auburn hair." The article added that McKenzie was "esteemed for her uniform good nature and kindness of heart."[10]

But a popular misconception about women soldiers is that, because they passed as men, they all must have been ugly or excessively masculine in appearance. Some probably were. When Mary Ann Pitman, alias Molly Hays, alias Lieutenant Rawley, CSA, arrived at Alton Military Prison on November 1, 1864, another prisoner said she "was a very hard case." Later that month, the same prisoner got a better look at her, and wrote that "she was still arrayed in masculine attire. Her features are coarse . . . hands and feet small. She has rather a masculine appearance, and is by no means a pleasing object to look upon." A newspaper reporter opined that Molly Mooney of the 7th Iowa Infantry "would scarcely be admired in feminine dress."[11]

The stereotype of the unattractive woman soldier was not universally accurate, however. Loreta Velazquez was said to be beautiful in her youth. The woman who served as Frank Martin in Michigan and Tennessee regiments was deemed "pretty" by the popular press, owing to her blue eyes, auburn hair, and fair complexion. The press also declared that Martin was amiable, patriotic, and determined. General Sheridan, who thought that Ella Reno was coarse, had a different opinion of Reno's friend Sarah Bradbury, alias Frank Morton, whom he described as rather prepossessing. Although she was "necessarily bronzed and hardened by exposure," Sheridan believed that she was so "comely" that passing for a man must have been difficult for her.[12]

A woman's looks either helped or hindered her male masquerade, and there was little she could do about her appearance beyond concealing obvious female physical attributes. A high-pitched voice and lack of facial hair, however, could not be concealed. An officer in the 59th New York Infantry testified that although Harriet Merrill looked just a like a male in her uniform, she possessed a "voice a little strange for a man's." Fortunately for women soldiers, the presence of adolescent boys in the ranks of the Civil War armies provided camouflage for the likewise beardless and high-voiced females. Women unable to pass for full-grown men easily

played the part of pubescent boys or young men just emerging from ado-
lescence. While the official minimum age of service was eighteen for both
the Union and Confederate armies until 1864, when the Confederacy
dropped its conscription age to seventeen, younger boys routinely lied
about their age in order to enlist, and there was no official minimum age
for drum and bugle boys in the Union army until 1864, when it was set at
sixteen. Despite such regulations, thousands of boys aged sixteen and
under served in the armies.[13]

Women in the ranks were routinely described as having a boyish appearance. Two girls from Maryland who were about sixteen and eighteen
years old, respectively, and had enlisted with their boyfriends were discovered at Culpepper Courthouse in the summer of 1862, having done duty
on the ammunition train and in the Signal Corps. When they were exposed as females, comrades remarked that they "really resembled two fine
looking boys." An unidentified drummer boy who was wounded at Gettysburg was not the "lad of fifteen" he appeared to be, but a girl of eighteen
who refused to give her real name or any other personal information. One
newspaper reported that "She wore a neat suit of soldier-clothes, and
made a pretty boy." Two women sent to the Washington, D.C., provost
marshal in 1861 were described as "boyish-looking." A Secret Service
agent who interviewed them remarked that "the deception was perfect."[14]

Lou Morris, alias William Morris, who served in two Missouri Union
regiments, was described as good-looking, sprightly, and active, present-
ing "the appearance of a hardy boy of eighteen." Jane Short, alias Charley
Davis, who enlisted with Lou, was tanned, "thick-set," and in her uniform
looked "much like an unsophisticated country lad of twenty years."
Frances Hook possessed heavy features, high cheekbones, and abundant,
close-cropped black hair. Although she was in her twenties, in her uniform
she looked just like a beardless boy. Similarly, Malinda Blalock, aged
twenty at her enlistment, served one month in the 26th North Carolina
Infantry as Sam Blalock, during which time her compatriots viewed her as
just another boy, albeit an attractive one. Only when the regiment learned
that Blalock was a woman did they understand why she never went swim-
ming with the others.[15]

Lizzie Compton, who was a little over five feet tall, stoutly built, and
fair complexioned, resembled "a rosy boy of fifteen." Another observer
said that Compton "appeared to be a boy still in school." Still another contemporary vowed that the "slight" soldier was no more than seventeen

years old. He was correct. Compton first enlisted in the Union army at the age of fourteen and was still a minor when the war ended. Charlotte Hope, who passed as Charlie Hopper in the 1st Virginia Cavalry (CSA), appeared to her comrades to be a boy about sixteen years of age.[16]

One newspaper article related that Rebecca "Georgianna" Peterman was "rather slenderly formed, but with somewhat masculine features, though with a very small and delicate hand. In walk and carriage she has every appearance of a boy." Another reported that "in her soldier's clothes [she] has the appearance of a rather good looking boy of sixteen. She is of medium height, with dark eyes and hair. . . . She is very quiet." Yet another article about Peterman declared that "all who have seen this military specimen . . . agree that she is unusually good looking." Peterman's former schoolteacher even chimed in with his opinion of her masquerade, noting, "I remember seeing her in her uniform—she was a fine looking soldier in fact looked better as a soldier than as a girl." Indeed, Peterman so looked like a soldier that no one in her regiment, other than her cousin and step-brother, ever suspected her sex over the course of several years.[17]

Fannie Wilson served in the 3rd Illinois Cavalry, was nineteen years old, "of a masculine voice," and described as tanned and smart and "somewhat educated." She was "easily able to pass herself off for a boy of about seventeen or eighteen." Similarly, Pvt. John Thompson of the 1st Kentucky Infantry (U.S.), whose real name is unknown, "looked as manly as most boys at eighteen." Thompson feared that her lack of an Adams apple might give her away, so she always kept her coat buttoned to the chin.[18]

Pvt. Albert Cashier had a similar worry, because she, too, always kept her shirt buttoned to the collar regardless of the weather. She hid the fact that she had no Adam's apple, but she could not hide the fact that she had no beard or other facial hair. Her fellow soldiers often remarked upon it. Additionally, Cashier carried the distinction of being the smallest soldier in her company. Nevertheless, Cashier was viewed by her fellow soldiers and commanding officers as "a short well built man." With her light complexion, blue eyes, and auburn hair, she resembled the many other Irish-Americans who served in the Union army.[19]

After the war, comrades of Sarah Edmonds, alias Pvt. Franklin Thompson of the 2nd Michigan Infantry, testified that although she was an effeminate-looking soldier, she had concealed her sex admirably. Twenty years after Edmonds left the Union army, Gen. Orlando M. Poe, for whom Franklin Thompson acted as orderly during the Battle of Fredericksburg, asserted that during the war no one suspected that Thompson might be a woman. Maj. Byron Cutcheon of the 20th Michigan Infantry disagreed, saying that some of the soldiers did suspect that Thompson might be a woman, but the matter was not publicly discussed. Cutcheon also stated that to most observers, Thompson looked like a "small and delicate appearing boy of apparently eighteen years of age." It is a credit to Edmonds' masquerade that when she accidentally met with a fellow Canadian who was serving as a lieutenant in the Union army, and whom she had known from childhood, he did not recognize her.[20]

Successful women soldiers were perceived as modest boys or shy young men because their voices were higher pitched, because they lacked beards or mustaches, and because they were particularly retiring about personal matters and bodily functions. Other women made their deceptions more perfect by engaging in activities that were considered distinctly unfeminine and reserved mainly to the masculine realm in the nineteenth century. These women took up drinking, tobacco, cursing, gambling, fighting, and other bad but primarily male habits. Because many women who entered the army hailed from working-class or farming backgrounds, they may have been acquainted with some of these activities prior to the war. Even so, any woman who could hold her liquor or hold her own at the card table enhanced her chances of being taken for a man.

Some women soldiers seemed to enjoy these pleasures and for perhaps the first time in their lives were able to engage in them without social censure. Frances Clayton took up all the manly vices. To better conceal her sex, she learned to drink, smoke, chew, and swear. She was especially fond of cigars. She even gambled, and a fellow soldier declared that he had played poker with her on a number of occasions. An unnamed Confederate woman who served in the Army of Tennessee was turned out of her Louisiana regiment "for her bad and immoral conduct." It is unclear exactly what constituted "immoral conduct," but when sent to the guardhouse, a sergeant noted that "she and the other prisoners play[ed] cards together just as if she was another man."[21]

In August 1861, Nellie Williams, who claimed to be a soldier in the 2nd Iowa Infantry, was arrested in Louisville "unhappily under the influence of liquor." She was described as having black eyes, short black hair, and "features very feminine indeed, and a woman's voice beyond all question." A woman called Canadian Lou also betrayed herself while intoxicated. Coming off a march with her Missouri regiment, she apparently decided to unwind a bit in Memphis. Jailed for public drunkenness, she was recognized as a woman because she had previously lived in the city. A "wretched looking woman" in male attire was arrested while drunk in St. Louis in October 1861. Having served in a three-month regiment at Cairo, she had been discharged two months prior to her arrest. She told the police that she "got hard up, and being friendless and homeless and destitute, took to drink." In April 1863, Margaret Catherine Murphy of the 98th Ohio Infantry was also discovered to be a woman while she was inebriated. Loreta Velazquez, on the other hand, established a reputation for temperance when she was serving as Lieutenant Buford. She was afraid that if she drank, she might reveal her true identity while under the influence.[22] Her fear was clearly justified.

Elvira Ibecker, alias Charles Fuller of the 46th Pennsylvania Infantry, not only drank whiskey but also chewed tobacco. Confederate "Captain Billy" kept a tobacco bag tied on a button of her coat. Melverina Peppercorn likewise chewed tobacco and could spit ten feet. Loreta Velazquez learned to smoke cigars while in the Confederate army. Martha Parks Lindley smoked a clay pipe, as did Mary Brown, who had smoked since the age of eleven.[23]

Some women soldiers brawled with their messmates when necessary. In January 1864, Rosetta Wakeman got into a fight with another private in her regiment. Wakeman proudly wrote home that "Stephen Wiley pitched on me and I give him three or four pretty good cracks and he put downstairs with him Self." Even though Wiley was seven inches taller than Wakeman, he was clearly no match for her.[24]

Not only did female soldiers sometimes fight, but they cursed, too. Ella Reno was jailed for two weeks as punishment for verbally insulting a superior. In colorful language, she told him that he was not loyal, that he did not deserve his stripes and commission, and she suggested that he go home. The three Confederate women prisoners in Cairo were described as "reckless and profane with their profane and vulgar comrades." In other words, they fit right in. Writing about two female Confederate corporals confined at Carroll Prison in Washington, D.C., a contemporary said, "They are a tough couple and talk far more worse than any degraded witch possibly could. They are very impudent and can beat any private in the oath uttering line."[25]

In acting the part of one of the boys, at least three distaff soldiers courted civilian women. Loreta Velazquez felt that to truly portray Harry T.

Buford as a dashing young Confederate officer, she should flirt with women. She even took a few out on dates, and reported that she was "tolerably successful" with the "opposite" sex. Albert Cashier apparently reported having a girlfriend for about two years. Throughout the war Cashier corresponded with the Morey family of Babcock's Grove, Illinois. Three of the Morey's letters to her inquire about a "sweetheart," wondering if Albert would bring her home at the end of the war, and asking if Albert had bought her a new dress. The Morey family, like the soldiers with whom Cashier served, did not know that Cashier was a woman. Since Cashier's letters to the Morey family have not been found, further information about the relationship between Cashier and the "sweetheart" is unavailable. Whether this was a lesbian relationship, a platonic courtship designed to bolster Cashier's male persona, or a complete fabrication is not known. Prior to the war, Sarah Edmonds, who enjoyed a successful career as a door-to-door Bible salesman using her persona of Franklin Thompson, owned a horse and buggy and took women out on dates. As with Cashier, the nature of these relationships is unclear. Although Edmonds admitted to them, she never explained them. From all accounts her postwar marriage was a happy one, so it seems likely her prewar courtships were merely designed to enhance her male masquerade.[26]

Other women soldiers relied on the assistance of the loved ones with whom they enlisted to help maintain the fiction that they were men. The presence of a companion who knew her secret sometimes proved critical to a woman soldier's ability to preserve her masquerade. A case in point was the woman discovered in the ranks of a New Jersey regiment because she gave birth to a baby boy. "It was as much surprising to the Company that she belonged to as it is to me or you," wrote a soldier. "The Company had noticed that she always tented with one person, and many times when it was her turn to come on duty that her tent mate would take her place." The assistance of this loved one obviously helped the woman soldier conceal her pregnancy and thus her sex.[27]

Another example is Mrs. Watkins and Mrs. Epping, who served with their husbands in the 2nd Maryland Infantry (U.S.). Their captain remembered them: "It was while the regiment was being formed on the beach at Roanoke Island . . . that the officer of the guard detected two women in the ranks of Company G. . . . [T]hey were pointed out to me, the most pitiful objects that one could imagine. They were in new full uniforms of the United States soldier, with hair knotted under their caps, fully armed and equipped, with muskets in hand. These poor trembling weak creatures held their places in line however, being held up by the soldiers in the secret, who stood by them." Mrs. Watkins and Mrs. Epping, with the help of their husbands, lasted six months in their regiment before the captain noticed they were women.[28]

The main reason that other women soldiers were successful in maintaining male disguises for long periods of time, however, is that the majority of the Civil War distaff soldiers were working-class and farm women. This background enabled them to make the transition from civilian to soldier more easily. Adapting to the hard life of a soldier was not so difficult for them because notions of idealized womanhood were hardly applicable to their lives. These women were accustomed to hard work and well acquainted with manual labor and drudgery before their army careers began. Farming and frontier women were generally adept at using firearms and working with horses. The working-class women, especially those from urban areas, were also quite used to poor living conditions.

When Melverina Peppercorn enlisted in the Confederate army, she could shoot as well as the twin brother she joined with and was "strong as a man," and no one in her family doubted that she could do the job. The woman who enlisted as John Thompson in the 1st Kentucky Infantry (U.S.) was equally hardy. One reporter noted that "She performed camp duties with great fortitude, and never fell out of the ranks during the severest marches." She was never heard to complain, either. Lucy Gauss of the 18th North Carolina Infantry was a tall and masculine-looking woman who could hunt, ride, and shoot long before she enlisted. A fellow soldier in the 95th Illinois Infantry remarked that Albert Cashier could "do as much work as anyone in the Company."[29]

In addition to strength and endurance, some women possessed useful talents. Frances Clayton was an "accomplished horse-man." Frank Martin was another "first-rate horsewoman," so she often worked as a scout. Frank Martin may also have had some musical training, for she initially enlisted as a bugler. Martha Lindley was good with horses and rather fond of the animals before her enlistment. Life in the cavalry came naturally to her. Sarah Edmonds learned horseback riding as a child, but perhaps equally important in her life as a soldier, she wore trousers and learned to use firearms while she worked on the family farm.[30]

Loreta Velazquez prepared for her army service by drawing on her experiences as an army wife before the war. Her first husband was an officer in the United States army, and they lived at a variety of forts. She easily adapted to life in the Confederate army because she knew the military argot and was familiar with army organization and drills. Just as importantly, she knew how to procure a tactics manual and use the forms needed by an officer to raise and maintain a regiment, such as recruiting papers and muster rolls.[31]

For those who passed as men and held masculine jobs prior to enlisting in the army, their experiences held them in good stead. Sophia Cryder had worked as a teamster, so she had some notion of what she might encounter in the service. Lizzie Compton worked on a steamboat. Albert Cashier was a farmer, a shepherd, and a laborer before joining the army, having passed as a man for several years prior to the war. Even though Rosetta Wakeman only passed as a man for a few weeks before enlistment, her job as a coal handler on a Chenango Canal boat proved a valuable introduction to the world of men. She had also worked as a domestic, and she grew up on a farm in Afton, New York. Being the eldest child, she probably assisted her father as a farmhand. Indeed, having labored all her life, Wakeman was clearly prepared to take on the life of a soldier.[32]

When telling his wife about a woman in his regiment in March 1865, Sergeant Weiss wrote, "I suppose she was tough." Such sentiments were expressed about a number of women soldiers. Sarah Collins of Wisconsin was in good physical health and "could easily have borne the hardships incident to a soldier's life." Albert Cashier was rigorously healthy during her three years in the Union army. Sarah Edmonds was so hardy that while at training camp in Fort Wayne, Michigan, she not only performed all the regular tasks of a soldier, such as drilling and fatigue duty, but in her off-duty hours she also volunteered as a nurse for her sick comrades. It was the tough women, the strong women, and the hardworking women who boasted the most successful military careers, especially once they grew accustomed to portraying men. Loreta Velazquez wrote that after she learned to act and talk like a man, and after she grew comfortable with her new wardrobe, she no longer feared detection and she no longer needed to work so hard at her persona.[33]

The women soldiers of the Union and Confederate armies underwent a rapid and necessary transition from a female to a male identity. While their sex remained female, their gender identity increasingly became male oriented as they adopted male behaviors and attitudes. They enjoyed the freedom that living as men gave them, and they especially enjoyed wearing male attire. The unidentified drummer girl who was wounded at Gettysburg vowed that "they may do what they please with her, but she [would] never wear women's clothes again." Perhaps she was swearing off the tortures of corsets and hoops, or perhaps she was referring to the relative freedom and independence that adopting a male identity provided her. She was not alone in feeling this way. Having served eighteen months in the Union army, Lizzie Compton expressed a determination never to live the life of a woman again.[34]

Some women retained their female perspective on life even as they internalized the male role of soldier. Loreta Velazquez professed "a thorough distaste for vulgarity of language and profanity," and her experiences in army camps "tended to increase [her] disgust at the blackguardism which many men are so fond of indulging in," particularly with respect to women.[35]

Ultimately, societal expectations and idealizations of women, whether or not those expectations and ideals had any basis in reality, played a major role in enabling so many women to maintain the myth that they were males and contributed to the longevity of many women soldiers' army careers. The role of soldier was so closely identified with masculinity that the wearing of a uniform and the performance of military duties often blinded a woman soldier's comrades to her true sex. Nineteenth-century society "defined power, initiative, and assertion as 'masculine.'" Soldiering was the very antithesis of idealized Victorian womanhood. That romantic ideal of the weak and timorous female made many individuals, both civilian and soldier, incapable of recognizing the women hidden away in the ranks, for surely no woman could perform the hard, sometimes horrifying, and indisputably masculine duties of a soldier. "Of course no one in the regiment suspected a woman to be among us and that made her more secure from detection," wrote Sergeant Weiss to his wife. Likewise, Gen. Orlando M. Poe, reminiscing about Sarah Edmonds, wrote, "A single glance at her in her proper character caused me to wonder how I ever could have mistaken her for a man, and I readily recall many things which ought to have betrayed her, except that no one thought of finding a woman in soldier's dress."[36]

Nevertheless, for women soldiers to be fully successful in the ranks, it was not enough to look like a man, act like a man, and be as strong and tough as a man. Just like their male compatriots, women had to learn how to be soldiers. The United States did not have a large standing army prior to the Civil War, so professional soldiers were a minority in both the Union and Confederate armies. The fighting forces of the Civil War were primarily composed of citizen volunteers, who were supplemented by draftees later in the war. These citizen soldiers, male and female, were amateurs ignorant of army life, often led by officers who were learning the military ropes at the same time as their commands. In camp, the citizen soldiers learned complex drills and maneuvers, were instructed on the use of their weapons, and became accustomed to following orders. Women soldiers learned their lessons well, given that a large number of them remained in the military for long periods of time. Some women were even promoted up the ranks to noncommissioned and commissioned officer status. Significantly, no soldiers are known to have been detected as women because they were a danger to themselves or others on the parade ground or because they were inept on the battlefield.

The weapons and equipment employed by the Civil War–era military were not overly burdensome, and that helped women soldiers. The predominant infantry weapons were rifled muskets that generally weighed no more than ten to fifteen pounds. The increased weight that soldiers carried on the march likewise was not problematic for even a small or light-framed woman. The average load of weapons, ammunition, and supplies was thirty pounds, or the weight of a small child.

Rosetta Wakeman eagerly learned her soldiering lessons and evinced great pride in her accomplishments. In March 1863, she wrote to her family back home, "How would you like to be in the front rank and have the rear rank load and fire their guns over you shoulder?" In October of the same year, Wakeman bragged, "I have got So that I Can drill just as well as any man there is in my regiment." She had not bragged to them the previous June, however, when she damaged her bayonet scabbard and lost twenty-five cents in wages as a result.[37]

Like the men with whom they served, the women evolved into soldiers in both form and function. Frances Clayton not only became "a capital swordsman," but also commanded attention with her "masculine stride in walking" and her "erect and soldierly carriage." Of Marian McKenzie it was said that "no soldier has been more dutiful or is better drilled." Lizzie Compton loved being in the army and took immense pride in understanding the soldier role perfectly and using her musket well.[38]

Like all civilians who left the relative comfort and security of home to join the military, women soldiers embarked upon a new career filled with adventure, danger, excitement, and hardship. Traditionally, soldiers have relied on comradeship to cope with the stresses, perils, and long periods of inactivity and boredom that characterize wartime. Female soldiers of the Civil War were no different. Even though they often were, by necessity, more reserved and retiring than the men they served with, they nevertheless formed lasting friendships with their fellow soldiers. Indeed, women soldiers formed bonds of comradeship that became as much a motivation for them to remain in the ranks as were their patriotic ideals. Those who enlisted with their husbands, brothers, or friends began army life with a close associate who kept them company and assisted them with assimilation. But women who enlisted by themselves soon found friends as well. In a number of cases, women soldiers forged friendships with other women combatants they encountered in camp or in the field. While a male soldier might not recognize a woman soldier in his midst because he did not expect one, a woman soldier was more likely to be on the lookout for someone she could confide in and rely on to keep her secret.

Mollie Bell spent most of her service in the Shenandoah Valley, and she stated that she knew of six other women serving in Confederate Gen. Jubal Early's army. Rebecca "Georgianna" Peterman said that she knew of two women from her home county serving in the Union army. An unnamed woman soldier who was arrested at Fort Walker/Welles at Hilton Head, South Carolina, in 1865 told her captors that there were at least two other women serving in her squad. The guards, however, were unable to locate them. Mary Ann Clark "said she never slept with the boys, having a female chum who bunked with her."[39]

Two women, identified only as Kate and Eliza Frances, served together in the 1st West Virginia Cavalry. In September 1864, they "reported that they have another companion, if not several, of the same 'persuasion.'" When Ella Reno and Sarah Bradbury were called to account for a drunken escapade, neither would tell their interrogators, including General Sheridan, how they came to know one another. The woman soldier known only as Frank Martin made friends wherever she went during her three separate army stints. When she served in the Army of the Cumberland, she was acquainted with three female soldiers. While stationed in Louisville, she became the friend and confidant of an unnamed woman lieutenant. In November 1864, Frank Martin was keeping company with a female private known as George Smith.[40]

Women soldiers not only made friends with other women, but they developed deep and lasting friendships with men, too. Jerome Robbins of the 2nd Michigan Infantry highly prized the friendship of Franklin Thompson but was shocked and felt betrayed when he finally learned that Thompson was really Sarah Edmonds. Despite these feelings, he kept her secret. Robbins did note prior to the discovery that Thompson acted "strangely," and he confided in his diary, "Foolish as it may seem a mystery appearts to me connected with him which is impossible for me to fathom." He described Thompson as possessing "a nature to willful to be pleasant—to jealous to be happy or lend happiness to those whom he has a warm friendship for." Their friendship flourished nevertheless, with Robbins mentioning it seven times in his diary. He referred to their relationship as a "consolation" and "a blessing," and even declared, "This friendship [is] one of the greatest events of my life." The two soldiers spent much of their free time in conversation, especially in their first year of service together, and Robbins felt quite lonely when Thompson ultimately made friends with her other tent mates and began spending less time with him. Their friendship never completely waned, though. Robbins nursed Edmonds through one of her bouts of malaria.[41]

Albert Cashier also formed friendships with her compatriots. When comrade Amos Morton was injured and sent to Gayoso Hospital, he wrote to his "Dear friend Albert" to report on his health, to request that Cashier "take care of [his] clothes" and to let Cashier know that he "had not forgoten [Cashier] intierly." Morton was so fond of Cashier that he wanted Albert to join him and his wife when they moved to Iowa after the war. Another comrade, John D. Caswell, corresponded with Cashier after he left the infantry. Caswell wanted news of the regiment, requested that Cashier collect on debts owed to him, and most importantly, wanted Cashier to visit him on furlough. Cashier and Samuel Pepper, also of the 95th Illinois Infantry, got along so well that they established a business after the war, briefly operating a plant nursery in Belvedere, Illinois. The closeness of their relationship is indicated by the fact that, on an 1866 trip to Chicago, Cashier bought a ham and carpeting to send to Pepper and Pepper lent Cashier money. Cashier was illiterate; therefore one or more of the men in her regiment read to her the letters she received and wrote down her dictated replies. But the most telling testimonial to the bonds Cashier forged with her comrades is how, more than forty years later, they rallied to her defense when her sex became publicly known, when the Pension Bureau investigated her, and when the State of Illinois committed her to an insane asylum.[42]

Cashier was esteemed by more than just the men with whom she served. She enjoyed a wide circle of acquaintances, friends, and loved ones, both in and out of the army. Cashier's relationship with the Morey family on the home front extended beyond correspondence. Cashier sent them money, blankets, and other gifts, and in turn, they wrote to her with news of mutual friends and reports on crops and sent her care packages and postage stamps. The Moreys worried about Cashier's health and diet, continually encouraged Albert to come to them after the war and attend school, and exclaimed over the photographs she periodically sent them. The family scanned published casualty lists, anxiously looking for Cashier's name. The Morey children often added postscripts to their mother's letters, and they were always excited to hear news about Albert. Cashier also corresponded with two other friends in Belvedere, Michael Murphy and Lauren Hamlin. Cashier sent Murphy Confederate postage stamps as souvenirs, as well as a photograph. Hamlin was the sister of another soldier in the 95th Illinois Infantry, and when he died, Cashier wrote a condolence letter to the family. Hamlin responded to this kindness by requesting that Albert come to them "as if you were coming home for we shall always be glad to see you."[43]

Both during and after the war Cashier's circle of friends did not know that Albert was a woman. Similarly, there is no evidence that the soldiers of the 153rd New York Infantry had any inkling that Lyons Wakeman was actually Rosetta Wakeman. But others in the army did know Wakeman's secret. While stationed in Washington, D.C., she found out that two childhood friends were serving in a regiment not far from her. On October 13, 1863, Wakeman wrote home: "I went to my lieutenant and got a pass for today and this morning I Started for Georgetown, and when I got there . . . I got a man to row me across the River to the island and then I found Henry Austin and Perry Wilder. They knew me just as Soon as they see me. You better believe I had a good visit with them. I stayed about two Hours and Started back for Camp again." It seems unlikely that Wakeman had the time or opportunity to purchase and put on a dress before visiting her friends, meaning that she called on Austin and Wilder in her uniform. Like her family in New York, they knew her secret, and they kept it.[44]

Some male soldiers eventually realized that they had female soldiers in their midst. Some of the men reported their discovery to commanding officers, which usually brought a swift end to the woman's service, at least in the regiment where she was detected. But others kept the secret. Elvira Ibecker, alias Charles Fuller, apparently had a few male soldier confidants who did not tell the officers about her. One of the men serving with Annie Lillybridge in the 21st Michigan Infantry knew about her sex but did not turn her in. At least two soldiers in addition to Jerome Robbins eventually learned that Franklin Thompson was a woman.[45]

Men who went to war with their wives, sisters, or sweethearts had obvious personal reasons for keeping their loved one's secret. The motivations of those male soldiers who maintained silence about a female soldier when they were not related to, or enamored of, the women in their regiments is less clear. Respect might have been the reason. Courage, bravery, valor, and honor were qualities cherished by and expected of soldiers. Any individual who displayed these qualities in the performance of military duties and especially on the field of battle was accepted as a comrade in that special fraternity formed by soldiers and combat veterans. For some male soldiers, bravery and patriotism were far more important in a comrade than gender.

The military career of a woman soldier was usually safe if her comrades learned of it, so long as the commissioned officers were kept ignorant of the matter. It was the officers who were concerned about compliance with army regulations, and it was the officers, rather than the enlisted men, who usually expressed irritation or anger over a woman found in the ranks. Keeping the officers in the dark was not very difficult. An enlisted man seldom had personal dealings with commanding officers other than brief encounters relating to routine army matters. Military duty did not necessitate that commissioned officers pay singular attention to the individuals in their command. And the massive, elbow-to-elbow troop formations required by Civil War tactics guaranteed that the individual soldier was rarely the focus of attention, either during drill or on the battlefield.

The very nature of Civil War armies played a role in keeping the existence of women soldiers a secret from the commissioned officers. Particularly in the early years of the war the armies were amazingly democratic and disorganized, with officers elected by the rank and file. Throughout the war it was difficult for officers to maintain firm control and authority over the independent-minded citizen soldiers who volunteered or were conscripted to fight for their country. Officers were commonly as inexperienced as their soldiers. Disorganization, insubordination, and ignorance were yet additional factors that helped women soldiers keep up the pretense that they were men.

The women who served as soldiers in the Civil War went to extraordinary lengths to reinvent themselves as males, but their new personas were essentially means to an end. These women wanted to be soldiers in a society that reserved the warrior role for men. They desired an active and independent life in a world that insisted women be passive and dependent. So they transformed themselves, and once the world perceived them to be male, the army taught them how to be soldiers. Their experiences in camp and the personal bonds they forged with their comrades molded them as warriors. Relying on cleverness, hard work, and a little luck, women soldiers not only performed their assumed duty to their country to the best of their ability, but they also found a level of personal freedom and self-determination unavailable to them in their true identities as women.

4

"FAIRLY EARNED HER EPAULETTES"
Women Soldiers in the Military Service

The life of a Civil War soldier was filled with more than drilling, marching, and fighting. Army life for enlisted men and officers was full of responsibilities both dull and dangerous, and women soldiers performed all of them alongside their male comrades without asking for or receiving special consideration because of their sex. In the 18th North Carolina Infantry, for example, Lucy Thompson Gauss was detailed as a sharpshooter, a role given to her because of her keen eye, steady hand, and sure aim.[1]

Guard duty was a more common occupation of infantry soldiers. From October 1862 to February 1864, Sarah Rosetta Wakeman, alias Pvt. Lyons Wakeman, performed guard and provost marshal duty in the defenses of Washington, D.C., along with the other members of her regiment, the 153rd New York Infantry. For part of that time Wakeman was stationed in the capital city guarding prisoners at Old Capitol and Carroll Prisons. She was also based in Alexandria, Virginia, a southern city under Federal occupation. Troops stationed there guarded against Confederate attack and enforced martial law. In the Confederate army, the woman called Captain Billy commanded an infantry company. In 1863 that company was charged with transporting and guarding the prisoners captured at the Battle of Chickamauga.[2]

For infantry soldiers in the field, round-the-clock picket duty was necessary to maintain security. Pickets were the outposts of a camped army who kept a watchful eye and sounded the alarm in the case of enemy attack. They also checked passes for anyone, suspicious or not, who entered or left camp. For the most part, standing picket was unremarkable and tedious duty, and like the men, women soldiers resigned themselves to it. A more exciting job was scouting. In the 7th Wisconsin Infantry, Rebecca "Georgianna" Peterman spent part of her service detached from her regiment on this duty. Scouts were often sent out from camp to ascertain the position and the strength of any enemy in the vicinity. Scouting, sometimes referred to as spying in contemporary parlance, was more commonly a job for the cavalry, however. By her own request Charlotte Hope of the 1st Virginia Cavalry (CSA) was detailed for most scouting expeditions. She was more likely to encounter Union troops while performing this dangerous duty, and she was anxious to engage the enemy at every opportunity.[3]

Frank Martin served in a number of capacities during the war. She began her career in the infantry and later reenlisted in a cavalry regiment. She also performed clerical work at headquarters. Contemporary newspapers delighted in recounting her wartime story. Of her stint in the cavalry, one reporter gushed, "She is represented as an excellent horseman. . . . She has seen and endured all the hardships and privations incident to the life of a soldier, and gained an enviable reputation as a scout, having made several wonderful expeditions, which were attended with signal success."[4]

The cavalry performed functions other than scouting. Cavalry raiding parties often were sent out. When Union Col. Henry C. Gilbert led a raid on Beersheba Springs, Tennessee, on April 13, 1864, five of his thirty-five troopers were women. Dragoons were also employed as escorts to the generals, working as bodyguards and couriers. Sarah Bradbury, a private in a cavalry company, performed escort duty at Gen. Philip Sheridan's headquarters.[5]

Infantry, cavalry, and artillery soldiers were sometimes pulled from their regiments for medical duty. Regimental surgeons often found themselves short of medical staff, particularly in field and regimental hospitals. Both Union and Confederate regulations dictated that surgeons detail soldiers from the ranks as necessary to assist them in tending to the sick and wounded. While serving under the alias of Frank Deming, a female private in the 17th Ohio Infantry was detailed for hospital duty in November 1861 by order of the surgeon. Similarly, Martha Parks Lindley, alias Pvt. Jim Smith of the 6th U.S. Cavalry, spent ten months of her enlistment detached on hospital duty as orderly for the surgeon. Soldiers also were drawn out of their regiments to remove or tend to the wounded on the field while battles raged around them. Lizzie Compton performed this task during one of her seven enlistments. A comrade said that she did the work "fearlessly" under fire.[6]

In other cases, women enlisted directly for medical service. Frances Jamieson, alias Frank Abel, left her Union cavalry regiment after the death of her husband at First Bull Run and joined the Hospital Corps as a nurse, where her responsibilities included the grim task of assisting with amputations as well as other surgical theater nursing chores. In the 12th Indiana Cavalry, the assistant surgeon was a woman.[7]

The responsibility of nursing comrades and working in field hospitals might appear to modern audiences as traditional woman's work, and therefore it seems ironic that women in the guise of men were cast in such a stereotypical female role. However, such was not the case during the Civil War, when most military nurses were men. Indeed, not until the Spanish-American War did females outnumber males as U.S. army nurses. During the Civil War, fewer than four thousand women served as paid nurses for the Union army. Neither the number of paid Confederate nurses nor the women on both sides who nursed without compensation is recorded with any accuracy, but even so, male nurses always outnumbered female nurses in army hospitals. Civil War soldier women who worked in the Medical Corps were doing a traditional man's job.[8]

There were still other military occupations for soldiers. Some enlisted directly for service as teamsters or mule drivers and worked the wagon trains supplying the armies under the aegis of the Quartermaster Department. Edmonia Gates spent six months as a U.S. teamster. Similarly, during one of her three enlistments, Ella Reno was a teamster in a division wagon train. At one point, she "was ordered to take a train of wagons across a river at night which she accomplished." This feat earned for her the admiration of at least one Union captain. Indeed, he was impressed with Reno the soldier. In writing of her previous stints in both the infantry and cavalry, he declared that Reno had "done all the duties of [an] ordinary private—made long marches—been in hot battles, stood guard—been out on picket duty." Throughout her army career, Reno maintained her record as a good and faithful soldier.[9]

In addition to serving in the ranks, in wagon trains, and in hospitals, women also served in various headquarters commands. One woman soldier was rumored to have served with her husband at Gen. Robert E. Lee's headquarters. Union soldier Ida Remington spent part of her two-year service detailed as an officer's servant. Two girls from Pennsylvania also served in regimental headquarters as personal aides to officers. One of these was Charles Norton of the 141st Pennsylvania Infantry. Attached to Company E, she was the jack-of-all-trades for the captain. She cooked, nursed, kept guard over the property of the officers, and did whatever other jobs came to hand or were assigned to her. The other girl was just a child of twelve when she ran away from home and joined a Pennsylvania regiment under the name Charles Martin. Her regiment saw five battles during her service, but she was never a combatant. Rather, because of her obvious education and fine handwriting, she was commandeered by officers as a regimental clerk.[10]

Frank Martin ended up at departmental headquarters in Louisville, Kentucky. While still in the cavalry, she arrived there in 1863, acting as aide to a captain. Detailed to clerical duty at Barracks Number 1, she won the esteem of her superiors, being "possessed of more than ordinary intelligence." Yet another scribe in the Union army was Mary Jane G., a "handsome, fresh-looking 'detailed man' acting as . . . clerk" to an unspecified general.[11]

Soldiers considered it an honor to work for a general or to win assignment to some special duty. Near the end of the war, Maria Lewis was designated a member of an honor guard that presented to the War Department seventeen captured Confederate battle flags. Lewis, an African American, impersonated a white man in order to serve for eighteen months in the 8th New York Cavalry. As one contemporary noted, Lewis "wore uniform & carried sword & carbine & rode & scouted & skirmished & fought like the rest."[12]

Sarah Edmonds, alias Pvt. Franklin Thompson of the 2nd Michigan Infantry, not only shouldered a musket when her regiment engaged the enemy, but she also pulled nursing and mail carrier duty. During the Battle of Fredericksburg, she served as an orderly to General Poe. Of all the female Union soldiers known to have served, Sarah Edmonds enjoyed military duties more varied than those of any of her female contemporaries. Like most privates, Edmonds spent the first two months of her service in the school of the soldier and on drill, picket, and guard duty. Private Thompson was then assigned as a nurse in the regimental hospital by order of the regimental surgeon. She served in that capacity for five months and then was detailed to a general hospital at Georgetown, near Washington, D.C. A little more than a month later she was allowed to return to her regiment. One of Edmonds' patients in the regimental hospital later testified to the "care, kindness, and self-sacrificing devotion of 'Frank' to the sick soldiers of the regiment." Of her tour in the Georgetown hospital, Edmonds wrote that she was "simply eyes, ears, hands and feet. It does seem as if there is a sort of stoicism granted for such occasions." After the Battle of First Bull Run, Edmonds volunteered to nurse the wounded. She recalled that she "was obliged in many instances to use [her] teeth in order to tear the thick woolen garments stiffened with blood." That early in the conflict, medical supplies were crude and in short supply, but service in field and general hospitals remained extremely grim throughout the war.[13]

Carrying the mail was no easy duty, either. Private Thompson served in that capacity from April 1862 through the Battle of Antietam in September. During the Peninsula campaign she carried mail and orders from the troops camped near Richmond to the supply depot established at White House Landing, her path often crossing the river and the swamp that both bear the name Chickahominy. She contracted malaria as a result. Years later she described these ordeals: "I was more than once obliged to swim my horse across the [Chickahominy]. . . . Those cold baths . . . fastened the chills and fever upon me, which eventually drove me from the Army." Yet despite the hardships, despite "sitting drenched in the saddle . . . shivering by the roadside watching for daylight to pick . . . through the dangerous mud holes," Edmonds never resigned the unhealthy and dangerous duty. Rather, she so enjoyed the mobility and freedom that courier service entailed that she volunteered for work as a spy. After passing loyalty interviews and firearm tests, she was accepted as a volunteer for spy duty. She then spied intermittently for the duration of her mail carrier detail. In her memoirs, she related that she was often successful in penetrating enemy lines and obtaining useful information.[14]

Of all the female soldiers known to have served the Confederacy, Mary Ann Pitman and Loreta Velazquez faced the most danger and engaged in the wildest adventures. The careers of the two women were similar in two respects. Both of them raised a company of soldiers, and both became spies after their tenure in the army. Mary Ann Pitman came from Chestnut Bluff, Tennessee. At the outbreak of the war, she disguised herself as a man, went to Union City, and with the help of a male friend, recruited a full cavalry company. She became second lieutenant under the alias of Rawley. Similarly, Loreta Velazquez spent the first part of her Confederate career raising and equipping an independent company using her own funds and then briefly serving as the lieutenant. Like many units recruited at the beginning of the war, her term of enlistment was only three months. Velazquez turned command of her independent company over to a trusted associate and, in the summer of 1861, headed for Virginia.[15]

Velazquez fought in several engagements during the first two years of the war. Twice during her military career, in Mississippi and later in Virginia, Velazquez was a courier carrying dispatches between various Confederate commands. She also worked as a passport agent and military conductor on southern railroads for three weeks in 1862. During this time she rode the trains, examining military passes and furlough documents of passengers and arresting any suspicious characters. During the two years that Velazquez proffered her services to Confederate armies, she did so with the self-appointed rank of lieutenant. Only for three months did she serve as a private in the 21st Louisiana Infantry.[16]

When Velazquez published her memoirs in 1876, Maj. John Newman of that regiment stated, "I have been personally acquainted with her for the past thirteen years. She . . . served under me with distinction as a soldier . . . and was afterwards promoted for her great efficiency and integrity to the position of 1st Lieutenant. . . . I therefore take great pride in recommending her." Actually, Velazquez was unsuccessful in seeking a real officer's commission from the Confederate War Department. On June 16, 1863, "Williams, Mrs. Lauretta Fennett, alias H. T. Buford, Lt. CSA," applied for a formal commission in the Confederate army. Her application was received in Richmond on July 27, but it appears that the War Department never acted upon her request. Rather, her letter was returned to her. On September 15, 1863, however, a Richmond newspaper reported that "in consideration of her services" the Confederate government had bestowed upon her "the rank of Captain" and that she promptly drew over one thousand dollars in back pay, though in her memoirs Velazquez wrote that she never received a regular commission.[17]

While the authenticity of Velazquez's rank is subject to debate, her devotion to the Confederate cause is not. She was an ardent supporter of the South. After her army service she devoted her energies to the Confederate Secret Service. Her patriotism was surpassed only by her sense of adventure and desire for action. When questioned by a newspaper reporter in

1861, she said she was "determined to fight the battles of her country." Even as a little girl Velazquez had fantasized about being a heroic military officer. The Civil War gave her a chance to realize her childhood dreams, and she was "elated . . . at the prospect . . . of being able to prove [herself] as good a fighter as any of the gallant men who had taken up arms in behalf of the cause of Southern independence."[18]

Throughout her military career Velazquez detested inactivity and constantly sought excitement. She thoroughly enjoyed battle but hated the drudgeries of camp life. Her restlessness, impulsiveness, and impatience were serious character flaws in a soldier, especially in an officer, and these traits impinged on her military career. The woman had no tolerance for boredom. Rather than submitting to the dreary lot of the common soldier, she pined for the perceived glory of serving as an officer, so she moved from place to place, never staying with one military job for very long. She wrote in her memoirs that perhaps she could have controlled her restlessness and stayed in one command had she received her long-sought-after commission. Apparently it did not occur to her that if she had been more patient or persistent in pursuing one course of action, perhaps she might have received that coveted official commission. She did, however, finally see that she "was doing no very material service by plunging into the thick of a fight, as much for the enjoyment of the thing as anything else," so she put aside her martial ambitions and spent the last two years of the war as a spy.[19]

Mary Ann Pitman never evinced the personal ambition or the need for glory that plagued Velazquez. She was, nevertheless, a successful soldier and Confederate operative. After she raised her cavalry company and fought with it at the Battle of Shiloh, the company was assigned permanently to the command of Gen. Nathan Bedford Forrest. Still using the alias of Lieutenant Rawley, Pitman served under General Forrest for a year, during which time she was promoted to first lieutenant. She was then detailed by Forrest to smuggling and spying on behalf of his command.[20]

General Forrest was "a good quartermaster and commissary," with a "practical talent in seeing that his men and his horses were looked after." Not content to rely on army bureaucracy for necessary sustenance, Forrest detailed officers to obtain any supplies that were not issued by the Confederate government. As his biographer noted, "he went out and supplied himself." After receiving orders to garner guns and ammunition for the command, Pitman decided to do so dressed as a woman, thinking she could more easily evade Union troops if she was perceived as a civilian woman rather than a Confederate officer. Using the alias of Molly Hays, she went to St. Louis to make her purchases. Pitman was quite successful at procuring supplies for Forrest, spending a year purchasing and transporting musket caps, pistols, cartridges, black powder, revolvers, and clothing, and making at least three journeys between St. Louis and her command.[21]

Pitman also spied for Forrest. Molly Hays often slipped through Union lines by pretending to be a loyal citizen who had information that she would impart only to the commanding officer. Once inside the lines, Pitman "found no difficulty in bamboozling the younger staff officers into showing her the defenses and positions of troops and fortifications." Pitman then conveyed this intelligence to Forrest's headquarters. Pitman's career as a Confederate soldier, smuggler, and spy ended in April 1864. While on the last of her supply trips, she received a dispatch from Forrest ordering her to return to her place in the field. On the way back to her command she was captured in the vicinity of Fort Pillow, Tennessee. Thus ended her service in the Confederate army.[22]

Just as women soldiers were found in every facet of military life throughout the war, they also held every rank from musician to major. Nearly all the women soldiers known to have served as musicians were drummers in Union infantry regiments; one exception was Frank Martin, who was a bugler in the cavalry. Edmonia Gates, the teamster, also served a term as drummer boy in Wilson's Zouaves, the 121st New York Infantry. Charles Martin, the child who became a regimental clerk, initially enlisted as a drummer boy. Rebecca "Georgianna" Peterman, who was about seventeen years old when she enlisted, was a drummer during the first year of her service in the 7th Wisconsin Infantry. In her second year, she abandoned music and "did good service with the musket," along with her scouting details.[23]

Jane Short enlisted in the band of a Missouri infantry regiment, where "she performed excellent service on the base-drum." The unnamed Union woman wounded at Gettysburg served as a drummer boy during her second army enlistment. Fanny Harris of Indiana was yet another drummer, said to have "passed through a dozen battles." Since many women soldiers looked like teenaged boys too young for the regular enlistment age, their only possible entry into the army was through the ranks of the musicians. At least half a dozen women went through the war as drummer boys.[24]

Promotions among women soldiers were not uncommon. The un-named woman soldier from New Jersey "was a private when she enlisted but [was] promoted to corporal." She was then promoted to sergeant for gallant conduct shortly before she gave birth to her child. An anonymous woman soldier in the Army of the Cumberland was promoted to sergeant "owing to his good qualities." This sergeant "always attended to his various duties with promptitude and care—and nothing out of the way was discovered of him until . . . he gave birth to a large boy." These two cases notwithstanding, pregnancy was not a prerequisite for women becoming sergeants. A female orderly sergeant in the cavalry was captured at the Battle of Chancellorsville, and a female orderly sergeant in the artillery was captured at the Battle of Cold Harbor, both Confederates. On the Union side, Katie Hanson enlisted in 1861 in an Ohio regiment and rose to the rank of sergeant. Martha Lindley temporarily served as a sergeant in late 1861 and again in the fall of 1862, but both times was demoted back to private. Alfred J. Luther mustered in at Leavenworth into the 1st Kansas Infantry as a corporal on May 30, 1861. She was promoted to first sergeant almost a year later. Frances Day, alias Frank Mayne, enlisted in the Union army on August 5, 1862, and was mustered into the 126th Pennsylvania Infantry four days later with the rank of sergeant. Although Frank Mayne was a complete stranger to everyone in camp, "in a few days he had . . . ingratiated himself with his comrades and officers" and was therefore elected to the position.[25]

On June 23, 1865, Sgt. Jennie R. Gregg was discharged from the 128th Ohio Infantry at Johnson's Island, where elements of her regiment were employed as guards for the military prison. Her discharge paper gave her age as twenty-two and described her as four feet ten inches tall, with a dark complexion, black eyes, and auburn hair. It is unclear when Gregg was promoted to sergeant, just as it is unknown when her sex was discovered or what alias she originally used. All Civil War Union discharge documents provided the civilian occupation of the soldier, and Gregg's discharge stated that her occupation was "Lady." Perhaps Gregg was discharged when her true identity became known, or she may have been discharged at the expiration of her term of enlistment and then revealed the truth about herself.[26]

A Union woman soldier known only as Margaret, who was killed during the Battle of Second Bull Run, held the rank of color sergeant. Color sergeants commanded the guard that carried the regimental flags into battle.

This position was vastly important. Battlefields soon became covered in smoke, and soldiers' sight lines were impaired just as if they were in a heavy fog. The brightly colored regimental flags stationed in the middle of a line of battle anchored soldiers to their command. If the flags fell back, so did they. If the colors advanced, they followed. Carrying the colors was a high honor, but it was dangerous because the enemy could easily target flag bearers.[27]

Women soldiers advanced into the echelon of commissioned officers as well, serving as lieutenants and captains. Mary Dennis was commissioned a lieutenant in a Minnesota regiment early in 1861, but her service was brief. In 1863, Frank Martin made friends with a woman lieutenant in Louisville but refused to disclose her identity, most likely to protect the officer from expulsion. In September 1863, a female lieutenant in the Union army was one of three hundred prisoners of war held in Atlanta.[28]

Mary Ann Clark was promoted to the rank of lieutenant after she was captured, paroled, and returned to the Army of Tennessee. In August 1863, another Confederate soldier wrote home about her:

> Pa among all the curiosities I have seen since I left home one I must mention, a female Lieutenant. I had heard of her deeds of bravery in several battles and a few evenings ago, I went to the Station about a quarter of amile distant from camp. I discovered quite a crowd, approaching the crowd I inquired what was up. One of the soldiers directed my attention to a youth apparently about seventeen years of age, well dressed with a Liutinants badge on his collar. I remarked that I saw nothing verry strange, he then told me that the young man was not a man, but a female. [I]t is said . . . she fell a prisoner into the hands of the Yankees, her sex was discovered by the federals and she was regularly paroled as a prisoner of war, but they did not permit her to return until she had donned female apparel. She has since her return I suppose been promoted to the office of Lt.

There was at least one other female Confederate lieutenant. During the 1862 Shenandoah Valley campaign, an anonymous woman from Alabama served as a first lieutenant. Her husband was also her captain, and he no doubt played a role in her commissioning.[29]

Four Confederate women were captains. Two of them may have received their commissions through the influence of their husbands. Captain Billy, whose full name remains unknown, entered service as a lieutenant under the command of her husband. When he was killed, she was given his rank and command. Had she been an incompetent officer, however, her superiors surely would have sent her home instead of promoting her when her husband died. Nepotism gave another woman her rank, but just like Captain Billy, she proved herself worthy of it. An Englishman traveling in the Confederacy in late 1863 and early 1864 encountered "a Confederate captain in one of the ladies" on a train between Augusta and Atlanta. He admiringly recorded her story: "Her husband was a major in the Confederate army, and she had taken an active part herself in the war, and fairly earned her epaulettes. She was no longer in uniform, having lately retired from the service, was young, good-looking, and lady-like, and told her adventures in a pleasant quiet way."[30]

In 1864, "a beautiful, dashing lady, in the uniform of a Captain, passed on the Northern train towards Richmond." She traveled in the company of a major, who may or may not have been her husband. A native of Mississippi, she was a battle-hardened veteran "promoted on the field for gallantry." Near the end of the war, Confederates Mary Wright and Margaret Henry were captured while burning bridges in Tennessee and incarcerated in Nashville. The newspaper that reported their capture exclaimed that "one of them rejoices in the rank and uniform of a captain."[31]

At least one woman reached the rank of major, the highest that any woman soldier in the Civil War is known to have held. There are no reports of women becoming colonels or generals. In the summer of 1863, an impressed Rosetta Wakeman wrote to her parents, "Over to Carroll Prison they have got three women that is Confined in their Rooms. One of them was a Major in the union army and she went into battle with her men. When the Rebels bullets was acoming like a hail storm she rode her horse and gave orders to the men. Now She is in Prison for not doing aCcordingly to the regulation of war." Did Wakeman mean that the woman major was imprisoned for improperly doing her duty, or did she mean that the major was incarcerated for being a woman? If the major was sent to prison because of discovery of her sex, it is ironic that one of her prison guards was also a woman soldier in disguise. Since the records of prisoners held at Carroll Prison are incomplete, the name of the Union woman major remains a mystery.[32]

The fact that some women were promoted into the officer ranks is testament to how well those individuals performed their military duty. Evidence suggests that most of the women, regardless of their rank, felt a keen sense of their duty and performed admirably as soldiers. The comments of comrades and superiors of female soldiers confirm this, for they generally spoke or wrote of the women found among them in favorable terms. "She stood guard, went on picket duty, in rain or storm, and fought on the field with the rest, and was considered a good fighting man," according to one report about Frances Clayton. A former comrade of Rebecca "Georgianna" Peterman said that she was "one of the most gallant soldiers he ever saw" and swore "that she was a 'good fellow.'"[33]

When Frances Hook was revealed to be a woman, the officers and men of her regiment expressed "great indignation . . . and hastened to protest, that, although she had been with them for more than a year, not one in the regiment suspicioned that she was a woman." They further admitted that during her tenure in the ranks, not only did she do full duty on the picket line and in camp, but also that she was a good fighter. Similarly, after one of the many times Lizzie Compton was discovered to be a girl in military guise, her colonel admitted that her conduct as a soldier was above reproach. After the war, when Sarah Edmonds applied to Congress for a soldier's pension, a number of her comrades testified on her behalf, including First Lt. William Turner, whose affidavit stated that Pvt. Franklin Thompson "bore a good reputation, behaved as a person of good moral character, and was always ready for duty." No less a personage than the secretary of war concurred, writing that Edmonds was "a female soldier who . . . served as a private . . . rendering faithful service in the ranks."[34]

Of course, not every woman soldier was a paragon of military virtue. In reminiscing about the woman soldier in the 14th Maine Infantry, a comrade wrote that "she was small and slightly built and for that reason was excused from some heavy fatigue duty." Since her commanding officers did not know that she was a woman until the end of the war, her sex had nothing to do with her special treatment. In contrast with this woman was Pvt. Albert D. J. Cashier, whose officers often chose her for foraging and skirmishing duties, as she maintained a reputation as a hardworking soldier. Just as the officers of the 14th Maine Infantry did not know they were excusing a woman, the officers of the 95th Illinois Infantry did not realize they were relying on one.[35]

In a postwar newspaper story about Martha Lindley's Civil War career, the reporter glowingly wrote that she "was a good soldier . . . and never shirked any of the unpleasant duties of the men at the front." Lindley herself was more modest in assessing her days in the cavalry. "I did the best I could in the service of my country," she was quoted as saying. "Although

I am only a woman, I think I can say without egotism that there were worse soldiers than I in the service."[36]

Rosetta Wakeman also showed a determination to do the best she could. In January 1863, after surviving a case of measles and watching thirty of her comrades succumb to the disease, Private Wakeman wrote to her father, "If it is God will for me to die here it is my will to die here." Soldiers naturally thought of death, and the subject preyed on Wakeman's mind in August when she wrote, "I don't know how long before I shall have to go into the field of battle. For my part I don't Care. I don't feel afraid to go. I don't believe there are any Rebel's bullet made for me yet. Nor I don't Care if there is. . . . If it is God will for me to fall in the field of battle, it is my will to go and never return home." Like many a soldier, Wakeman relied on her religious beliefs to buoy her commitment to the army.[37]

Confederates Mary and Mollie Bell seemed equally committed to their army, but apparently lacked Wakeman's philosophical nature. Their attitude was sheer bravado. They insisted "that if all the women of the Confederacy were as patriotick as they the country would have been free long ago." Jane Perkins, who served in the Confederate artillery, bragged about her service and was proud of her abilities. When she arrived at Point Lookout Military Prison in June 1864 and was questioned by the provost marshal, Perkins defiantly "said she could straddle a horse, jump a fence and kill a Yankee as well as any rebel."[38]

Women soldiers capably performed the military duties assigned to them, never asked for special consideration, and from all accounts were competent and obedient soldiers. Not one woman soldier is known to have been court-martialed for failing to perform her duty, for committing a military crime, or for disgracing her uniform. Only three women soldiers are known to have deserted their regiments, and two of these later reenlisted. Taken as a whole, the record of women's military service during the Civil War is a proud one.

5

"WHY THEY DETAINED HER I CAN'T IMAGINE"
The Prisoner of War Experience

A soldier's feeling of obligation, duty, and patriotism was severely challenged if he or she fell into the hands of the enemy. Second only to wounds and disease, becoming a prisoner of war was the most serious threat to the health and well-being of a Civil War soldier, especially after the parole and exchange system collapsed in 1863. About thirteen percent of Civil War POWs died as a result of their incarceration. Indeed, a soldier was less likely to die on the battlefield than in prison; only about 5 percent of Civil War soldiers were killed in action. Prison facilities, both North and South, were deplorable, and POWs suffered greatly from exposure to the elements, lack of food, overcrowded conditions, and inadequate sanitary arrangements. The conduct of women POWs as they endured the deprivation, starvation, filth, and pestilence of the prison camps demonstrated their serious commitment to cause and country.[1]

Capture was not a significant worry for women soldiers early in the war because most prisoners were paroled and exchanged in short order. For example, the woman soldier serving in the 1st New York Cavalry who was captured at the Battle of Savage's Station was a prisoner of war for less than two months. She fell into enemy hands on June 29, 1862, and by mid-August, she and her husband were safely at Camp Parole in Annapolis, Maryland. A Confederate woman who enlisted in a guerrilla regiment was captured in December 1862 near Thibodauxville, Louisiana. She pledged not to take up arms against the United States until properly exchanged and was immediately paroled. When prisoner exchanges ceased, however, capture became a vexing problem not only for women POWs but for their captors as well.[2]

Since women were not supposed to be soldiers, army regulations did not address the treatment of female prisoners of war. So Union and Confederate military authorities handled the existence of women prisoners on a case-by-case basis. Therefore, the prisoner of war experiences of women soldiers varied widely. The treatment of female Union POWs by Confederate authorities hinged on whether or not the prisoner was recognized as a woman. In nearly every case, the prisoner was released when her sex was revealed. After the widowed Frances Jamieson, alias Frank Abel, went to work as a spy for General Banks in September 1862, she was captured on October 1 by Confederate cavalry and imprisoned in Richmond. Two months later, Confederate authorities exchanged her for southern spy Belle Boyd.[3]

During a December 11, 1863, scouting operation near Florence, Alabama, Union soldier Frances Hook, alias Frank Miller, was captured by civilians when she went into a house looking for food. Her captors turned her over to Confederate cavalry under the command of General Roddey, and she was sent to Atlanta along with other Union prisoners. Somewhere between Alabama and Georgia, Hook attempted to escape. She was shot in the thigh, and the Confederate surgeon who tended her wound discovered that she was a woman. In Atlanta, Hook was not housed with the rest of the Union prisoners but in deference to her sex was given a separate room. By February 1864, Confederate authorities were evacuating Union prisoners from the city, but some of the incarcerated could not be removed by rail because they were too sick or badly wounded. Confederate authorities arranged a special exchange of prisoners, and on February 17, 1864, Frances Hook, along with twenty-seven other POWs, was sent to Union lines under a flag of truce at Graysville, Georgia.[4]

Two other Union women were not so quickly discovered. Captured at different times and different places in 1863, they decided to share the fate of their fellow prisoners rather than confess their sex. Mary Jane Johnson and Madame Collier, as she was dubbed by a fellow prisoner, were sent to the POW camp on Belle Isle, Virginia, an island in the James River across from Richmond. Belle Isle consisted of a six-acre lot and lacked sufficient tents to shelter the prisoners from the summer sun or the winter cold.[5]

Collier was from east Tennessee and had followed her lover to war. At Belle Isle she continued to hide her sex in the hope that she might ultimately be released through a prisoner exchange. As another POW noted in his diary, she found herself "in durance vile . . . [with] nothing to do but make the best of it." There is no record of how long Collier had been incarcerated before a fellow captive discovered her sex. On December 23, 1863, he turned her in to the lieutenant in charge of the camp, who promptly released her and sent her across the river to Richmond; from there she was sent North under the first flag of truce. Before Collier left Belle Isle, however, she informed the lieutenant that there was another woman still in the prison.[6]

Mary Jane Johnson served in the 11th Kentucky Cavalry (U.S.), the same regiment in which Lizzie Compton briefly served. She arrived at Belle Isle in late November or early December, and she and Collier quickly saw through each other's disguises. After Collier was liberated, and before the prison guards could find Johnson, she fell sick in January 1864. She went to the camp hospital, where she confessed her sex. She would not talk about herself, however, or divulge her reasons for joining the army, stating only that she had served a little more than a year before falling into Confederate hands. Johnson was released from Belle Isle and presumably sent home. Another prisoner wrote of her in his diary, "She is a young girl of seventeen or eighteen years of age, of prepossessing appearance, and modest and reserved demeanor." Male POWs usually reacted favorably to the women who shared their plight.[7]

Florena Budwin's incarceration did not end as happily as Collier's and Johnson's. She and her husband were captured by Confederates and sent to Andersonville Prison, arriving there sometime after February 1864, when the prison was established. Florena Budwin did not reveal her sex even after her husband was killed by a prison guard. All Civil War prisons were overcrowded and deplorable, but Andersonville, a stockaded pen, arguably was the worst. One historian called Andersonville "a filthy zoo not even fit for animals." Nonetheless, Budwin kept her secret, and perhaps kept the faith that she might one day see freedom. In the face of the increasing threat from Union forces advancing into Georgia, Confederate authorities moved some of the prisoners to Florence, South Carolina, in the fall of 1864.[8]

Budwin was among the thousands of prisoners transferred, arriving at Florence in September. Conditions at Florence were not much better than at Andersonville. Indeed, the swampy stockade at Florence had a higher mortality rate. Budwin continued to conceal her sex at Florence, but how she accomplished this feat is a mystery. By the winter of 1864, Budwin was ill. There was practically no medicine available at Florence and only one doctor to minister to all the sick prisoners. Dr. Josephus Hall must have been a conscientious or an observant physician, however, because it was he who finally recognized that Budwin was a woman. She was immediately given a private room in which to recuperate, and she received the best medical care available. Civilian women living near the prison donated clothing and much of her food and medicine. Despite these kindnesses, all those months of living in wretched conditions finally took their toll on Budwin. She died of pneumonia on January 25, 1865, only one month before all the sick prisoners at Florence were paroled and sent north. She was twenty years old. Budwin was buried in the prison cemetery, which is now a national cemetery. Approximately 2,300 Union POWs were laid to rest there, but Budwin's grave was the only one marked with a headstone.[9]

Budwin's decision to keep her sex a secret during her POW ordeal probably cost her life. Her reasons for doing so are not known. Actually, very little information is available about this woman soldier, except for her prisoner of war status. Even her name is questionable. She probably provided a fictitious identity when discovered at Florence—the first name perhaps suggested by the name of the prison. The surname Budwin cannot be linked with any Union officers or enlisted men. The woman soldier who called herself Florena Budwin took nearly all her secrets to the grave. "Who she was before the war or whence she came when she answered the call to service" are unanswerable questions.[10]

In contrast to Budwin's secrecy, the Union woman captured at Catlett's Station on August 22, 1862 tried to gain immediate release by confessing her sex. A Confederate officer recounted that

> there was a good deal of merriment among the young staff-officers at headquarters concerning one of our Catlett's Station prisoners . . . who, just as we were sending off the main body of these prisoners to Richmond, had been discovered to be a good-looking woman in full Federal uniform. In order that she might follow to the field her warlike lord, she had enlisted as a private soldier in the same company with him, and now claimed to be excepted from the rest of the prisoners as a privilege of her sex. It was decided, however, that this modern Jeanne d'Arc must share the fate of her comrades for the present, and further decision in the case was left to the Richmond authorities.[11]

Extant Confederate records do not show how Richmond authorities dispensed with this soldier. It is also unknown how Confederate authorities ultimately dealt with an anonymous female lieutenant who was discovered among the three hundred POWs held in Atlanta in September 1863.[12]

Of the women soldiers known to have been captured, there were far more Confederate women than Union women. Were Union women more adept at eluding the enemy? Perhaps, but a more likely explanation is that instances of captured Union women were seriously underreported. Confederate authorities kept inadequate records of Union prisoners. Furthermore, near the end of the war, Confederates destroyed many of the records that they did keep. Union authorities kept a better, although far from complete, record of the Confederates they incarcerated.

Treatment of female Confederate POWs by the Union military was inconsistent, but the majority of them were kept in prison regardless of whether their sex became known. This held true in all theaters of the war, although women captured in the west sometimes received more lenient treatment. Mary Ann Clark is an example. After being captured at the Battle of Richmond, Kentucky, she was held in a variety of places for almost four months, finally arriving in Cairo in December 1862. Clark's sex was known to her guards, and this may be the reason she was ultimately exchanged, even though Clark expressed a willingness to stay with her comrades in prison. Clark was allowed to send letters during her incarceration, and she hastened to assure a friend that she was "treated like a lady." Clark also requested that her mother be informed of her status, writing, "I never expect to see her again—as I may get killed in battle—there is a battle impending at Vicksburg and I expect to be in it—our officers here tell me that they will exchange me for a man."[13]

The officers told her the truth. Union authorities gave her a dress to wear and paroled her, after she promised to go to friends in Vicksburg and resume the life of a civilian. But she changed her mind by the time she reached Jackson, Mississippi. Having been in the service for a total of eleven months, Clark decided to go for the war. She put her uniform back on and returned to the Confederate army and General Bragg's command, where she quickly rose to the rank of lieutenant. The details of Clark's military career after her promotion are not known, and whether she survived the war is a mystery.[14]

The train that carried Clark and about forty other prisoners to Cairo included two more women who had been captured in Kentucky in October 1862. It is unclear what happened to these anonymous women, but most likely they were exchanged like Mary Ann Clark. A newspaper correspondent who got a good look at the prisoners when they first embarked filed this report: "Walking about the group, a friend with me called my attention to two personages among the prisoners, dressed like the others . . . the regular features, small heads and hands, swelling and round chests, and limbs of whom, pronounced their possessors not men, but women. . . . I was soon convinced that, among the thirty or forty lame and halt, sick and convalescing rebels before my eyes, there were at least three women included."[15]

Another Confederate POW, referred to as Mrs. Stone in the press, was about twenty years old and served with her husband for three months before she was wounded and captured at the Battle of Perryville. Recognized as a woman, Mrs. Stone was initially treated at a Union hospital and then sent to a private home to recover. Meanwhile, her husband, who had also been captured, obtained a parole through the intercession of a Northern officer so that he could search for his wife. Mr. and Mrs. Stone were reunited, and both were released from Union custody when they agreed to take the oath of allegiance and leave the South. They accepted the conditions and moved to New York City.[16]

The kindness shown to the Stones was not an anomaly. Union officials tried to be kind to Mary Jane Green, but her patriotism ran deeper than Mrs. Stone's, and she refused to give up her male clothing or to renounce the Confederacy. Green was imprisoned seven times during the war. She was first captured in Braxton County, Virginia, while carrying Confederate military mail. When she promised to return to civilian life, she was released. But Green returned to the Confederate army, became a spy, and was captured a second time while reconnoitering near Union lines. Union authorities paroled her after a brief imprisonment in Wheeling, West Virginia. But they did not give her a pass to return to Confederate lines, and she was once again picked up and imprisoned. She explained that she was just trying to go home, so they freed her. On her way back to Braxton County, she was incarcerated yet again for being publicly and loudly pro-Confederate. Authorities relented, and Green finally made it home. She promptly resumed spying for the Confederates and was arrested for a fifth time and imprisoned in Wheeling on January 20, 1863.[17]

In the Wheeling jail Green was given a set of women's clothes to wear, but she refused to put them on because she was not given hoops to wear under the dress. The Wheeling *Daily Intelligencer* vacillated on the issue of Green. At one point, she was termed "very rebellious," but later she was described as "the gentle maiden." In any event, she was rather quickly released from jail. Green then joined a band of guerrillas and was captured by Union forces in the act of cutting telegraph lines. The Wheeling provost marshal had had enough of Green and sent her off to Washington, D.C. She arrived there on May 5, 1863. The Washington provost marshal, however, returned her to rebel lines. Green could not leave well enough alone, and she tried to return to Washington to claim her baggage. When she was arrested a seventh time, the Washington provost marshal sent her to Annapolis, Maryland, and she arrived there by the end of the month. The Annapolis provost marshal did not want her and sent her to the Old Capitol Prison in Washington, D.C., where she stayed until the end of the war.[18]

Other Confederate women POWs did not receive as many chances as Mary Jane Green. They were incarcerated for long periods, even though in most cases their sex was discovered in short order after their capture. A woman captured near Savannah, Georgia, arrived at Hilton Head, South Carolina, with a squad of prisoners on April 8, 1865. Her sex was detected the next morning in the yard of Fort Walker/Welles. The guards arrested her and removed her from the general prisoner population. Arresting someone who was already a prisoner may seem bizarre, but the presence of women soldiers often led to irrational behavior on the part of the provost marshals.[19]

In other cases, women soldiers were simply sent to the nearest prison. In November 1864, a Confederate woman was captured by members of the 7th New York Cavalry while she was alone on picket duty. The major of that regiment briefly interviewed her before sending her to prison at Fortress Monroe. She said she enlisted to be with her husband. The major later remarked that "she was the second woman, in Confederate uniform, I saw during the war." The female orderly sergeant captured at the Battle of Chancellorsville was sent to Baltimore as a prisoner. She was probably confined at Fort McHenry, where other Confederate POWs as well as civilian Confederate sympathizers and unruly Union soldiers were also incarcerated.[20]

When Ellen Levasay of the 3rd Missouri Cavalry (CSA) surrendered at Vicksburg, she was sent to either the Gratiot or Myrtle Street Prison in St. Louis. On August 1, 1863, she was transferred to Camp Morton, Indiana, arriving on August 14. A soldier named William Levasay of the same regiment arrived at Camp Morton the same day. William and Ellen were probably related; they may have been married, or perhaps they were siblings or cousins. William Levasay "galvanized" immediately, meaning that he renounced the Confederacy and enlisted in a Union regiment. Ellen Levasay, on the other hand, remained a prisoner at Camp Morton for eight months. Originally the Indiana State Fairgrounds, Camp Morton was an overcrowded facility, and throughout the winter of 1863–64, prisoners lived in unheated, ramshackle buildings originally intended for livestock. By the spring of 1864, Levasay obviously could not stand being a prisoner any longer. On April 19, 1864, she took the oath of allegiance to the United States and was liberated.[21]

Mary Wright and Margaret Henry were captured in March of 1865 with a squad of Confederate bridge burners. Their imprisonment in Nashville did not last long, as the war was nearly over. One northern newspaper described them as "dashing young creatures." Indeed, female prisoners evoked admiration not only on the part of their fellow POWs but sometimes on the part of their enemies as well.[22]

At least two Confederate women were captured and incarcerated without their sex being detected, which was unusual given the crowded and closely monitored conditions of most prisons and the routine search for valuables when a new prisoner arrived. Even more amazing, Union authorities did not realize that they were women until they gave birth. In April 1864 at Rock Island Prison in Illinois "a portly young fellow in Confederate grey, was . . . delivered of a fine boy." A fellow POW happily noted that the baby was "a new recruit for Uncle Jeff." About eight months later, on December 12, 1864, the Sandusky *Commercial Register* reported that "one of the rebel officers . . . in one of the barracks . . . on Johnson's Island . . . gave birth to a 'bouncing boy.' . . . [T]he officer . . . was undoubtedly a woman." Yet the partisan newspaper took little joy in the occasion and broadly hinted that the southern officer was a prostitute rather than a patriot. Rock Island and Johnson's Island were similar environments, where crudely constructed and poorly heated barracks housed prisoners within a stockade. Given the generally abhorrent conditions of these two military prisons, especially the minimal rations, it was remarkable that the mothers and their babies survived the ordeal. Their ultimate fates are not known.[23]

Similarly, the fates of two of the three Confederate women serving in the Army of Northern Virginia who were captured within a week of each other in the late spring of 1864 remains a mystery. On Thursday, May 26, 1864, a Confederate cavalry woman was captured at the North Anna River. She was briefly held at Baldwin's Mill and attracted quite a crowd of curious onlookers. She was so livid at being captured and being stared at that she threw rocks at any soldiers who came near her. The next day, Jane Perkins of a Virginia artillery regiment was captured at Hanover, Virginia. And a few days later, at the Battle of Cold Harbor, a female Confederate artillery sergeant was captured.[24]

On May 28, the anonymous cavalry woman was seen in a train of prisoners under the protection of a Union provost guard. On May 30, Perkins was seen in another prisoner convoy crossing the Pamunkey River heading towards City Point, a Yankee base of operations. She was still in the convoy the next day when she made the acquaintance of Capt. Thomas L. Pinckney of the 4th South Carolina Cavalry. Pinckney reported that Perkins received much attention from the officers in charge of the prisoners and seemed unconcerned about her predicament. She told Pinckney, "I have the advantage of you in that they cannot hold me for long, and when I get back to Gen. Lee's quarters I will make known many things." Perkins obviously expected that her captors would release her. That evening, however, Perkins was removed from the prisoner convoy headed to City Point and placed with a different group of prisoners whose destination was White House Landing.[25]

She arrived there on June 2, 1864, one of about nine hundred Confederate POWs. A sergeant at White House Landing said that she was dressed in an officer's uniform, and he speculated that Perkins was a lieutenant. He wrote to his wife that Perkins had commanded her battery and was "a good looking girl under 25 years and very intelligent looking."[26] Actually, Perkins was exactly twenty-five, having enlisted in the Confederate army when she was about twenty-three years old. Another Union sergeant at White House Landing also said that Perkins was a lieutenant, but the War Department later recorded her rank as private. A fellow POW said that Perkins was the driver for her artillery company.[27]

The Confederate cavalry woman was also among the prisoners who arrived at White House Landing on June 2. On June 5, the female artillery sergeant captured at Cold Harbor arrived at the same location in the company of other prisoners from that battle. The Union sympathies of nurse Anna Morris Holstein did not keep her from noting with more than a bit of female pride that the sergeant was "the *last* to leave the gun when captured."[28]

Many Confederate prisoners captured during the spring 1864 campaign in Virginia were sent to the prison at Point Lookout, Maryland. Perkins arrived there on June 8, 1864. The other two Confederate women POWs who were at White House Landing at the same time as Perkins were not sent to Point Lookout. Indeed, it is not known what happened to them. They may have escaped, died of disease, or been exchanged. But if they were exchanged, why did Union authorities retain Perkins? Perhaps the other two women swore the oath of allegiance, but Perkins refused. By all accounts, Perkins was a defiant prisoner, and maybe her Union captors did not find her attitude endearing.[29]

Others were puzzled by Perkins' incarceration at Point Lookout. "Why the Yanks detained her I can't imagine," wrote a fellow POW. But detain her they did. She was given her own tent while in the camp, and news of her arrival quickly spread. One prisoner vowed in his diary that Perkins was "purely virtuous." Another prisoner wrote in his diary that "the young rebel lady prisoner . . . has given birth to a little artilleryman." This was probably an unfounded rumor, as no other record concerning Perkins mentions her being with child. A War Department medical inspector was conducting a review of Point Lookout when Perkins arrived. He noted her in his report but did not mention that she was pregnant. Even so, the medical inspector wanted Perkins removed from the camp. Accordingly, the Commissary General of Prisoners ordered her released from Point Lookout but not from custody. On July 12, 1864, Perkins was transferred to Washington, D.C., and imprisoned at Old Capitol. There she stayed until October 1864, when she was transferred to the House of Correction in Fitchburg, Massachusetts, even though she was a prisoner of war, not a convicted criminal. Originally a state institution, the Fitchburg prison had a separate wing for female prisoners. The United States government used the facility during the war for confining particularly troublesome women. Perkins appears to have been the only POW sent there. She arrived on October 17.[30]

Despite Perkins' ardent Confederate sympathies, she had been born in Massachusetts, and thus it was quite ironic that she was imprisoned there. Perkins was in bad shape when she arrived. Blockade runner Mary Terry, a fellow prisoner at Fitchburg, recorded in her diary that "Jane Perkins . . . is paralyzed in the right arm and leg." Terry offered no explanation for

Perkins' condition, whether it resulted from accident or abuse, and it is not known whether this condition came about in Washington or in Massachusetts. Equally unclear is whether Perkins' paralysis was temporary or permanent. One thing is clear. According to all reports, Perkins was in good health and good physical condition when captured. Her paralysis was a direct result of her confinement. Like so many male POWs, Perkins emerged from her prison ordeal in far worse shape than she entered it. In March 1865, after spending ten months as a prisoner of war, military authorities sent Perkins from Fitchburg to Fortress Monroe and exchanged her for a Union prisoner held by Confederates.[31]

Like Jane Perkins, women POWs generally did not claim special privilege because they were female. While some of them received kinder treatment or early release when their sex was discovered, rarely did the women request it. Rather, the majority of women POWs, Union and Confederate, accepted their fate as a misfortune of war just as their male comrades did. POW status rarely caused a woman soldier to waver in her support for her cause or to reject the flag under which she had fought. A singular exception is Mary Ann Pitman. Upon her capture by Union soldiers, she became a traitor to the Confederate army.

Mary Ann Pitman was captured on or about April 1, 1864, while she was returning to her command from a procurement trip to St. Louis. Taken to Fort Pillow, Tennessee, she immediately threw herself on the mercy of the garrison commander, offering to tell him anything he wished to know about Confederate troop movements. She was sent to Memphis and finally to St. Louis, arriving there sometime in the middle of May. In St. Louis, Pitman was repeatedly interrogated by Col. J. P. Sanderson, provost marshal general of the Department of the Missouri. She was most cooperative. She told Sanderson everything she knew about Confederate war plans and about citizens throughout Missouri who secretly assisted the Confederacy in procuring munitions and medicine. Since Pitman previously purchased ordnance from Confederate sympathizers in St. Louis, she clearly had a great deal of valuable information to supply to the colonel.[32]

At the close of the war, Pitman claimed to have allowed herself to be captured and said, "I had become sick of serving in such a cause and I determined to turn and assist in putting down the rebellion." This was a somewhat different story than what she told Colonel Sanderson in June 1864. At that time Pitman had explained that she "found the Union officers & soldiers not to be the desperadoes who I had been taught to believe them to be." Even though her hatred of Yankees evaporated as the war progressed, she added, she had never considered leaving the Confederate army because desertion was a dishonorable act. Pitman may have been trying to appease and flatter Colonel Sanderson and portray herself as a truthful and trustworthy individual.[33]

In fact, upon her capture, Pitman feared for her life and worried that her role as a Confederate supplier might be considered a treasonous act by the United States government, punishable by death. She admitted this, forthrightly telling Sanderson, "I had been performing services, which placed my life at the mercy and disposal of the Federal Government." To protect herself, Pitman said that she "gave such information as [she] could to indicate [her] personal integrity and show the authorities [her] determination to act in good faith." In St. Louis, as in many other areas of the United States that were under martial law during the war, the Union army court-martialed civilians, and anyone suspected of aiding and abetting the Confederacy could be tried before a military judge advocate. The Union army was even known to court-martial captured Confederate soldiers, so Pitman's fears were not unfounded. By cooperating fully, Pitman did indeed save herself from a military tribunal.[34]

During the summer of 1864, Pitman remained in St. Louis under the protection of the Provost Marshal's Office, during which time she was contacted by Colonel Ferris of the Confederate army. Ferris was in St. Louis to garner supplies, but he was also detailed to look for Lieutenant Rawley (Pitman). Ferris asked Pitman to return with him to Gen. Sterling Price's headquarters and delivered a letter to Pitman from General Forrest that requested she return to the army "at all hazards." Forrest must have learned of Pitman's whereabouts through information provided by Confederate spies in Missouri. Pitman told Ferris to inform Forrest that she was doing more for the Confederate cause in St. Louis than in the army, that she would rejoin her command when they came to Missouri, and that it was too dangerous for her to attempt a return to the Confederates at that time. During her meeting with Ferris she also gathered information about Price's plans for raiding Missouri. She promptly relayed this information to Colonel Sanderson.[35]

Shortly after her meeting with Ferris, Pitman was incarcerated in the St. Charles Street Prison for Women. Her imprisonment seems to have been for her own protection. The provost marshal probably feared that her life would be in jeopardy if Confederates learned that she was a Union agent. He may also have sent her to St. Charles Street to spy on the inmates. While there she learned about a number of rebel operations being carried out both inside and outside the prison. She dutifully passed along all the details she heard.[36]

Conditions at St. Charles Street were terrible. Pitman testified before a Union board of inquiry about the inedible food and lack of heat. She also reported that the keeper and his wife demanded bribes from prisoners, sold care packages sent to the women, and burned letters that prisoners wrote to friends and family. Even worse, the keeper and his wife physically abused their female prisoners. They beat a pregnant woman, forced another into prostitution, and locked a third woman in her room on half rations without toilet facilities. Pitman was horrified by the conditions that she and the other women endured at the facility.[37]

But Pitman did not stay at the prison long. On October 21, 1864, Pitman and several other women tried to escape and were caught. That evening, Pitman took the oath of allegiance to the United States. The attempted escape apparently was staged and meant to bolster Pitman's reputation as a Confederate sympathizer. On the evening of the jailbreak, Pitman was sent to Union forces in the field, carrying a letter from Joseph Darr, who had become the department provost marshal upon Colonel Sanderson's death. Darr planned for Pitman to infiltrate the headquarters of General Price.[38]

It is unclear whether Pitman performed this mission or was sent back to St. Louis and Provost Marshal Darr. Her next stop was the military prison at Alton, Illinois. She arrived there on or about November 1, 1864, and was put to work as assistant letter inspector for the prison. It is not known why Union officials sent her there. Her assignment inspecting prisoner letters suggests that she was doing more espionage work for the Union. On the other hand, Pitman wrote several letters of her own to the Provost Marshal's Office in St. Louis, begging for clemency. Perhaps she was sent to Alton, just as she was sent to St. Charles Street, to make sure no one discovered that she was really a Union operative. Or maybe she did something to anger Darr and was sent to Alton as punishment.[39]

Even more mysteriously, Pitman used two aliases at Alton, Molly Hays and Charles Thompson. The commandant of Alton ordered Charles Thompson transferred to St. Louis on November 11 but immediately changed his mind, or received orders to the contrary, because Pitman was not released on that date. Rather, she was released at the end of the month. Probably because of the intercession of Darr, and no doubt based on the continuous information she provided to his office, Mary Ann Pitman was pardoned by the president of the United States on November 24. Regardless of whether this pardon was the result of her pleas for mercy or a reward for services rendered to the Union, it brought an end to her incarceration. Officials at Alton released her on November 29, 1864.[40]

Pitman returned to St. Louis and again went to work as a spy for the Provost Marshal's Office. A pass dated January 7, 1865, stated that Pitman was "on a secret mission connected with the service . . . and . . . entitled to the protection and assistance of our forces everywhere." Resuming her old Confederate identities of Molly Hays and Lieutenant Rawley, she went into the Missouri countryside ostensibly to purchase necessities for the Confederate army. She then turned in the Confederate sympathizers who offered to give or sell such supplies. Her work ended when the war did. In May 1865 the United States War Department approved payment of the incredibly large sum of five thousand dollars to Mary Ann Pitman for services rendered during the war. The secretary of war noted that the payment "would indeed be a moderate compensation for her extended disclosures."[41] Then Mary Ann Pitman simply vanished from the historical record.

With the exception of Malinda Blalock, who engaged in pro-Union bushwhacking after her brief stint in the Confederate army, Pitman is the only woman soldier known to have switched sides during the war. Other Confederate women took the oath of allegiance to gain their freedom, but they did not take up arms or otherwise turn against their former comrades. The remainder of the captured women soldiers of the Civil War were devoted to their flag and to their country and never wavered in their convictions, even when they fell into the hands of the enemy.

6

"I Would Rather Have Been Shot Dead"

Women Soldiers as Casualties of War

The Civil War exacted a heavy physical toll on the citizen soldiers who
served in the Union and Confederate armies. Death, disease, dismemberment, and disfigurement stalked them. In the most costly conflict
on record in America's history, more than 600,000 military deaths were
recorded by the end of four long years of internecine warfare. Women
soldiers numbered among the battlefield casualties, including those killed
in action at First Manassas, Shiloh, Second Manassas, Antietam, Gettysburg, Resaca, Dallas, the Crater, on the Petersburg front, and at Appomattox Station.[1]

The deaths of women soldiers often elicited a compassionate response
from male soldiers, even if the dead woman had been their enemy. Pvt.
Mark Nickerson of the 10th Massachusetts Infantry recalled finding a
southern woman killed during the Battle of Antietam:

> A Sergeant in charge of a burying party from our regiment reported to his Cap-
> tain that there was a dead Confederate up in the cornfield whom he had reason
> to believe was a woman. He wanted to know if she should be kept separate, or
> brought along with the others. The Captain after satisfying himself that this
> Confederate was a woman ordered that she be buried by herself. The news soon
> spread among the soldiers that there was a woman among the Confederate
> dead, and many of them went and gazed upon the upturned face, and tears glis-
> tened in many eyes as they turned away. She was wrapped in a soldier's blanket

and buried by herself and a head board made from a cracker box was set up at her grave marked "unknown Woman CSA."

Nothing in my experience up to that time affected me as did that incident. I wanted to know her history and why she was there. She must have been killed just as the Southerners were being driven back from the cornfield.[2]

More women paid the ultimate price for their devotion to country and cause. Charlotte Hope, alias Charlie Hopper of the 1st Virginia Cavalry (CSA), was killed in a raid. An unnamed corporal in the Union cavalry, described as quiet and retiring by the army surgeon who tried to save her, died from a saber wound to the head in 1864. A Confederate woman was shot in the chest at the Battle of Peachtree Creek. The Union soldier who found her after the battle noted that she was still alive and "full of pluck," but it is unlikely that she survived such a severe wound.[3]

The woman soldier known as Frank Martin said that on three separate occasions during her military service she assisted in the burial of women soldiers. Their sex was unknown to anyone but her. Martin did not, however, divulge where or how they were killed.[4] Given the state of mid-nineteenth-century medical care, death was probably more merciful for soldiers killed outright on the battlefield than for soldiers who lingered after incurring mortal wounds. Such was the case of three Union women, all badly wounded in action, all of whom lived just long enough to tell their life stories to either the surgeon or their comrades.

While walking the field looking for wounded after the Battle of Antietam, Sarah Edmonds, alias Franklin Thompson of the 2nd Michigan Infantry, spotted a youthful soldier badly injured in the neck. She called a surgeon over to the soldier, but after a cursory examination, he said there was nothing he could do to save the soldier from dying, and he left to attend other cases. The soldier then whispered to Edmonds that there was something "he" needed, and confessed to being a female, apparently recognizing that Edmonds was a woman, too. The soldier said that she had enlisted with her brother and that they were orphans. She had witnessed his death earlier that day, about an hour before she was wounded. She told Edmonds that she had fulfilled the duties of a soldier faithfully, and that she was willing to die for the Union. She asked Edmonds to bury her, so that no one would ever know her secret. Edmonds stayed with the soldier until she died and then honored the woman's final request. With the help of two unwitting soldiers, Edmonds buried her, wrapped in a blanket, under a tree.[5]

Frances Day, who briefly served as Sgt. Frank Mayne in the 126th Pennsylvania Infantry, joined another regiment not long after she deserted the 126th. This regiment was sent west, where Day was seriously wounded in the spring of 1863. Her sex was discovered by the surgeon, so Day told her story. Then she died. A letter was sent to the officers of her first regiment, informing them of the true identity and the death of their former sergeant.[6]

A woman soldier identified only as Emily served with a Michigan regiment and was shot in the side at the Battle of Lookout Mountain. She was carried to the surgeon's tent, and her sex was discovered when the wound was examined. The surgeon told her that nothing could be done to save her. Emily's colonel happened to be in the same tent, and he convinced her to tell who she was, so her parents could be notified of her death. Accordingly, Emily dictated a note to her father: "Forgive your dying daughter. I have but a few moments to live. My native soil drinks my blood. I expected to deliver my country, but the Fates would not have it so. I am content to die. Pray, pa, forgive me. Tell ma to kiss my daguerreotype." Emily was buried near the battlefield.[7]

Both wounds and disease often proved fatal to Civil War soldiers. Yet some women soldiers who were sick or injured refused medical care, not because of distrust of the medical profession as was the case with many of their male compatriots, but because they feared that the scrutiny of doctors might reveal their sex and bring about the end of their service. This fear was well founded. Nearly all of the women who were discovered as a result of wounds or disease and managed to survive and recover were dismissed from the service. While there were some women soldiers who kept their sex a secret while availing themselves of medical care, one can only ponder how they contrived to do so.[8]

Annie Lillybridge of the 21st Michigan Infantry was shot in the arm and discovered to be a woman when she sought medical treatment. She was sent home when her arm healed. Likewise, the lieutenant wounded in the shoulder at the Battle of the Wilderness was discovered to be a woman when she arrived at Satterlee Military Hospital in Philadelphia. She told her nurse that she had enlisted with her lover. She, too, was discharged from the Union army.[9]

Another Union soldier, Mary Ellen Wise, was wounded twice but somehow escaped discovery both times during her two years of service in an infantry regiment. When she received a third, severe wound at Lookout

Mountain, however, her secret was betrayed. She took a minié ball in the shoulder. When she recovered from her injury, Wise went to Washington to garner her back pay. The paymaster general, however, refused to release her wages, arguing that army regulations did not authorize payment of women soldiers passing as men. In August 1864, her case was brought to the attention of President Abraham Lincoln, who "'blazed with anger'" at the injustice done to Wise. He ordered that she be paid immediately. Upon hearing the good news, Wise presented herself at the offices of the paymaster general, and her back pay was finally handed over to her.[10]

Another wounded woman soldier also went to Washington. Shot in the leg and shoulder at the Battle of Shiloh, she was still recovering from her wounds two years later as a resident of the Ladies Home for the Friendless. Two more Union women soldiers were discharged from the service after they were wounded, but they did not go home, either. Instead, they traveled to other locations and reenlisted. Frank Martin was shot in the shoulder at the Battle of Stones River and was subsequently discovered by the surgeon. When she left the hospital, she went to Bowling Green, where no one knew her, and enlisted in another regiment. Similarly, Lizzie Compton took a minié ball in the shoulder at Green River. A surgeon in the field hospital detected Compton's sex when he cut away her uniform jacket and shirt. He removed the bullet from Compton's shoulder, bound up the wound, and then called for a chaplain to watch over her. Compton was later sent, under escort, to Bardstown, Kentucky, where she convalesced in a Union hospital and eventually was mustered out of the army. Compton quickly returned to the Green River area and joined a regiment encamped there. Martin and Compton clearly felt such devotion to the Union cause that nothing, not even painful wounds, deterred them from serving their country. Both women bragged of multiple wartime enlistments.[11]

Women soldiers were also wounded at the Battles of Antietam and Gettysburg. The female casualties at Antietam benefitted from the attentions of two rather prominent individuals. Governor Curtin of Pennsylvania assisted Catherine Davidson, and Clara Barton cared for Mary Galloway. Galloway, shot in the neck and not found until the day after the battle, was taken to a shed behind one of the farmhouse hospitals but was not seen by a surgeon until another day had passed. Galloway, however, would not let the doctor near her, so he summoned Clara Barton, who succeeded in calming the frantic soldier. With Barton's help, the surgeon finally examined the wound. The bullet had entered the left side of her neck and lodged in the right side of her back. Galloway was still alive because the ball miraculously missed all her vital organs. Unable to provide anesthesia to the patient, the surgeon nevertheless removed the bullet from Galloway's back and then turned her over to the care of Barton. Galloway finally consented to tell the story of how she had dressed as a soldier to seek out her lover, and she confessed that she was only sixteen years old. Barton kindly located Galloway's sweetheart in a hospital in Frederick, Maryland. The pair were ultimately reunited and later married.[12]

Catherine Davidson, serving with the 28th Ohio Infantry, was shot in the arm at Antietam. Shortly after the battle, the governor of Pennsylvania arrived and took to the field to help with the wounded. Davidson was one of the soldiers he consoled, and it was he who put her in an ambulance. Davidson thought she was dying, so she gave him her ring. Davidson did not die, but she did lose her right arm when surgeons amputated it halfway between the shoulder and the elbow. After her dismissal from the service, Davidson called upon the governor at the Continental Hotel in Philadelphia. She rushed over to him, kissed him on the forehead, and poured out her thanks for his kindness to her. The governor was quite surprised, for he had not realized that the soldier who gave him the ring was a woman. He was wearing the ring that day in the hotel, and Davidson showed him her initials inside it. Governor Curtin offered it back to her, but Davidson wanted him to keep it, saying, "The finger that used to wear that ring will never wear it any more. The hand is dead, but the soldier still lives."[13]

In addition to one Confederate killed in action, three women are known to have been wounded at Gettysburg, one Union and two Confederate. They all were discovered to be women because of their injuries. The Union woman was quietly turned out of the service upon her recovery and, like Frank Martin and Lizzie Compton, immediately reenlisted. The Confederate woman wounded in Pickett's Charge laid on the field screaming all night. Whether she survived her ordeal is unknown.[14]

The other Confederate woman shot at that battle did survive, but only because surgeons amputated her leg after she was captured and sent to a U.S. military hospital. A Union soldier recovering in the same hospital wrote to his parents:

> I must tel you we have got a female secesh here. she was wounded at gettysburg but our doctors soon found her out. I have not seen her but the[y] say she is

very good looking[.] the poor girl [h]as lost a leg. it [is] a great pity she did not stay at home with her mother but she get good care and kind treatment. it [is] rather romantic to have a female soldier in the hospital and her only to have one leg and far a way from home but I hope she will soon get better and get home to her friends.[15]

Union officials must have felt as charitable towards the Confederate amputee as did the enlisted men in the hospital. They apparently sent this woman to her home in the South rather than retaining her as a prisoner of war.

Soldiers too severely wounded to be moved during or after engagements often found themselves in the hands of the enemy. Wounded Confederate women soldiers were captured at the Battles of Richmond, Perryville, and Allatoona. Union soldier Frances Hook was wounded after her capture by Confederates when she attempted an escape and was shot in the leg by a guard. Earlier in Hook's army career, she had sustained a minor wound that led to her discovery and dismissal from the service, but like so many other women soldiers, she simply reenlisted in another regiment. Her wounding by the Confederate guard was far more serious, as the bullet lodged deep in her left thigh. Confederate authorities exchanged her on February 17, 1864, and the Union soldiers who received her took her to General Hospital No. 2 at Chattanooga the very next day.[16]

Hook was treated in Ward 2 of the Chattanooga hospital until the end of the month. She gave her age as twenty-five but refused to reveal her true identity, so hospital personnel continued to refer to her as Frank Miller, the alias under which she had most recently enlisted. While in this hospital, Hook met Dr. Mary Edwards Walker, who was so excited about the presence of a female soldier that she notified the press. As a result, several newspaper reporters contacted Hook, who consented to interviews but steadfastly refused to give her real name. She said that the reason she enlisted in the service was to be with her brother, but she stayed in the service after his death because she enjoyed being a soldier. Despite this love of the army, she told reporters that she would willingly leave the service when she sufficiently recovered from the bullet wound.[17]

On March 1, 1864, Hook was transferred to General Hospital No. 17 in Nashville, a facility usually reserved for officers. She convalesced there for a little more than two months and then was transferred to General Hospital No. 1, also in Nashville, on May 5. By June, the doctors there decided that Hook's leg was finally healed and that she could go home. The officers arranging for her transportation to her hometown prevailed upon her to tell them who she really was, and at last, Hook gave in and told them. She even allowed the hospital attendants to take a photograph of her. Although Hook had promised the newspaper reporters that she would go home, the hospital personnel did not believe it, since she seemed upset to be leaving her soldier life behind. Accordingly, the officers in charge of sending her home also alerted recruiting authorities, advising them to be on the lookout for her trying to rejoin the service. On June 10, 1864, Frances Hook left the Nashville hospital, bound for an unrecorded location north of Tennessee.[18]

Loreta Velazquez was also wounded more than once, sustaining three injuries during the course of the war. Shortly after her stint at Fort Donelson, while working as a scout for General Johnston, she was wounded in the foot during a skirmish. She sought medical attention but feared that constant surveillance by the surgeon might result in her discovery, so she deserted the hospital. She was next wounded at Shiloh by shrapnel. Her third injury was again to the foot, sustained while running dispatches between Richmond and Atlanta. Lieutenant Buford (Velazquez) was treated at the Empire Hotel Hospital in Atlanta, admitted on July 26, 1863.[19]

Despite her injuries and the medical attention she sought for them, Velazquez successfully kept her secret. For nearly all female soldiers, the nature of the wound dictated whether its recipient was detected as a woman. The sex of a soldier killed in action may or may not have been discovered, depending on the care or haste that burial parties employed after a battle. But the sex of a woman soldier badly or mortally wounded would almost certainly be discovered. A woman shot in the shoulder, upper arm, chest, back, groin, or thigh was detected as soon as the surgeon removed clothing to gain access to the wound. Women wounded in the face, hands, calves, or feet often escaped detection because their medical care did not require extensive disrobing for treatment. Rebecca "Georgianna" Peterman sustained a wound slightly above the temple. It left her with a bad scar but her army career still intact. Confederate soldier Mollie Bean of the 47th North Carolina Infantry was wounded twice during her two years of army service. Neither of the wounds led to her detection, so they were probably minor injuries that required noninvasive treatment. Mary Ann Pitman was wounded in the side at the Battle of Shiloh. Such a wound should have led to Pitman's discovery, but perhaps the doctor who treated her kept her secret, or maybe the wound was not serious and Pitman attended to it herself.[20]

Mary Owens fought in three battles with her Pennsylvania cavalry regiment and was wounded each time. One of these wounds was above her right eye. Another was to the arm. Owens dressed this second wound herself, fearing that a visit to the regimental hospital might end her service. Both of these injuries were probably cuts from an enemy saber. Owens' third wound was to the chest and required that she be taken to a hospital, where her sex was finally revealed. She was treated, discharged from the hospital and the army, and sent home.[21]

Like Mary Owens, Sarah Edmonds attended to her own injuries rather than seek medical care. Also like Owens, she was hurt on three occasions during her service. Only one of her injuries was combat related; the other two were accidents. In August 1862, while carrying mail between Manassas and Washington, Edmonds tried to jump a ditch with her mule. The animal threw her and she landed hard on her left side. She suffered multiple contusions to her leg, leaving her lame for quite a while. More seriously, she suffered a lung hemorrhage. She coughed blood for more than a week but never sought the attention of an army doctor. On another occasion, Edmonds was bitten in the arm by a vicious horse. She treated the bite wound herself and continued with her duties. Her third injury came when her horse was shot from under her and she broke a bone when she fell. Again, Edmonds refused medical care.[22]

These injuries plagued her for the rest of her life. In 1896, an arthritic Edmonds requested an increase in her monthly soldier's pension, saying that her wartime injuries were the cause of her failing health. The Pension Bureau retorted that there were no medical records to prove that she was ever injured during the war, and therefore her claim held no merit. Edmonds responded, "Had I been what I represented myself to be, I should have gone to the hospital. . . . But being a *woman* I felt compelled to suffer in silence . . . in order to escape detection of my sex. *I would rather have been shot dead*, than to have been known to be a woman and sent away from the army." The Pension Bureau was not swayed, and Edmonds never received an increased allotment.[23]

Neither injuries nor detection drove Edmonds away from the Union army. Rather, disease ended her military service. During the Peninsula campaign, Edmonds contracted malaria. She survived the first bout of chills and fever and, typically, did not seek medical treatment, even during the worst of the illness. In March 1863, the 2nd Michigan Infantry transferred to Kentucky, where Edmonds suffered a recurrence. By April, Edmonds had a severe malarial fever and was often delirious. Comrades repeatedly urged "Frank" to go to the hospital, but to no avail. In lucid moments, Edmonds realized that the illness might result in a revelation of her sex, whether or not she was hospitalized. She also realized that if she did not seek some type of medical care, she would never fully recover from the disease. Edmonds applied for a leave of absence, but the request was denied. The illness and fear of discovery drove her to a mild nervous breakdown. She later wrote of the episode, "I now became discouraged, and fearing that if I remained longer my sex might be discovered, I left the Army." Her regiment listed Pvt. Franklin Thompson as having deserted April 19, 1863, from their camp near Lebanon.[24]

Edmonds was not the only woman who survived injury only to lose her military career due to illness. Jane Short, alias Charley Davis, served more than a year in the Union cavalry, during which time she was wounded in the hand at Shiloh. Only when she fell ill and was sent to a hospital, however, was her sex detected, and she was then discharged. Similarly, illness was the undoing of an unnamed woman soldier in the 2nd Indiana Cavalry. One of her comrades wrote to his wife, "We discovered last week a soldier who turned out to be a girl. She had already been in service for 21 months and was twice wounded. Maybe she would have remained undiscovered for a long time, if she hadn't fainted. She was given a warm bath which gave the secret away."[25]

The woman who served as Alfred J. Luther in the 1st Kansas Infantry, was wounded at Wilson's Creek, but not detected as a woman. Nineteen months later in Louisiana, Sergeant Luther contracted "variola"—a nineteenth century term for smallpox. She was admitted to the regimental hospital on March 10, 1863, and transferred to a general hospital at Lake Providence nine days later. Luther died of the disease on March 22, 1863. Even though she spent almost two weeks in the hospital, her sex was not discovered until her body was prepared for burial.[26]

The revelation of sick and dying women soldiers commonly evoked feelings of compassion, sympathy, and admiration on the part of their male compatriots. The death of Sergeant Luther was a prime example. A soldier in the 1st Minnesota Artillery wrote to his sister:

> One of the members of the 1st Kansas Reg't died in the Hospital. . . . After
> death the somewhat startling discovery was made by those who were preparing

the body for burial, that their companion, beside whom they had marched and fought for nearly two years was a woman. You can imagine their astonishment. The Reg't is camped near us and I went to the Hospital and saw her. She was of pretty good size for a woman with rather masculine features. She must have been very shrewd to have kept her secret so long when she was surrounded by several hundred men. . . . This girl enlisted after they went to Missouri, so they know nothing of her early history. She doubtless served under an assumed name. Poor girl! who knows what trouble, grief, or persecution drove her to embrace the hardships of a soldier's life. She had always sustained an excellent reputation in the Regiment. She was brave as a Lion in battle and never flinched from the severest fatigues or the hardest duties. She had been in more than a dozen battles and skirmishes. She was a Sergeant when she died. The men in the company all speak of her in terms of respect and affection. She would have been promoted to a Lieutenancy in a few days if she had lived.[27]

Other women soldiers succumbed to disease, which is not surprising since twice as many Civil War soldiers died from disease than died of wounds. Death or dismemberment from battle wounds was a soldier's biggest fear, but illness was the most common killer. Diseases like smallpox, measles, and typhoid fever ran rampant through the armies and prison camps, preying on the citizen soldiers, many of whom were from farms or rural areas and therefore lacked immunities to contagious viruses and bacteria as a result of their lack of previous exposure. Opportunistic infections like pneumonia frequently struck soldiers weakened by other illnesses, wounds, or wretched living conditions. Chronic diarrhea and dysentery, both untreatable by Civil War–era medicine, plagued the soldiers, who often drank contaminated water, ate contaminated food, and practiced poor sanitary habits in camp and on the march.[28]

Among the female soldiers who died of disease was an unnamed woman killed by an unidentified fever at Overton Hospital in Memphis in 1863. She originally joined the army at the beginning of the war to follow her lover and then reenlisted when her original term expired. She was not discovered as a woman until shortly before her death. A St. Louis newspaper published her story and asked, "Can any of our cavalry men tell us who the unfortunate girl was?" No answers were forthcoming.[29]

A northern woman identified only as Charlie H. died of measles at a general hospital in Tullahoma, Tennessee, in the spring of 1865. Described as a "frail and fair" private about eighteen years old, Charlie became a favorite of the medical staff because "he was grateful for the smallest attention and kindness." No one at the hospital suspected that Charlie was a girl, for "there was nothing about him different from other boy-patients except his extreme fairness." After days of seeming to improve, Charlie's condition deteriorated, and it became apparent that the soldier was destined to die. Charlie sensed that the end was near and sent for the surgeon to hear a deathbed confession. After telling him that she was a woman, she explained that she was an orphan who had been abandoned by the man she loved. Having "nothing to live for but [her] country," she joined the Union army and "fought to defend its rights and maintain its honor." Charlie then requested that the surgeon personally place her body in the coffin because she did not want anyone to know her secret. When she died, the surgeon honored her final request by privately dressing the body, supervising its move to the dead house, and personally nailing down the lid of the coffin. The surgeon then waited seventeen years before telling Charlie's story.[30]

Rosetta Wakeman, alias Lyons Wakeman of the 153rd New York Infantry, also contracted measles while in the army. On January 1, 1863, she was admitted to the regimental hospital for care. She fought the disease well and returned to duty a week later. Like Charlie H., she also successfully hid the fact that she was a woman during this illness. After her bout with the measles, Wakeman remained healthy until the Red River campaign, when she became debilitated by chronic diarrhea. Wakeman entered the regimental hospital at Alexandria, Louisiana, on May 3, 1864. Four days later, the regimental surgeon ordered her transferred to New Orleans. Her voyage down the Red River took fifteen days. She was admitted to Marine USA General Hospital on May 22, 1864, still suffering from "diarrhoea acuta." The condition never improved, and on June 19, 1864, Rosetta Wakeman died. She was twenty-two years old. She was buried at Monument Cemetery, now known as Chalmette National Cemetery, under her assumed identity of Lyons Wakeman. Her comrades back in the regiment were notified of her demise in August.[31]

Private Wakeman spent two weeks traveling from the regimental hospital to the general hospital. She then lingered nearly a month in the hospital before dying. Even though she suffered from a wasting disease that must eventually have left her too weak to move from her bed, and therefore incapable of attending to her own sanitary needs, it appears as if no one ever realized that Wakeman was a woman, or if they did, they made no written record of the fact. No one will ever really know what transpired during the final month of Private Wakeman's life. What is known is that she occupied one of the 5,808 Union army hospital beds in New Orleans. Perhaps the medical staff was so overwhelmed with sick and wounded soldiers that Wakeman received little individual attention. With a soaring death rate in New Orleans that summer from an outbreak of yellow fever as well as casualties from the Red River campaign, the dead were probably hurriedly put in coffins and buried as quickly as possible. The case of Private Wakeman raises the question of how many other women soldiers died of disease, their sex not discovered by nurses or surgeons.[32]

Other women soldiers survived their illnesses. Charles Martin, the runaway child turned regimental clerk, was taken ill with typhoid fever and sent to a Philadelphia hospital. When she recovered, she was sent home to her parents, who thought she was dead. Yet another Charlie, a veteran of both Battles of Bull Run, was stricken with typhoid when her regiment transferred to Tennessee. Sent to a Memphis hospital, she was happy to go home when she recovered. She had enlisted with her betrothed, but he had died previously.[33]

In some cases, the exact cause of a woman soldier's illness was not known, or at least not recorded. Fannie Wilson and Nellie Graves, who had followed their sweethearts into the 24th New Jersey Infantry, caught the same unspecified illness and were sent to Cairo along with other sick and wounded from their brigade. Discovered in the hospital, they were discharged from the service and sent home when they recovered. On November 7, 1862, Pvt. Charles Freeman, listed as serving with the 52nd Ohio Infantry, was admitted to a hospital in Lebanon, Kentucky, suffering from a fever. She was transferred to General Hospital No. 11 in Louisville, where a flustered hospital clerk recorded that Freeman was suffering not only from a fever but also from "sextual incompatibility," giving the term a whole new meaning. Private Freeman was in reality Mary G. Scaberry of Columbus, Ohio, who had been in military service for four months before falling ill. She was discharged from the service on December 13, 1862, for being "a woman in disguise as a soldier."[34]

Not every sick woman soldier was detected as a result of her illness, however. The stalwart Albert Cashier of the 95th Illinois Infantry was admitted to her regimental hospital on April 28, 1864, complaining of diarrhea. She was released the next day. While this was her only visit to a hospital for the condition, it plagued her for much of the war and she occasionally sought help from the regimental surgeon. Indeed, chronic diarrhea was Cashier's unwelcome companion for much of the rest of her life. In 1899, when Cashier sought an increased pension payment, Dr. Charles F. Ross deposed that he had treated the veteran for that illness for ten years. Also in 1899, Cashier submitted to an examination by surgeons of the Medical Division of the Bureau of Pensions. Those doctors concurred that Cashier suffered from chronic diarrhea and inquired about "his" eating habits. Cashier swore that the condition was the result of the war. Astonishingly, neither Dr. Ross nor the Pension Bureau doctors realized that Albert Cashier was a woman.[35] The state of medical care in the late nineteenth century was clearly different than it is today.

Wounds and illness were two physical risks that all soldiers faced, regardless of their sex. Women soldiers faced the additional physical risks inherent in pregnancy and childbirth. Six soldiers are known to have performed their military duties while pregnant. Incredibly, none of their comrades noticed their condition until the women went into labor and delivered their babies. Two Confederate prisoners of war gave birth while incarcerated, and babies were born to Union women as well.

The most sensational case was the unidentified corporal from New Jersey who gave birth to a baby boy while on duty in winter camp on the Rappahannock River in Virginia. Col. Adrian Root of the 94th New York Infantry recorded the event in a letter to his mother, writing, "When I was last on duty as General Officer of the Day I came across a very singular case of illness out on the picket line. . . . A corporal of a New Jersey regiment who was on duty with the pickets complained of being unwell, but little notice was given his complaints at first. His pain and other symptoms of severe indisposition increased, becoming so evident that his officers had him carried to a nearby farmhouse. There the worthy corporal was safely delivered of a fine, fat little recruit for the . . . regiment!" The farmhouse where she delivered her child was in use as an army hospital. Another soldier reported that when she was taken to the hospital and looked at by the surgeon the "examination caus[ed] a great commotion among the doctors and hospital attendants."[36]

There is little wonder that the event created a sensation. The New Jersey woman had served nearly a year in her regiment, and "no one had suspected anything wrong up to the very hour of the picket line denouement." The birth became the primary gossip of the Army of the Potomac that winter and spring, with many soldiers writing home with the story, expressing surprise, wonderment, and often humor. One soldier even sent the news to the press. The New Orleans *Daily Picayune* belatedly reported, in May 1863, that "the army has increased some lately, not by conscription but by birth." Another soldier who told the story to his mother wrote, "The other night the Corporal had a baby, for the Corporal turned out to be a woman!" Yet another soldier worried that his family would not believe the tale, writing, "You may perhaps think that this is a big story. It is, but it is a true one." One more soldier opined that "it Is not a bad move of the government if they can make the corporals bear children and serve as a soldier they may keep the stock up."[37]

The soldiers of the Army of the Potomac who recorded the incident seemed overjoyed by the news of the birth, and they expressed good wishes for the woman and her child. In late February, a squad of New York soldiers obtained a pass to travel throughout the encampment to find the mother and baby and pay their respects. Perhaps the birth was so compelling to the soldiers because it was an affirmation of life in the midst of the death and destruction of the war. Some soldiers were so taken with the news that they said the woman was not from New Jersey, but from a regiment from their state. Others established a "contribution fund . . . to give her boy a military education."[38]

The excitement and good wishes of the comrades of the soldier-mother were not diminished by the fact that the woman apparently was not married to the father of her child. The relationship between the parents was that of "intimate friends," as one officer euphemistically wrote. In fact, the commanding officers seemed as concerned about her welfare as were the enlisted men and reportedly demanded to know the identity of the father. "She swore it on one of the Seargants of the Company who messed with her and they toke $8.00 out of his monthly pay while he is in the service and that is to go to support her and her child." About three months postpartum, the mother and baby were separated from the father and sent home to her parents. One soldier was "sorry for the girl—forced to leave him at last & in much worse condition."[39]

It is a mystery how she concealed her pregnancy until she went into labor. Extant reports of the birth relate that the baby was fat, an indication that the soldier carried the child to term. She must have worn a truly oversized uniform coat. Similarly, a sergeant in the Army of the Cumberland must also have possessed some large clothing. On April 17, 1863, while news of the birth of a baby in the Army of the Potomac was still making the rounds of Union campfires in Virginia, a baby was born in the camp of the 20th Army Corps in Murfreesboro, Tennessee. One of the soldiers in that camp related the story of the sergeant-mother to his hometown newspaper, adding, "This lady . . . has been in the war for more than two years; and she disguised herself so perfectly that no person mistrusted her for a female." The editor humorously noted, "He says no one has suspected this soldier of being a female. It strikes us that the tent-born boy's paternal relative must have had a pretty strong suspicion."[40]

General Rosecrans did not find the birth of a child at all funny. Upon hearing the news, the outraged general sent the following telegram to the commander of the 20th Army Corps: "The Medical Director reports that an Orderlie Sergent in Brig Gen *Johnsons* Division was to day delivered of a baby—which is violation of all military law and of the army regulations[.] No such case has been known since the days of Jupiter. You will apply a proper punishment in the case, and a remedy, to prevent a repetetion of the act."[41] General Rosecrans was mistaken. Nowhere in the U.S. Army regulations did it state that a soldier could not have a baby. As for the proper remedy to prevent a repetition of the act, was Rosecrans referring to the birth or the conception?

Yet another baby was born to a Union soldier. On March 2, 1865, Sgt. Joseph Cross of the 29th Connecticut Infantry (Colored) wrote to his wife, "One Question I wish to ask Did you Ever hear of A Man having a child[?] there is such a case in our regement & in Company F she played man Ever since wee have been [out] the child war Born feb 28 it rained hard all day and now she is in the hospital." The identity of this African American soldier who became a mother in the trenches near Petersburg remains unknown.[42]

Less than a week later, on March 6, 1865, a corporal in the 6th New York Heavy Artillery delivered early in the morning at Bermuda Hundred, Virginia. Like the New Jersey woman two years earlier, this corporal went into labor while walking the picket line. Her sergeant, Herman Weiss, happily related the incident to his wife: "What was our surprise when . . . we heard that the corporal had been taken very sick so that the doctor had send him right off to the division hospital and that then and there this . . . good looking corporal had been relieved of a nice little boy and that the corporal and the boy was doing first rate."[43]

Upon receiving his letter, Adeline Weiss immediately wrote back to her husband, exclaiming, "What a woman she must have been. I cant contrive how she hid it." Her letter continued, "She must have been more than the

common run of woman or she could never [have] stood soldiering especially in her condition." Her husband replied that it was fairly easy for the
corporal to hide her pregnancy, because their uniforms did not fit very
well, and besides, "there is a great many women that dont show much anyway." Sergeant Weiss also reported that the birth caused a great deal of
merriment in the regiment.[44]

The ultimate fates of the soldiers who became mothers while in the service are not known. They went home with their babies and disappeared
from the historical record. Indeed, childbirth is the only reason that these
women were ever detected. Had they not gotten pregnant, they presumably would have served their term of service, barring any wounds or disease, and then gone home without anyone ever knowing they were
women—no one, that is, except the loved ones with whom they went to
war in the first place. Why did these women elect to stay in the service
after they realized they were expecting? The two Confederate women in
POW camps may not have had the choice to go home, but the Union
women most certainly did. Maybe the pregnant Union women wished to
stay with the fathers of their babies. Or perhaps their sense of duty and
patriotism compelled them to carry on despite the discomforts and added
burden of pregnancy. One thing is certain. Unlike wounds or disease,
which only sometimes led to the discovery of a woman soldier's sex, childbirth inevitably gave away a woman soldier's true identity.

Fear of revelation must have been an extra source of anxiety for the
women soldiers of the Civil War. Both male and female soldiers faced
the very real possibilities of death and disease, and the women, just like
the men, accepted the fact that their military service might cost them their
lives. But unlike their male comrades, women soldiers dealt with the additional worry of discovery, knowing that if their sex was detected, their
carefully contrived army careers would end.

7

"A CONGENITAL PECULIARITY"

Women Discovered in the Ranks

In August 1861 at Lancaster, Ohio, a student aged eighteen enlisted for a term of three years in the 17th Ohio Infantry. Pvt. Frank Deming, described as five feet six inches tall, with a dark complexion, gray eyes, and black hair, served until May 18, 1862, when the soldier was discharged for disability near Corinth, Mississippi. The certificate of disability for discharge noted that Private Deming was unfit for duty "no days" during the previous two months, but nevertheless cited the soldier as being "incapable of performing the duties of a soldier" because of "a congenital peculiarity which should have prevented her admission into the Army—being a female." This was despite the fact that Deming had indeed been performing assigned army duties for nine months. The clerk of Company A dutifully noted on the next muster roll that Deming's "disability" was "being a woman."[1]

While some women soldiers served out their entire enlistments without official discovery during the Civil War, others startled their comrades and irritated their officers when their identity as females was revealed while they were serving in the ranks. Most discoveries resulted from women becoming casualties of war. Being taken prisoner, for example, usually assured that a woman serving as a soldier would be found out. Wounded women soldiers were discovered after the Battles of Shiloh, Richmond, Perryville, Murfreesboro, Antietam, Fredericksburg, Gettysburg, Green

River, Lookout Mountain, Peachtree Creek, Allatoona, and the Wilderness, among others. Additional female warriors were revealed by burial parties in the aftermath of battles such as First Manassas, Second Manassas, Shiloh, Gettysburg, Resaca, Dallas, and the Crater, as well as along the lines at Petersburg and Appomattox.

The bodies of two of these women were not discovered until after the war, when the federal government attempted to find the graves of all Union soldiers and rebury them in newly created national cemeteries. In June 1866, it was reported that "in disinterring the Federal dead near Resaca, Ga., a body was discovered which excited considerable attention from the smallness of the feet. On examination it was found to be that of a woman, shot through the head." That woman soldier, like so many of her comrades, had been hastily buried after the battle, with a wooden marker placed on the grave. The reburial crew mistakenly deciphered the woman's weathered grave marker as reading, "Charles Johehons, private, Sixth Missouri Volunteers." The War Department held no record of such a soldier, and thus neither her true identity nor the name under which she served may ever be known.[2]

Similarly, the identity of another woman soldier, who was unearthed from the mass grave at the Crater may also never be known. Gravediggers discovered her body in September 1866, and noted that she had been shot through the head, just like the body unearthed at Resaca. The workmen also noted that her body was in a "remarkable state of preservation," and they described her as having "a delicate face." She was reburied alongside the men with whom she fought and died.[3]

Illness, too, was a threat to women soldiers cloaked in male disguise. A number of women fought in hard battles and endured hard marching only to be dismissed from the service or lose their lives to typhoid, measles, malaria, pneumonia, dysentery, and smallpox. Going into labor and delivering a baby was another sure way for a woman in uniform to disclose the fact that she was not a man. Other women, however, inadvertently divulged their sex through some accident or incident that occurred in camp or in the course of regular army life. Theft of an officer's boots was the downfall of Charles Norton, the "faithful and efficient helper" of the 141st Pennsylvania Infantry. Investigation into the theft exposed this "general favorite" to be a she, who "was speedily mustered out of the service."[4]

Sarah Bradbury, the dragoon, and Ella Reno, the teamster, gave themselves away in the spring of 1863, as General Sheridan recorded in his memoirs: "While out on the foraging expedition these Amazons had secured a supply of 'apple-jack' by some means, got very drunk, and on the return had fallen into Stone River and been nearly drowned. After they had been fished from the water, in the process of resuscitation their sex was disclosed, though up to this time it appeared to be known only to each other." The colonel who forwarded the two drunk and soaked women to Sheridan was said to be "mortified" by the discovery.[5]

Only a small number of women betrayed themselves through stereotypical feminine behavior or appearance. Mary Smith joined the 41st Ohio Infantry sometime in August or September 1861 and was sent to Camp Wood near Cleveland. She was described as intelligent and good looking but was suspected of being a woman because of her "peculiar wring of the dish cloth" and her ability to sew as well as a professional seamstress. She may have been smart, but she could not hide her ingrained feminine habits, and her soldiering career came to a swift end. Perhaps she was not so clever as a woman soldier in the 14th Maine Infantry who explained away her expert sewing by informing her captain that she was a tailor prior to the war. He did not learn that she was a woman until the war was nearly over.[6]

Old habits betrayed more than one woman. Two were discovered in the 95th Illinois Infantry, Albert Cashier's regiment, when an officer threw apples to them. They were dressed in their military uniforms, but reflexively made a grab for their nonexistent aprons in order to catch the apples. They were discharged immediately. A woman trying to enlist in the spring of 1863 was suspected when she gave "a quick jerk of her head that only a woman could give." Having a distinctly female manner also gave away a girl in the 3rd Ohio Infantry. She enlisted with her brother but became separated from him after their brief training was complete. She spent a couple of weeks on duty in Camp Dennison, near Cincinnati, until she approached the commanding officer to request a transfer to Pennsylvania, where she thought her brother might be. He suspected her sex immediately.[7]

Nancy Corbin confessed that she was a woman when she was questioned by a colonel. Although she was dressed as a male, the colonel observed that she was "rather a fine looking girl." Obviously, Corbin was a rather poor study of male appearance and behavior. An unnamed female nurse who joined a Pennsylvania cavalry unit was also unsuccessful at acting her male role. She became separated from her husband and thought that by enlisting as a soldier she could travel to the front and find him. Hers was a thin disguise, so much so that another dragoon made sexual advances toward her. Jennie Robertson was another who was not adept at male pretense. She enlisted twice in the United States regular army, but was discovered within three months each time.[8]

A woman from Iowa who enlisted under the alias of Charles H. Williams was discovered in August 1861 while walking down a street in St. Louis. Two police officers were suspicious of Williams, noticing the soldier's fair complexion and small hands. They turned Williams over to the provost marshal, who released her when she promised to leave the army. Pvt. John Thompson of the 1st Kentucky Infantry (U.S.) "first excited suspicion by her feminine method of putting on her stockings; and when handed over to the surgeon proved to be a woman."[9]

At Harper's Ferry in 1864, a young soldier "was sitting under an apple tree when a club, thrown at an apple, fell upon her head, causing her to give a woman's squeal. She was arrested and examined by the doctor, who declared, 'He bears unmistakable evidences of being a woman.'" Her comrades assumed that she was a spy, even though she was only about sixteen years old. Two women with the 49th Georgia Infantry caused "considerable excitement" in the Shenandoah Valley in 1864. As one soldier wrote, "They were dressed in men's clothes, or rather in a soldier's garb, and were following the Brigade on foot. It was soon rumored all through the Brigade that they were of the fair sex, and their face and hair also betrayed them." Assuming that the women were "disreputable characters," officers ordered them to stay behind while the regiment moved on.[10]

Unfamiliar clothing ended several army careers. For those who had worn nothing but dresses their entire lives, the switch to pants and shirt was perplexing. A recruit in Rochester, New York, was discovered to be a woman when she tried to put her pants on over her head. Since she had arrived in camp already wearing male attire, one wonders why she had not already learned this lesson. Sarah Collins of Wisconsin was discovered shortly after enlistment by the way she put on her shoes and socks.[11]

Close quarters were the culprit in the revelation of two more female recruits. In January 1864, a woman soldier was detected at winter barracks in Covington, Kentucky. The episode "created a great sensation," and the officers at headquarters gave the woman "an unceremonious and dishonorable discharge." The confined nature of a transport steamer was the undoing of a woman discovered in St. Louis in September 1862. This "rather good looking individual" was then summarily arrested by the police.[12]

Some distaff soldiers revealed their true identities to obtain a discharge when they decided they wanted to leave the military. For example, in 1862, an unnamed Union woman soldier of Scottish descent grew weary of the drudgery of a soldier's life, so she turned herself in, was discharged, and went home. Lou Morris enlisted in a cavalry regiment and served nine months before deserting and going to Memphis. There, she encountered another former woman soldier, Jane Short, who had been mustered out of the Union army after she was discovered while sick. The two women reenlisted together in a Missouri infantry regiment and served undetected until August 1864, when Jane heard that their regiment was being sent to fight Confederate forces under General Forrest. A frightened Jane not only revealed her secret to authorities but also turned in Lou. Both women were discharged. Jane, "content to return to the paths of peace again," was happy to go home. Lou, however, "said that she was not frightened," and vowed to join another regiment when an opportunity presented itself.[13]

A few women were given away by the loved ones with whom they served. Marian Green left home in the summer of 1862 and enlisted in the 1st Michigan Mechanics and Engineers to be near her fiancé. She spent the summer rebuilding bridges on the Memphis and Charleston Railroad but did not let her fiancé know she was in the regiment until that fall, when he became ill. Green requested a transfer to hospital duty so that she could care for him. The fiancé was not pleased by her presence, however, so he wrote to her parents, who immediately informed military officials. Green was sent home. Her fiancé survived the war, and Green must have forgiven him for his betrayal, for they married when he was mustered out of the service.[14]

In other instances, women soldiers were discovered because someone recognized them. One volunteer in the 66th Indiana Infantry, who "conducted herself in the most proper manner after enlistment," was discharged from the service after her uncle visited Camp Noble, near New Albany, and recognized the young soldier as his niece. Sophia Cryder served in the 11th Pennsylvania Infantry for about a week before she was recognized while on guard duty by two farmers visiting camp. Cryder was so angry about her dismissal that two weeks later she burned down the barn of one of the farmers who had reported her. Mary Dennis of Minnesota "baffled even the inspection of the surgeon of the regiment in discovering her sex," but was recognized by a printer in St. Paul. Dennis made threats against the man should he expose her, so he fled but later related the incident to a newspaper reporter. Molly Mooney of the 7th Iowa Infantry served nearly six months before she was recognized in St. Louis by a policeman who had known her before the war.[15]

The reasons for some women's discovery are unknown. At a camp of instruction in Raleigh, North Carolina, one of the recruits was suspected of being a woman in August 1862. When confronted, she confessed and was sent home, but the reason for her detection is unrecorded. Sarah Smith was discovered in April 1862, having briefly served in the 2nd Indiana Cavalry. Yet another young woman from Indiana was found out shortly after she enlisted. While the details of her discovery are unrecorded, the reactions of those involved were noted. She was much chagrined at being discharged, while the captain was very indignant about her presence in his regiment.[16]

Elvira Ibecker, alias Pvt. Charles Fuller, enlisted in the 46th Pennsylvania Infantry on September 2, 1861, in Harrisburg. Fuller was described as eighteen years old, nearly five feet four inches tall, with a sallow complexion, black eyes, and light hair. She was discharged from the Union army early in October 1861 at Camp Lewis, Maryland. The company muster roll merely stated that she "was discovered to be a *female*." Pvt. John Williams enlisted in the 17th Missouri Infantry (U.S.) on October 3, 1861, in St. Louis. By the end of the month, Williams was discharged. "Proved to be a woman" was noted on the company muster roll next to Private Williams' name. Both Ibecker and Williams were discovered within a month of their enlistments. While the records are silent on how they were detected, it seems plausible that menstruation may have been the cause.[17]

Other women soldiers served out their enlistment terms incognito only to be discovered once they were out of the army. In September 1863, two female veterans who were still dressed as men were detected and jailed when they applied for work at the U.S. government arsenal in Indianapolis. Ida Remington was arrested in a saloon in Harrisburg after receiving her honorable discharge. She was put in jail for being drunk in public as well as for impersonating a man. Ida Ellison, a Virginia girl who served a stint in the Confederate army, was caught when she tried to return home. Unsympathetic Union authorities sent her to Old Capitol Prison in Washington and then sent her to Baltimore on release. Ellison unwisely returned to Washington "on a spree," and wound up in jail once again.[18]

Army officers found just as many ways to deal with women discovered in the ranks as there were ways in which women were revealed. No regulations, Union or Confederate, dealt with the presence or disposition of women soldiers. Individual officers, therefore, handled the discovery of women soldiers in a variety of ways, often making snap judgements under pressure from the embarrassment of learning that a woman had served in their command. Those women who experienced the misfortune of being discovered by their officers while serving in the army found themselves discharged, honorably or dishonorably; arrested and jailed; or detailed as nurses, laundresses, or spies. In some cases, most commonly in the Confederate army, women soldiers were allowed to continue their service despite their sex.

Those women who were wounded in battle or found out while sick most often earned kind treatment and were discharged and sent home only when they recovered from their injuries or triumphed over their disease. Soldiers who were suddenly and unexpectedly exposed as women, however, often met with a far less sympathetic reaction from army officials. These women were often summarily discharged, sent out of camp to the nearest city or town, and there left to their own devices. For example, when a woman was discovered in the command of Confederate Gen. Joseph Wheeler, he peremptorily "ordered that she should be immediately put beyond our lines." He admitted after the war that he "never asked her name, or the name under which her sex was concealed."[19]

When two female privates were detected in the 2nd Maryland Cavalry (U.S.) while camped near Harper's Ferry in August 1862, they were drummed out of their regiment. When Fanny Harris of Indiana was discovered in the fall of 1864, she was sent to Chicago and discharged, even though she was a veteran drummer boy who had withstood nearly a dozen engagements. In October 1864, a Massachusetts private on provost duty in Baltimore noted that two Union women arrived in the city as prisoners, having been "detected in the army in mens clothes." The women were housed in the city jail overnight, then "sent away" in the morning. The very next month, the same soldier recorded in his diary that "2 more young girls with soldiers clothes on . . . had been down to the front and sent here to be discharged."[20]

Officers undoubtedly thought that, by discharging women soldiers and sending them away, they were ridding the service of females. They were wrong. Some women were so determined to be soldiers and found army life so attractive that when discovered and discharged from one regiment, they promptly found another one in which to enlist. Union soldier Frank Martin was a classic example. She originally enlisted in a Tennessee regiment in 1862 and was discovered when wounded at Stones River. She then joined a Michigan cavalry regiment as a bugler and served through the spring of 1863, rising to the position of clerk and aide-de-camp. While in Louisville, she was exposed by a soldier who had grown up in her hometown. Martin "begged to be retained in the position to which she had been assigned, since, having been in the service ten months, she wished to complete her term of enlistment." Her wish may have been granted temporarily, but she was soon mustered out. A year and a half later, Martin was detained by the provost marshal for Gen. William T. Sherman's army, who wrote to his counterpart in Nashville, "I send herewith two young women dressed in soldier's uniforms calling themselves Frank Martin and George Smith." Three days later a follow-up order was sent instructing that "the two women sent you . . . will be provided with wearing apparel befitting their sex and sent to their respective homes."[21]

Many women soldiers were just as devoted to country and cause as was Frank Martin, and they claimed service in two or more regiments over the course of the war. Their determination to make a substantial contribution to the war effort enabled them to overcome every barrier placed between them and their objective of aiding their country in its hour of need. For these soldiers, ejection from a regiment was merely a temporary setback. The Union woman soldier wounded at Gettysburg "was turned out of the army in a quiet way after she recovered." Just as quietly, the woman reenlisted. She was discovered the second time "by accident" and was "sent on the boat to Fortress Monroe to be dismissed." Sallie Curtis of Indiana served a first enlistment of twenty months before being discovered and discharged. She promptly enlisted again, in the 2nd Kentucky Heavy Artillery (U.S.) She was discovered after a week and received her second discharge paper.[22]

When Fannie Wilson recovered from the illness responsible for her expulsion from the 24th New Jersey Infantry, she went to Cairo and found a job as a ballerina. This shift from masculine to feminine employment did not please her, so she joined the 3rd Illinois Cavalry. Her career as a dragoon ended swiftly, and Wilson found herself jailed on charges of being a spy. She swore her loyalty to the Union and was sent north. Louisa Hoffman enlisted three times and served in all three branches of the Union

army. She was with the 1st Virginia Cavalry (U.S.) at the Battle of First
Bull Run and later briefly served as a cook in the 1st Ohio Infantry, a regiment mustered in for only three months. In August 1863, Hoffman was
arrested by a provost guard shortly after signing up with the 1st Tennessee
Light Artillery (U.S.).[23]

Ella Reno enlisted on four separate occasions and was discovered and
dismissed each time. She served a total of eighteen months in infantry and
cavalry regiments. Upon one of these discoveries, Reno arrived in Cincinnati in May 1863, having been sent to that city by General Sheridan. She
was taken immediately to the offices of Gen. Ambrose Burnside, whose
secretary recorded that "this morning a bit of romance comes up to disturb
the regular routine of red tape. A cavalryman was sent to our Head Qrs
. . . on further examination *he* swore that *his* name was *Miss Ella Reno.*"
Burnside's secretary, Capt. Daniel Larned, was singularly impressed with
Reno, writing that she "was noted for her bravery & daring." Burnside
must also have been impressed with her, since he acquiesced when Reno
begged not to be sent home. He turned her over to the care of an officer's
wife, who was charged with finding her a dress to wear, and then he procured a job for Reno at one of the Louisville hospitals. Reno accepted the
position despite her desire to return to the army.[24]

Lizzie Compton, who sometimes went by the name Jack or Johnny, was
unusually persistent in her efforts to remain on active duty. Over the
course of the war, she served for at least a year and a half and was detected
seven times. One discovery occurred when Compton was thrown from a
horse. She was betrayed another time due to a shrapnel wound in her side
at Fredericksburg. In the spring of 1863, she was arrested in Louisville
while serving in a Minnesota regiment. Her colonel suggested she take a
job as a hospital attendant, but Compton said she would rather die. After
a brief confinement at Park Barracks, she was released and sent on her
way. She was discovered again after being shot at Green River. The inde-
fatigable Compton joined a fifth regiment when her shoulder healed. The
perceptive men in her new company quickly suspected that Johnny was a
girl. They allowed her to tend the wounded on the field but made her stay
behind in Lebanon when the regiment returned to campaigning. Compton left Kentucky and traveled to Rochester, New York, where she was
detected trying to enlist in a cavalry regiment in January 1864. Taken to
the city magistrate, she told her long story of army service. The magistrate
did not detain her, and a rejoicing Compton left the city on a train. Her

destination was Louisville, where she joined the 11th Kentucky Cavalry (U.S.) and was almost immediately detected. Ironically, Compton was last seen caring for Union soldiers wounded in the Atlanta campaign in Marietta, although only a year previously she had vehemently resisted that kind of work.[25]

Other soldiers revealed to be women were just as determined to stay in the army. Those who served by the side of loved ones often prevailed upon their officers to allow them to stay with their regiment, serving as nurses or laundresses. If they could not be soldiers, they reasoned, they would be useful in other ways while remaining with their loved ones and comrades. Confederate William Bradley, who served as a private in Miles's Louisiana Legion for more than two months in 1861, became attached to the regiment as a laundress after the regimental clerk declared that the soldier had been "mustered in through mistake, was of female sex." A year later, at Port Hudson, Mrs. Bradley, the "wife of a 2d sergeant in a company of Miles' Legion[,] was struck in the leg by a piece of shell. . . . She suffered amputation, but died soon after."[26]

Union Lt. Col. Jacob Duryee of the 2nd Maryland Infantry (U.S.) admitted after the war that two women were found in the ranks of his regiment. "I was thunderstruck," he remembered, "and instantly went to make an investigation." His inquiries revealed that the two women were married to Pvts. Lewis Epping and Wesley Watkins. Instead of being sent home, "these two interesting daughters of the Second Maryland, owing to the many important events and the great excitement at the time, passed muster as laundresses, and . . . these devoted young wives stood severe hardships, and remained with the regiment during many campaigns." Mrs. Watkins and Mrs. Epping enlisted in the regiment on August 9, 1861, and served as soldiers alongside their husbands for about six months before their discovery. Mary Watkins then served as a regimental laundress for about a year, until her husband received a medical discharge for syphilis on January 6, 1863. Mrs. Epping worked as regimental laundress for at least eighteen months, until her husband was discharged in August 1863 at the expiration of his term of enlistment. Lewis Epping reenlisted shortly thereafter. No record exists to tell whether his wife remained by his side.[27]

Elizabeth Finnern enlisted with husband John in the 81st Ohio Infantry in September 1861. After her sex was revealed, she stayed with the regiment, working both as a battlefield nurse and as a surgeon's assistant in the regimental hospital. Elizabeth was with her regiment for a full three

years, until her husband's discharge in September 1864. Her comrades recalled after the war that, in addition to nursing them when they were sick
or wounded, Elizabeth also was their seamstress and the laundress for her
husband's company. One veteran stated that Elizabeth "went though all
Marches and battles with us." Another declared that "*she* . . . was on every
march, and every battle field with the 81st Ohio." For practical reasons,
the hardworking Elizabeth stayed in male attire even after her sex was
known to everyone in the regiment. She was also a pragmatist who "in
times of danger . . . carried a musket just as did the soldiers and in all
respects shared the rough life of the men about her." Elizabeth Finnern
may have shared all the dangers and privations of a soldier's life, but she
did not share all the benefits. Mrs. Finnern drew no army pay for her work
as a nurse and surgeon's assistant.[28]

Satronia Smith enlisted in an Iowa regiment with her husband and remained undiscovered for about two months. Her commanding officer then
allowed her to stay with the regiment as a battlefield nurse. She left the
army after her husband died of wounds. Mary Brown, wife of Pvt. Ivory
Brown of the 31st Maine Infantry, also stayed with the regiment when she
was discovered to be a woman. Like Elizabeth Finnern, she worked as a
nurse and surgeon's assistant and, although she was only twenty years old,
became known as the "mother" of her regiment. Of course, not every
woman was lucky enough to stay with her husband after she was detected.
Mrs. Phillips, described as "an interesting little thing" and "a very good
looking girl," was prohibited from remaining with her husband when his
regiment was sent to the front. The colonel took pity on her, however,
and sent her to a boarding house in Alexandria, Virginia, where she found
employment.[29]

When Fannie Lee of Cleveland was discovered in Washington, D.C.,
while serving in the 6th Ohio Cavalry, she requested a nursing position in
one of the many hospitals in the city. An irate provost marshal refused,
stating that she had "so far unsex(ed) herself" as to be unworthy of the job.
Instead, she was sent home. Military officials sometimes took a different
view, however, deciding that a woman who wished to serve her country
should be allowed to do so, just not in the capacity of a soldier. Accordingly, some former women soldiers, like Ella Reno, did obtain jobs in army
hospitals. When Marian McKenzie was discovered in the 23rd Kentucky
Infantry (U.S.) because she had a stomach ache, her colonel registered surprise, declaring that Henry Fitzallen had been an excellent soldier. He

procured women's clothing for her and found her a job as a hospital nurse. McKenzie disliked the work, and after two months she left the hospital and reenlisted as a soldier.[30]

When Harriet Brown was discovered in 1862 after three month's service in an Illinois unit, she was sent to a Kentucky hospital to work as a nurse. Like Marian McKenzie, she disliked the position, so she put her uniform back on and headed for Chicago. She was arrested in Indianapolis and taken before the mayor to explain herself. After hearing her story, the Mayor ordered that Brown be given "suitable" apparel, and allowed her to go. She later decided that hospital work was a worthy pursuit, for in January 1865, Brown became an army matron at the U.S. General Hospital in Quincy, Illinois. She worked there for the next six months. In 1864, Sgt. Katie Hanson's captain confronted her with his suspicions about her sex, and she confessed. She was discharged and sent to work as a hospital nurse and "soon had in her care her captain, who had been wounded in a skirmish. Between them a strong affection was formed. At the close of the war they were married."[31]

A woman soldier identified only as "La Belle" Morgan was hired as a clerk to a provost marshal after her sex became known. Morgan had served about nine months before she was wounded, but unlike so many other female soldiers, she was only discovered after she transferred to the "Invalid Corps," properly known as the U.S. Veteran Volunteers. Other former women soldiers also went to work for provost marshals, but in a different capacity. They became spies, a job that was just as dangerous as soldiering and required intelligence and a talent for intrigue. In at least two cases, Union and Confederate officials reasoned that a woman who could hide her sex in the army was ingenious enough to be a successful spy.[32]

Frances Jamieson, alias Frank Abel, developed a checkered career as a detective for the U.S. government following her stints as a soldier and a hospital attendant. She worked as a spy for General Banks and then joined the Union detective force, teaming up with a man named George Fish. She and Fish were subsequently arrested by the provost marshal in Frederick, Maryland, for "misdemeanors in the discharge of their duties." Frank Abel was accused of harassing female refugees, and both detectives were censured for drunkenness and fornication. Abel was jailed in Old Capitol Prison for a time but was released in the summer of 1863 into the custody of Lafayette Baker, the head of the Union Secret Service. Baker employed her as a spy in Washington. She fulfilled this duty while disguised as a male hospital nurse. By January 1864, Abel was working as a spy in Norfolk, Virginia, but the provost marshal there recorded that she was also working part-time as a prostitute. He ordered her out of the city. Where Abel went, and what she did after complying with the order, are not known.[33]

Loreta Velazquez became an agent for the Confederate Secret Service upon her retirement from soldier life, spending about a year and a half in that capacity. She carried communications in and out of New Orleans when that city was under Union control and also traveled to Havana to procure much-needed supplies for the Confederate army. In the course of these duties, she was caught and jailed twice. After her second release, she was sent out of New Orleans as a "registered enemy." Velazquez then went to Richmond, where she was put to work "effecting important arrests of spies, and doing some very daring things," according to one of the local newspapers. A police officer in Richmond arrested her in June 1863, and she was thrown into Castle Thunder Prison, ostensibly for being a transvestite, but in reality on suspicion of being a spy. She was released when Confederate authorities made it known to local officials that she was, indeed, a spy, but for the Confederacy rather than the Union. From Richmond, Velazquez traveled to Atlanta carrying dispatches. After a brief hospitalization there, as well as a brief honeymoon with a Confederate officer she married while in Atlanta, Velazquez went to Washington, D.C., and landed a job working for Lafayette Baker. Using the alias Alice Williams, and earning two dollars a day as a "special agent," Velazquez was a successful double agent for about six months. She resigned that post in July 1864, fearing that if she stayed much longer, her real allegiance might be revealed.[34]

In her memoirs, Velazquez wrote that she became a spy because she realized that Confederate generals were not obtaining accurate information about the intentions and movements of the enemy. She also thought that she might find fame and prestige in the role and, at the very least, some of the excitement she constantly craved. Velazquez also wrote in her memoirs that, after leaving Washington, she became a Confederate operative in both Canada and Great Britain, selling counterfeit Federal bonds and securities in a desperate attempt to raise funds for the bankrupt Confederacy. Velazquez failed to admit in her memoirs, however, that in the winter of 1865, while in New York City, she plotted with other Confederate agents to assassinate President Lincoln. During the course of the postwar investigation into Lincoln's murder, a Union agent reported to the

Judge Advocate General, "My investigations have led to the discovery of another plot . . . for the murder of the late President quite as diabolical as the one which resulted in his death." One of the witnesses was "a Miss Alice Williams, who was commissioned in the rebel army as a lieutenant under the name of Buford, the would-be [assassin], except that she proposed to employ poison." Why Alice Williams was not arrested by the agent is a mystery.[35]

Spying was a serious and sometimes deadly affair during the Civil War. It is not surprising, therefore, that many women caught in uniform were suspected of being spies and were immediately arrested and imprisoned. When Tennessee Unionist Nancy Corbin was discovered to be a woman, she was sent to General Rosecrans. He determined that she was probably not a spy, but nevertheless ordered her escorted out of town. When Confederate Pvt. Mollie Bean of the 47th North Carolina Infantry was discovered in February 1865 after two years of faithful service, she was conveyed to Richmond and charged with being a "suspicious character." Confederate authorities remanded her "to Castle Thunder, that common receptacle of the guilty, the suspected and the unfortunate."[36]

While wearing a cavalry uniform, Mary Jane Prater was taken prisoner in the Kanawha Valley early in 1863 and was sent to Wheeling under charges of being a Confederate spy. She said that she was five months pregnant, but there is no record of her giving birth. On May 2, 1863, the commissary general of prisoners in Washington directed the Wheeling provost marshal either to bring disloyalty charges against Prater or let her go. The provost marshal released her, but rather than sending her back to Confederate lines or the Confederate army, he sent her to Pennsylvania "with other women of the same sort." Prater did not like the company, and she did not like Pennsylvania, so she immediately left for Wellsburg, West Virginia. Dressed in male attire, she was arrested there and sent back to Wheeling, where she cursed a colonel. She was sentenced to thirty days in jail. What happened to Prater after she served her sentence is not known, but she apparently did not further irritate Union authorities.[37]

Maggie Simpson was detected and arrested in the Shenandoah Valley in the fall of 1864 and then briefly jailed at Harper's Ferry. A soldier in the provost marshal's office said that Simpson was "another of the 'questionable characters' in the personification of a female woman clad so snugly in a soldier's uniform." He further declared that Simpson "was by no means an 'ornament to her sex.' On the whole, she was rather a scaly looking specimen" and had "a face similar to a crocodile and a voice as sweet as a cracked fiddle or an old cow bell or bellows!" On the morning of October 20, 1864, Simpson was sent to Fort McHenry. She arrived in Baltimore that same evening and was put in the civilian area of the prison. Her guard there also noted Simpson's lack of beauty, writing that "she was not a very good looking girl. She had curly hair." The Baltimore provost marshal sent Simpson to the city jail for thirty days. This sentence was levied not for her alleged Confederate sympathies, but for being a woman who dared to don male attire, specifically a uniform. As with so many other women soldiers, Simpson's ultimate fate is unknown.[38]

Margaret Catherine Murphy served in the 98th Ohio Infantry with her father, "the Orderly Sergeant of the Company." Murphy recounted to the Annapolis provost marshal that "a few days after I enlisted, I was detected by my laugh and was suspicioned of being a woman; my father reported to the Captain that he had examined me, and that I was a man." She served another six months in the regiment, as a corporal for a part of that time, before she irrevocably betrayed herself while drunk. Her captain ordered her put in women's clothes and turned her over to the jail in Wheeling, where she stayed for three weeks under suspicion of being a rebel spy. From there, army officials sent her to the Old Capitol Prison and then on to City Point, Virginia, to be transferred through to Confederate lines. At City Point, Murphy "was ordered to leave the boat and go ashore," she later testified. "I refused, cried, and tried to jump overboard and drown myself." Murphy said she "was sent to the Rebel lines on the suspicion of being a spy" and that she "never was a spy, never intended to be" and she loved her "country and the Union boys." She was nevertheless taken by a Confederate guard to Petersburg, where southern authorities jailed her with her hands tied behind her back because she cursed them. Not knowing what to do with her, Confederates returned her to City Point. Murphy was then sent to Annapolis, where she swore her loyalty, but the provost marshal did not believe her. He sent her once again to the Old Capitol Prison. Six months later, Murphy arrived at the prison in Fitchburg, Massachusetts, still mistakenly identified as a "rebel female prisoner." She apparently finished out the war there, paying a very high price for her patriotism.[39]

So did Sarah Mitchell, alias Charles Wilson, a sixteen-year-old soldier in a Union cavalry regiment. Arrested on August 8, 1864, at Sandy Hook, Virginia, she was sent to Washington, accused of being a spy for the Confederacy. Like Margaret Catherine Murphy, she was jailed at Old Capitol. In an attempt to gain her release, she told her captors that she was pregnant. The ruse failed. In October 1864, along with Confederate prisoner of war Jane Perkins, Mitchell was transferred to Fitchburg. There she stayed until March 1865, when she and Perkins were sent to Fortress Monroe to be exchanged. The Confederates gladly received Perkins but would not take Mitchell, stating that they had never heard of her and that she refused to swear loyalty to the South. At a loss for how to handle her case, Union officials sent Mitchell back to Fitchburg, despite the fact that she swore loyalty to the North and begged to be released and sent home.[40]

The Office of the Commissary General of Prisoners was occasionally more lenient than the district and department provost marshals. "If there are any charges of disloyalty against Marion McKenzie or Mary Jane Prather [sic], you will send them also. . . . Wearing soldiers clothing in camp is not an offense for which they can be sent south and if that is all that is against them, they must be disposed of in some other way,"ordered Colonel Hoffman in May 1863. After her brief tenure as a hospital nurse, McKenzie had joined another regiment but was discovered and arrested on December 20, 1862, in Charleston, West Virginia. Charged with being a spy, she was jailed in Wheeling, where she refused to wear the women's clothing provided for her. She explained to the provost marshal that she was a twenty-five-year-old Scottish immigrant. At one point, and probably under duress, McKenzie admitted to having served in a Confederate regiment as well as a Union one. She later retracted this statement, but it caused her to spend six months in jail before the commissary general of prisoners ultimately ordered her release.[41]

Of all the women soldiers accused of espionage, only one merited the charge. Pvt. John Thompson was proved to be a spy when a letter was found that she wrote to Confederate authorities describing Union troop movements. Thompson confessed but refused to reveal any further information about herself other than telling her commanding officers that she was not afraid to die. Instead of executing her, they sent her to Columbus, Ohio.[42]

Despite the opinion expressed by the commissary general of prisoners that women should not be jailed merely for dressing as men, a number of them nevertheless were. Even when not accused of being spies, some women soldiers were still turned over to the nearest provost marshal's office. For example, in 1864, the provost marshal in Harper's Ferry wrote to his counterpart in the Middle Department:

> I have the honor to forward to you, under guard *Two (2) Female Prisoners*, Bogus Soldiers, *entitled Kate alias James Johnson*, and *Eliza Frances alias Frank Glenn*. They were arrested for loitering about the camps dressed in the U.S. uniform, & claiming to belong to Co. "K," 1st W.Va. Cav. It is reported that they have another companion, if not several, of the same "persuasion" who will be "gobbled" as speedily as possible by the military authorities. I would respectfully recommend that you make a levy on some of the generous feminines of Baltimore, for a proper suit of wearing apparel, for the benefit of these wayward damsels.[43]

What became of these two and their undiscovered companions is unknown.

The treatment of women soldiers brought before a provost marshal varied from case to case depending on the temperament of the individual marshal. Some women were let go and others were sent to jail, even though their only crime was wearing a uniform. On May 18, 1864, a female recruit from Wisconsin called George Travis was detected on a train. To the surprise of everyone, "he was arrested and sent off that same evening, because the United States army does not enlist women." When Hattie Martin appeared before the Baltimore provost marshal, she told him that she had enlisted with her husband but now wanted to go home. She was allowed to do so. After Lizzie Hoffman was arrested while boarding a steamer with the rest of the 45th U.S. Colored Infantry, the Alexandria provost marshal sent her to the Central Guard House in Washington and ordered the commandant there to furnish her with a dress. Hoffman was an African American woman from Winchester, Virginia.[44]

Confederate Loreta Velazquez was jailed twice while she was serving as a soldier. In the fall of 1861, she was arrested in a Lynchburg, Virginia, hotel, "rigged out in a full suit of soldiers' clothes, and had registered her name . . . as Lieut. Buford." Her second arrest was in New Orleans, before it fell into Union hands. Confederate authorities in that city detained her for being a spy, but the provost marshal released her the next day for lack of evidence. Civilian authorities immediately arrested her for being a woman dressed in male attire. The mayor ordered her jailed for ten days and fined ten dollars for pretending to be someone she was not.[45]

Not uncommonly, women found in the ranks were sent to civilian authorities for punishment. Araminta Wilhelminia Smith was detected while trying to enlist in the 13th Indiana Infantry. She soon found herself in the mayor's court in Indianapolis. During her hearing, she flirted with the prosecutor, which enraged the mayor. He threw her in jail and ordered she be given nothing but bread and water. Eighteen months later, two more women soldiers appeared in the Indianapolis mayor's court, but they received very lenient treatment because of their ardent support of the Union; the mayor ordered both of these women released. One of the women, Sophia Thompson, was an Ohio farm girl who served two years before her superiors discovered she was a woman. When Mary Burns was discovered in the 7th Michigan Cavalry after only ten days in the service, she was placed in the city jail in Detroit and arraigned at the police court. Edmonia Gates was found serving in the 121st New York Infantry in March 1864 and was sent to the Washington, D.C., workhouse. Emma Black was arrested in Washington in August of that year, dressed in male attire and wanting to enlist in a regiment. She was sent to the Central Guard House, the same place that Lizzie Hoffman was incarcerated. In all of these cases, the only charge against the women was masquerading as men.[46]

⟨ Some women soldiers were quickly labeled prostitutes when found in the ranks. In these cases, the commanding officer usually made the charge, probably because of fear of censure from superiors for allowing a woman to serve. When Nellie Williams was arrested in Louisville in August 1861 after three months in the 2nd Iowa Infantry, her captain vowed that she was not a soldier, but rather "one of the inmates of a disreputable house on Seventh street." Confederate soldiers Mary and Mollie Bell were discovered after two years in the army. While their comrades vowed that they had "done good service as soldiers without at all exciting the suspicians . . . as to their sex," their "Captain assert[ed] that the women are common camp followers, and that they have been the means of demoralizing several hundred men in his command. They adopted the disguise of soldiers the better to . . . hide their iniquity." Mary and Mollie were remanded to Castle Thunder, and stayed there for nearly a month.[47]

Three women discovered in camp caused their male companions the distress of being court-martialed for assisting the women to enlist. Pvt. William Scott of the 13th Indiana Cavalry became acquainted with a woman in New Albany, Indiana, who followed him back to Camp Carrington in Indianapolis and enlisted as a soldier. "I told this woman that I had to go with the Regiment [and] the said woman told me that if I had to go she would go too," explained Private Scott to the court. "She told me if I did not allow her to go she would follow the Regiment wherever I went." Despite lack of clear proof that Private Scott was even with the woman when she was sworn into service, the tribunal found him guilty of assisting her and fined him two months pay. The colonel of the regiment was of the opinion that the woman was a prostitute. She was not called to testify, and the tribunal did not even bother to record her name. In August 1864, Pvt. H. C. Steel of the 3rd Illinois Cavalry kept the company of a woman "dressed in man's apparel." She spent at least one night with him in camp, and she rode "in the manner and fashion of a man" with him while he was in Memphis without a pass. He was court-martialed for both offenses. Again, the tribunal did not see fit to seek the testimony of this unidentified, "indecent" woman.[48]

On recruitment duty in Watertown, New York, Capt. Jerome Taft of the 59th New York Infantry made the acquaintance of a young prostitute named Harriet Merrill, who later arrived at the camp of the 59th and enlisted in Company G in November 1861. Although Taft promised Merrill that he would keep her secret, he discussed her with several other officers and rumors soon flew around camp. Within two months it was an open secret in the regiment that there was a woman among them. In January 1862, Taft was court-martialed for conduct unbecoming an officer and a gentleman, including inducing Harriet Merrill to "don the habiliments of a male, that she might enlist." Although he was found guilty of other charges, including stealing, "marauding," and lying, Taft was not convicted of persuading Merrill to become a soldier, as it was clearly her idea. Merrill was discharged prior to Taft's court-martial but was allowed to testify.[49]

Only one woman soldier appears to have been court-martialed in her own right for trying to serve as a soldier. Mrs. Jane Ferguson was tried on November 25, 1863 in Louisville, charged with being a spy. Specifically, the court charged that she "lurked" around the garrisons in several Kentucky towns, disguised as a man, in order to obtain military information for the Confederates. Ferguson was arrested one day after enlisting in the 13th Kentucky Cavalry (U.S.) under the alias John F. Findsley, but she had been in the area for about a year. When questioned by the provost marshal, Ferguson said that her husband was a Confederate soldier, and that she had formerly served in a guerrilla unit alongside him. Ferguson admitted that she had been sent to the Union camps by a Confederate captain, who ordered her to gain as much information as possible about Union intents and strength and then return with whatever information she acquired. Ferguson explained that she had no intention of returning to Confederate lines but had embraced the assignment in order to escape "illtreatment" by her husband and the "unbearable" life she lived with him. She swore that she enlisted in the Union army with "a desire for safety," in order "to avoid again coming in contact with [her] unnatural husband." In short, she was an abused wife seeking a new life. At her trial, the illiterate woman acted in her own defense, apparently eliciting no sympathy from her captors and never being offered any legal counsel. The military tribunal found her guilty of being a spy and sentenced her to hang. The finding and sentence were overturned by the judge advocate who reviewed the case, and Ferguson was released from custody. Where she went and whether she was ultimately successful in escaping her husband are not known.[50]

While most soldiers who were officially discovered to be women were ejected from the ranks, there were numerous instances in which an officer learned about a woman in his command but did not remove her. Thus some women soldiers continued to serve despite their sex, and a small contingent seem never to have concealed themselves at all. While the military experiences of Union and Confederate women soldiers were strikingly similar throughout the war, their experiences diverged in the arena of discovery. Union women were far more likely to be discharged from their regiments than were Confederate women upon being revealed as females.

In December 1864, a group of women in the Shenandoah Valley wrote to the Confederate secretary of war that they had organized an all-woman volunteer force for local defense. The secretary replied that the Confederacy was "not quite ready to call the ladies to our help in the field." He obviously did not know that southern women were already in the field, fighting and dying for the cause. From the beginning, Confederate women were in the ranks, with some not even bothering to pass as men. A Confederate soldier wrote to his wife from Texas in December 1861, "Even the women are patriotic. . . . I have seen women upon the battle field armed with pistols & bowie knives." He went on to say that he "saw one sitting on her horse within 10 paces of a cannon that was in operation."[51]

The captain of the 1st Virginia Cavalry (CSA) knew that Charlie Hopper was really Charlotte Hope and accordingly paid special attention to the young trooper. It is possible that the officers of Company D of the 18th North Carolina Infantry knew that one of their enlisted men was actually Lucy Thompson Gauss, wife of Pvt. Bryant Gauss. When Mary Ann Clark returned to the ranks of General Bragg's army after being a POW, she no longer worried about concealing her sex, and she even earned a promotion despite the general knowledge that she was a woman.[52]

Another southerner allowed to continue her military career despite her sex was Captain Billy. An observer at the Charlotte, North Carolina, railroad station saw her in command of her company there in 1863. Startled by the sight, he "ran over to where Gen. D. H. Hill was standing, and called his attention to the fact that a woman was over there in command of a company." Hill replied, "'My boy, that woman is an example for some of these men staying at home.'" Not only was she an example, but it was also an unaffordable luxury for a manpower-starved Confederacy to let any battle-tested officer or enlisted woman go home. Notions of gender propriety vanished in the face of unfilled ranks.[53]

Gen. Robert E. Lee himself apparently made accommodations for a woman in his command. As one soldier wrote in his diary, "A man and his wife went together, she putting on the uniform; Gen'l Lee when it came to his knowledge had them detailed so they could be together—I think to his Head Quarters." Confederate soldier Mary Ann Pitman, alias Lieutenant Rawley, also served with the full knowledge of her commanding officer. Rawley's real identity was never a complete secret, however, as two of her compatriots were men from her hometown. In 1863, she admitted to General Forrest that she was a woman and asked if he wanted her to leave. Pragmatist that he was, Forrest did not end her service.[54]

Because the Confederacy grew ever more desperate for soldiers, women in some rebel ranks gradually quit the pretense that they were men. The unidentified cavalry woman captured at the North Anna River was reported to be wearing her hair long, a clear indication that she was not trying to pass as a man. When Jane Perkins was captured, her hair was braided and tucked under her hat. One of her guards was surprised to see that she made no attempt to hide her sex.[55]

Like those spotted in Texas so early in the war, other Confederate women performed military duty without ever disguising their sex. In his memoirs, Lt. Col. Arthur Fremantle remembered that "a goodish-looking woman was pointed out to me in the cars as having served as a private soldier," and that the men in her regiment told him "that her sex was notorious to all the regiment, but no notice had been taken of it so long as she conducted herself properly. They also said that she was not the only representative of the female sex in the ranks."[56]

There were fewer instances of Yankee women continuing their military careers after their officers learned their secret. In the case of two Union women sent to the Washington provost marshal in 1861, a lieutenant had been privy to their disguise. One of the women was married and serving with her husband, and the other woman was engaged to an enlisted man. The lieutenant made a pass at one of the women, was rebuffed, and then reported both of them out of spite. Another woman soldier who served with her husband departed from the Peninsula campaign and returned home in August 1862 because she was pregnant. She was described by a nurse as "such a funny figure . . . her little feet and hands looked woman-ish—otherwise I never should have suspected it." Her comrades and her commanding officers did not have to suspect her sex, for as the nurse noted, "The whole regiment knew that she was a woman and she dressed as a man by the advice of the Col. and Adjutant."[57]

Duty for a woman soldier was a source of contention in the 116th Illinois Infantry. A woman identified only as Kate joined the regiment disguised as a man, but her sex was eventually noticed. The officers tolerated her presence because she was the girlfriend of one of the lieutenants, but they clearly did not expect her to continue to perform the regular duties of a soldier. Kate had other ideas and took her turn on picket. The colonel gave the lieutenant "fits" over the matter and then reprimanded the officer of the day for not stopping her.[58]

A very few Northern women served openly without concealing their sex, mostly in western regiments in the western theater. Frontier and mid-western regiments seemed more open to women serving undisguised in the ranks, perhaps because Victorian notions of women's proper place were not as firmly entrenched in the rough west as they were in the refined east. On September 20, 1862, the Butternut Valley Guards (Minnesota Militia) was organized, and served thirty days. One of the soldiers carried on the muster rolls and paid at the end of the tenure was Pvt. Jennie Jenkins, a female who felt no need to hide that fact. Mrs. Virginia French of Beersheba Springs, Tennessee, became positively indignant about a raid on her town conducted by Union Col. Henry C. Gilbert in April 1864, not because of the damage done, but because Gilbert had five women in his escort. "What in the name of common sense and common decency, the *mothers* of those girls could be thinking of?" she asked in her diary, observing, "Their conduct seemed to us very improper."[59]

As more and more women were found serving in the Union and Confederate armies, the knowledge of their existence rose from the ranks to army headquarters. Not only did the enlisted men and their commanding officers find out about women soldiers, but luminaries like Sherman, Sheridan, Burnside, D. H. Hill, Wheeler, Forrest, and Lee also became aware of women in their armies. When surprised or admiring male comrades wrote to their friends and relatives about the women in their midst, knowledge of women soldiers spread to the home front. And when news of women soldiers reached the press, it was disseminated to the rest of the reading public. When discovered, some women soldiers were treated fairly, and others were dealt with unjustly. Just as the treatment of women found in the army varied widely, so too did public opinion. Some women soldiers were lauded, and others were condemned.

Frances Clayton in female attire. *Courtesy of the Trustees of the Boston Public Library.*

Frances Clayton in uniform. *Courtesy of the Trustees of the Boston Public Library.*

Malinda Blalock, alias Sam Blalock. *Courtesy North Carolina Collection, University of North Carolina Library at Chapel Hill.*

Sarah Rosetta Wakeman, alias Pvt. Lyons Wakeman.
Courtesy Jackson K. Doane.

Sarah Edmonds in female attire. *Courtesy State Archives of Michigan.*

Sarah Edmonds in male attire. *Courtesy State Archives of Michigan.*

Loreta Janeta Velazquez in female attire, from
her memoir, *The Woman in Battle* (1876).

Lt. Harry T. Buford (Velazquez in uniform), from
The Woman in Battle.

"Starting for the Front," from *The Woman in Battle*.

"Riding for Life," illustration from Sarah Edmonds' memoir,
Nurse and Spy in the Union Army (1864).

Ohio cavalry veterans. The soldier in the middle appears to be a woman.
Courtesy Dr. Kathleen Dietrich.

Albert D. J. Cashier, photographed in 1864 (left) and 1913 (right).
Courtesy Illinois State Historical Library.

Lucy Matilda Thompson Gauss Kenney, alias Pvt. Bill Thompson.
*Courtesy Martha Cason Wilder. Reprinted, by permission of the author,
from Hoar,* The South's Last Boys in Gray.

Martha Parks Lindley, alias Pvt. James Smith.
Courtesy William Boldt.

1864 cartridge box and 1936 obituary of Union veteran Mary A. Brown.
Private collection of Lauren M. Cook.

John and Elizabeth Finnern's headstone, Greensburg, Indiana. Both were members of
Co. D., 81st Regiment, Ohio Volunteer Infantry. The bottom of the headstone reads,
"She served in male attire until her sex was detected, when she was detailed as a nurse,
serving 3 years." *Courtesy Philip Jackson, Jr.*

8

"ROMANTIC YOUNG LADIES"
Female Soldiers in the Public Consciousness

Although individual distaff soldiers for the most part endeavored to serve in secrecy, the fact that women adopted male identities and performed all the duties of soldiers in the armies of the North and the South was no secret during the Civil War. From 1861 to 1865, because of letters home from soldiers surprised by a woman found in their midst and newspaper articles written about women discovered in the ranks, the home front public became well aware that men were not alone in taking up arms against the enemy and that the legend of the Female Warrior from history and popular culture was being played out in a very real way in the camps and on the battlefields.

While the majority of news articles during the Civil War focused on individual women suddenly found out and turned over to authorities, at least one newspaper attempted to get a measure of the matter. The Detroit *Free Press* reported: "A Washington correspondent says the official records of the military authorities in that city show that upward of one hundred and fifty recruits have been discovered and made to resume the garments of their sex. . . . Curiously enough, over seventy of these martial demoiselles, when their sex was discovered, were acting as officers' servants. In one regiment there are seventeen officers' servants, in blue blouses and pants, who had to be clothed in calico and crinoline."[1]

One Civil War scribe declared, "We have had so many Mollie Pitchers that the disease may be said to have become almost an epidemic," while another noted, "We almost daily read accounts of the valorous deeds of females who have fought in the ranks." Early in the war, the Indianapolis *Daily Sentinel* reported that "romantic young ladies of late are frequently found in the military service." But less than two years later, the romance of reporting about women warriors had worn off for this paper, which by then reported matter-of-factly that yet "another female soldier was brought before his honor . . . yesterday."[2]

Yet women soldiers remained newsworthy. In 1865, the *United States Service Magazine* noted that "no editor can turn over a morning's 'exchange papers' without encountering authentic anecdotes of some fair and fast Polly or Lucy who, led by the spirit of patriotism, love, or fun, has donned the blue breeches and follows the drum." Women soldiers were so well publicized throughout the war that, in searching for the answer to who might be committing a series of petty thefts in the city, a Cincinnati reporter speculated that it was they who were responsible:

> It has leaked out that the robberies lately committed in most instances have been done by soldiers, or persons dressed in the garb of soldiers, and as the parties generally escape detection, it may be explained by the large number of females that are arrested who are passing as soldiers. A female thief, while dressed as a soldier, makes a friend of a stranger and robs him of his money, after which she drops the uniform and upturns in the habiliments of her sex; and they thus escape, as the police are on the alert for some soldier they cannot find.[3]

Like this Ohio reporter, Alfred Galpin of the 1st Wisconsin Infantry possessed an overactive imagination when it came to women in uniform. While serving as a hospital steward with General Sherman's army during the Atlanta campaign, Private Galpin developed a suspicion that Jacob Thurston of the 21st Ohio Infantry was actually a woman in disguise. Over the course of a week in April 1864, Galpin recorded in his diary his harassment of Thurston. "Bothered J. Thurston about being a female a good deal & circumstances do look very suspicious but still it is impossible," he wrote on April 21. The next day, he wrote, "Had more of my suspicions about Thurston's femininity confirmed. . . . (s)he is very sensitive on hands. . . . I am going to find out something for certain soon." Galpin further recorded that he was "getting to feel rather queer about Thurston. I'll find out his sex before long." The next day there was no let up for poor

Jacob Thurston: "Bothered Thurston a good deal again & found out that (s)he is not a *boy* whatever *it* may be." The relationship between the two deteriorated to physical blows, with Galpin and Thurston fighting for more than a week. Despite Galpin's harassment and a battle wound received on June 24, Jacob Thurston survived the war. He returned to Ohio and married, apparently giving the lie to Galpin's suspicions. Galpin also made note in his diary that he saw a "likeness" of female soldier Frances Hook that was passed around camp.[4]

Marsena Patrick, provost marshal of the Army of the Potomac, was hoodwinked by a male soldier who wished to go home and therefore presented himself as a woman in disguise at City Point in January 1865. Patrick wrote in his diary, "I had to examine a woman, dressed in our Uniform. Charley (or Charlotte) Anderson, of Cleaveland. . . . She has told me the truth, I think, about herself." There can be no doubt that general knowledge of women discovered while serving in Union regiments contributed to Patrick's decision to take this soldier's story at face value. Patrick read the newspapers, too, and probably listened to the gossip that circulated around the army camps. He sent Charlotte Anderson home to Ohio.[5]

Upon arrival in Cleveland, however, Anderson's ruse was finally revealed after an accusation that she was actually a he led to a physical examination. Anderson admitted that he had enlisted in the 38th Pennsylvania Infantry in July 1863 and left it a year later by dressing in women's clothes and "representing [himself] to Major Wells as a woman." He later enlisted in the 60th Ohio Infantry and left that regiment by the same means. When cornered in Cleveland, he claimed, "I adopted the course I have pursued to get home and was intending to go back to my regiment," adding, "I came through City Point on my way home; I saw General Patrick . . . I told him I was a girl; he told me to go home." Charlie Anderson had a feminine appearance. He took advantage of that, and of the common knowledge that women were among the men in the ranks, in order to take leave from active duty whenever he wished.[6]

Knowledge of women soldiers coupled with prejudices against the enemy were the salvation of Nancy Jenkins, alias John Smith, who was discovered wearing a Yankee uniform by the pro-Confederate Buck family of Front Royal, Virginia. When they found her taking water from their well, Jenkins claimed to have taken refuge with a black family near the town. The teenaged Jenkins said that Union soldiers had barged into her home, taken her prisoner, cut her hair, forced her to don a uniform, and enlisted her in the Union army. She also said that she escaped her captors, joined another regiment, and finally obtained a pass out of camp. Jenkins pleaded with the family to help her. They took her to a Confederate provost marshal who believed her story and issued her a pass to travel South. The Buck family gave her clothing and food and wished her Godspeed on her way home. Perhaps this bizarre tale was true, or maybe Jenkins fabricated the story to keep herself out of a southern prison. Jenkins might well have been a spy. In any event, she capitalized on the public familiarity with women's presence in the ranks.[7]

This public familiarity was largely brought about by the press. The women who went to war were often cast as real-life Female Warriors Bold if their stories closely matched the cultural icon of a patriotic or love-struck heroine. That conventional yet heroic image struck a cord with readers as newspapers and popular magazines enthusiastically and regularly reported the numerous instances of women found in the ranks. Especially in the early years of the war, when patriotic fervor was high, women soldiers were favorably viewed by the press, both northern and southern. Union supporter Araminta Smith was touted as "brilliant," "accomplished," and "beautiful." When a woman soldier from Lafayette, Indiana, was discovered, one newspaper hastened to assure readers that the woman in question was "virtuous." And when a southern woman was found in a Confederate training camp in August 1862, a Georgia newspaper dubbed her a "gallant heroine."[8]

Favorable press for women soldiers continued throughout the war, as reporters and editors lauded their patriotism as outstanding examples for their reading audiences. When Louisa Hoffman's story was told in August 1864, a Washington reporter called her "a very good-looking and respectable soldier girl" and observed, "She makes a very handsome soldier." The Lynchburg *Virginian* that same year called an unnamed Confederate captain "a beautiful, dashing lady."[9]

In September 1863, the *Missouri Democrat* published a long and sentimental story about an unnamed woman soldier whose origins and adventures conformed nearly completely to the Female Warrior motif. She was arrested in St. Louis in August 1863 after she had left the army to plan her wedding. She consented to a newspaper interview while jailed for wearing men's clothes. She claimed to be the orphaned daughter of a wealthy Michigan family who followed her older brothers to war. Initially serving as a nurse, she grew to dislike that work, so she joined her brothers' regiment as orderly to the major, who happened to be her second cousin. During the course of two years, she witnessed the death of both her brothers, was wounded herself, became ill, and fell in love with an officer. When she revealed her true identity to him, he asked to marry her. Most interestingly, this anonymous Union woman was the only distaff soldier to report that a comrade tried to rape her when he realized her sex. She shot him in the face. The reporter who recorded her story seemed fascinated by this woman's patriotism and virtue, and the romance and happy ending to her story was irresistible to Victorian readers. "Her appearance, manners, style of conversation, and the account she gives of herself, place her quite above the ordinary class of women who affect the garb of the opposite sex," he gushed.[10]

Other women soldiers became media darlings with their stories related in a number of papers. In some cases, newspapers were merely reprinting articles from other cities, but in others, a reporter actively pursued the story of an individual woman soldier to gather the details of her adventures in order to scoop the competition. On February 19, 1864, the Brooklyn *Daily Times* broke the story of Emily, who died at Lookout Mountain after dictating a note to her father. Although the paper reported that Emily was serving with a division that was not at the battle, the error did not diminish the sensation her story caused. Emily's tale was picked up by newspapers as far away as Wisconsin and reappeared in books and newspaper articles long after the war. It was retold as late as 1935, seventy years after her death, in the veterans' publication the *National Tribune*.

Emily's story was the perfect meld of patriotism and Victorian sentimentalism, accounting for its longevity. Newspaper stories about other women soldiers might have been more interesting, but Emily, with her determination to be a second Joan of Arc, was far more romantic. In reporting Emily's story, the Brooklyn *Daily Times* melodramatically editorialized that she suffered "a sad case of monomania, which had a terrible termination." Emily's deathbed letter was published verbatim, but the editors omitted the name of her parents and their address, presumably to preserve their privacy. All the reprinted articles about Emily were exactly the same, except that the Washington *Daily Morning Chronicle* further elaborated that the late Emily was "beautiful, educated, and refined."[11]

Frances Clayton was another woman soldier whose story was published in numerous papers when she came to the attention of reporters after her service ended. Clayton was discharged in Louisville in 1863, and initially she tried to make her way home to Minnesota. She then decided to return to the army to collect the back pay and bounty money owed to her deceased husband and herself, but a Confederate guerrilla party attacked her train, and she was robbed of her papers and her money. Newspapers chronicled her journey from Missouri to Minnesota to Grand Rapids, Michigan, and on to Quincy, Illinois, where a collection was taken up by well-wishers and former soldiers to aid her in her quest. Mrs. Clayton was last reported heading for Washington, D.C.

Half a dozen newspapers picked up her story, each one approvingly noting that she had done "full duty as a soldier" by the side of her husband. The articles also stated that she had been wounded at Stones River, the same battle where her husband died, and that her wound led to her discovery and dismissal from the service. When a reporter for *Fincher's Trades' Review* caught up with her in November 1863, however, Mrs. Clayton used the interview to set the record straight. She said that she was not discovered while in the service and that she was wounded at Fort Donelson, not at Stones River; unfortunately, Mrs. Clayton did not use the opportunity to clarify what regiment she served in. Each newspaper account gave conflicting military information, though most agreed that the Claytons had enlisted in a Missouri regiment despite their Minnesota roots. One paper reported her alias as "Jack Williams." Most reporters found the story of the faithful wife more appealing than the actual details of Clayton's life as a soldier.[12]

Newspapers around the country delighted in carrying stories of women found in the ranks or wounded in battle, and for the most part, the female soldiers who claimed patriotic zeal or love for a man as their reasons for fighting were rewarded with the longest articles and no little amount of praise. Mary Owens, who eloped with a man her father disapproved of and then fought by the side of her groom until he died, was "described as a woman of considerable beauty, and is said to be the heroine of the neighborhood," according to *Frank Leslie's Illustrated Newspaper*. As with Emily, Owens' story played to Victorian romanticism, and as with Frances Clayton, Owens' publicity did not begin until her military career was over.[13]

The story of Mary Ellen Wise's service, wounding, and determination to receive her wages was chronicled in newspapers from Washington, D.C., to New York to Indianapolis. But the District of Columbia papers held the advantage, since that was where Wise moved after her discharge from the Union army. In September 1864, the *Daily Morning Chronicle* happily reported that she had married fellow soldier Sgt. Lloyd Forehand at Lincoln Hospital in Washington, "Uncle Sam thereby losing a brave soldier and the Sergeant finding a good wife." But her marital bliss was short-lived. Less than five months later, the *Evening Star* announced:

> Ellen Forehand, once an enlisted soldier, but subsequently discharged and married to a sergeant of the 18th V.R.C., was arrested yesterday . . . on the complaint of her husband, who charged that she had followed him several days armed with a pistol and threatening to take his life. She is about 18 or 20 years old, and is considerably tanned by the sun during her service in an Indiana regiment. Her husband did not wish to prosecute her, but only wanted to be safe. Justice Handy dismissed her to leave the city in the first train, and she took her departure in the 6 P.M. train.

Where she went and what happened to her are not known, as the newspapers seemingly lost interest in Wise when she ceased conforming to the accepted female ideal. Apparently, Wise and Forehand divorced, for when Forehand applied for his veteran's pension after the war, he informed the government that his wife was named Flora and that they had married in 1870. He also lied and stated that he had not been previously married.[14]

Mary Ann Clark is another example of a woman soldier who became a newspaper heroine. Clark's story was reported sympathetically in northern papers even though she was a Confederate, while southern papers waxed eloquent in their praise of her. On December 30, 1862, the Jackson *Mississippian* hailed her as "heroic and self-sacrificing" and went on to relate that "Mrs. Clarke volunteered with her husband as a private, fought through the battles of Shiloh, where Mr. Clarke was killed—she performing the rites of burial with her own hands. She then continued with Bragg's army in Kentucky, fighting in the ranks as a common soldier, until she was twice wounded—once in the ankle and then in the breast, when she fell a prisoner into the hands of the Yankees. Her sex was discovered by the Federals, and she was regularly paroled as a prisoner of war, but they did not permit her to return until she had donned female apparel." Curiously, this article was repeated almost verbatim by Confederate Pvt. Robert Hodges in a letter home describing his encounter with Clark in August 1863. A Union colonel also wrote home about Clark, describing her as "somewhat brazen . . . but sharp as a steel trap."[15]

In this case both newspaper coverage and soldier correspondence served to inform the public, both North and South, about Mary Ann Clark's military service. But the story of Clark as presented by the press was wrong on several counts. She was referred to as "Amy," "Annie," or "Anna," and she was not a combatant at Shiloh. More importantly, Mary Ann Clark did not enlist to follow her husband into the army but rather joined due to the heartbreak her husband caused her when he left her and their children and took up with another woman. Neither northern nor southern newspapers mentioned Clark's temporary abandonment of her children. Whether Clark consciously shaped her story along the lines of the accepted romantic ideal of the Female Warrior or newspaper editors were selective in their reporting is not clear. But the publicity Clark received illustrates how the press often treated women soldiers with acceptance and respect, especially if their stories complied with popular romantic themes.[16]

Another southern woman who found favorable treatment in the northern press was Mrs. Stone. The writer who recorded her story declared that "she was in appearance the most modest and demure of dames, and certainly as handsome a woman as had ever been in the military service of the rebellion." Mrs. Stone's story was related in long, sympathetic detail, full of Victorian drama. Not only was Mrs. Stone a faithful wife, but she agreed to put aside the Confederate cause and pledge loyalty to the Union along with her husband, thus ensuring a warm news story north of the Mason-Dixon Line.[17]

Rebecca Peterman, renamed Georgianna by newspapers in Minnesota, Illinois, and Wisconsin, seemed none too pleased by the notoriety that accompanied her discovery in Chicago in February 1865. Following her discharge from the 7th Wisconsin Infantry, Peterman was on her way home to Ellenboro, Wisconsin, when she arrived in the Windy City. Her overcoat, which held her discharge papers and money, was stolen at the Soldier's Rest. Without funds and in a strange city, Peterman was reduced to wandering the streets looking for a warm and hospitable place to spend the night. She finally went to a police station and asked to sleep there. A policeman "detected something wrong in the appearance" of the soldier, and Peterman confessed to being a woman. The Chicago *Evening Journal* reported the incident immediately, and the story was soon reprinted in other papers. After praising Peterman for her "good service," the Chicago reporter appeared surprised that "she [seemed] to regard her past course as something not to be regretted."[18]

What Peterman did regret was finding herself in the spotlight. When she reached her home in Ellenboro, a local paper heralded her arrival. When she left home two weeks later after her older sister died in a freak accident, that, too, was reported in a state newspaper, although the reporter attributed Peterman's leaving home to the fact that her mother was pressuring her to don a dress. Wearing her uniform, Peterman first went to Prairie du Chien and checked into a soldiers' hostel. A few soldiers from her army days arrived and recognized her, so she was forced to leave. She next went to Boscobel and tried to reenlist. Unsuccessful there, she traveled to Portage and tried again. Because Wisconsin newspapers were charting her every move, officials in Portage quickly recognized her as the celebrated girl soldier from Ellenboro and remanded her to jail.[19]

For more than a month, the travels and travails of Rebecca "Georgianna" Peterman were printed and reprinted in Wisconsin newspapers. Reporters from the *Grant County Witness* interviewed her stepfather, who said that Peterman's "wild, erratic course" was a source of grief to her "staid, respectable" family. He further claimed, "The girl is perfectly uncontrollable."[20] The saga of Peterman's postarmy days ended with her leaving Portage. Perhaps the papers tired of hounding her, or she may finally have eluded them.

The press treated Peterman with far less compassion than other women soldiers received. Indeed, women like Peterman who admitted they joined the army for adventure as opposed to patriotism or love were often viewed with skepticism and derision by the press because their actions and motivations failed to conform to accepted romantic and cultural ideals. Another example was the "wretched" intoxicated woman who was picked up and jailed in St. Louis dressed in male attire. The *Missouri Democrat* reported that "as a matter of course she told the story of having been in the service at Cairo, but having been discharged a month or two ago, got hard up, and . . . took to drink." The distinctly unfeminine behavior of public drunkenness earned this former soldier no sympathy and in the reporter's eyes cast doubt on her story of having been in the military in the first place.[21]

The conservative Richmond, Virginia, newspapers pronounced uniformly harsh judgments on women found in the Confederate ranks but treated Loreta Velazquez rather mildly. When the *Enquirer* wrote about her in July 1863, she had been arrested in uniform and confined to Castle Thunder, and the tone of the article was mocking. Even though the paper admitted that her story of being a veteran soldier was "by no means improbable," they snidely stated that she "was not quite as pretty as the romance of her case might admit." But in September, the *Daily Examiner* was quite considerate, describing her as having "a history romantic in war as that of Joan of Arc" and declaring her to be "a devoted Southern woman." Perhaps this was due to the fact that Velazquez was recently married and had visited Richmond in her female identity of Mrs. DeCaulp, thus having resumed a more appropriate and socially acceptable role. The *Whig* was even more enamored of Velazquez, gleefully reporting that Union General "Butler denounced her as the most incorrigible she rebel he had ever met with."[22]

Other southern women were given poor treatment by the Richmond press. In 1864, when Mary and Mollie Bell were incarcerated at Castle Thunder, the *Daily Examiner*, after describing Mary as "seventeen and good looking" and Mollie as "twenty-four and scrawney," quoted their captain and asserted that the girls were harlots. The editor went on to blame the prostitutes who followed the army for General Early's failure in the 1864 Shenandoah Valley campaign. The captain's allegations were accepted by the paper, even though Mary and Mollie claimed patriotism as their only motivation for joining the ranks. The word of two unconventional young women did not, initially, outweigh the accusations of a male officer. In a follow-up article on Mary and Mollie, the newspaper reported that they were "released from the Castle and sent home to their fond parents. . . . They wore away the same toggery they came in, and seemed perfectly disconsolate at . . . being separated from their male companions in arms." This second article never mentioned that the women might be anything other than the soldiers they said they were, so apparently Mary and Mollie salvaged their reputations during their time in prison. The *Daily Examiner* was not gracious enough to apologize to the Bells or to print a retraction of the earlier allegations.[23]

In 1865, the *Whig* reported that Mollie Bean of the 47th North Carolina Infantry had been arrested and incarcerated at Castle Thunder. "This poor creature is, from her record, manifestly crazy," the article intoned. Had Mollie Bean been a man, her record of two years service and double wounding would have made her a war hero, but because the Richmond press deemed martial behavior unacceptable for women, Bean was judged suspect and insane.[24]

Some negative reporting about martial mesdames and mademoiselles was the result of partisan sentiment more than indignity over unconventional female behavior. The Washington *Daily Morning Chronicle*, which zealously cheered the exploits of Union women soldiers, informed its readers in 1864 that Confederate Ida Ellison was violent and suicidal. That same year, an Ohio newspaper related that a Confederate officer imprisoned at Johnson's Island was "the first case of a woman in rebel service that we have heard of," and concluded that the woman had joined the army for "profit, not patriotism, or love, as is the case with the girls that go into the United States service disguised as men." Given the fact that the officer was discovered when delivered of a baby boy, it seems possible that love played a role in her decision making.[25]

Regardless of a newspaper's editorial views on the propriety of women soldiers, the majority of reporters failed to record the facts about them accurately. In numerous newspaper articles, the numbers and even the states of the regiments to which women soldiers belonged were misidentified. Both real names and aliases were changed in print. Correspondents seemed largely unconcerned with correct details about women's service and more inspired by the romance of their stories, or lack thereof. It is also possible that individual women soldiers who were about to resume their private lives, reenlist in the army incognito, or return to their regiments, altered the facts of their identities and personal stories in order to protect their reputations or aliases or to guard against the real possibility of incarceration by military officials.

When the story of Frances Hook was carried by newspapers in 1864, most accounts related that she was captured after the Battle of Chickamauga. Only the Washington *Daily Morning Chronicle* accurately reported that she was captured during scouting operations near Florence, Alabama. But this paper and many others were wrong when it reported that Mary Ellen Wise had served under the alias James Wise in the 34th Indiana Infantry, because the records of that regiment do not show a soldier by that name. Neither was the 34th Indiana Infantry at Lookout Mountain, where Wise was so badly wounded.[26]

On May 8, 1863, the New Orleans *Daily Picayune* reported that a woman soldier called Charlie so loved a captain that she followed him to war in the 14th Iowa Infantry. When word leaked out that she was serving disguised as a man in his regiment and it dawned on her that she would be sent away from her beloved, she took his revolver and shot herself in the heart on the parade ground. The identity of this woman may never be known because the newspaper did not print her name and may not even have recorded her regiment correctly. While there were many soldiers named Charles in the 14th Iowa Infantry, regimental records do not reflect that any of them committed suicide. Similarly, when Ida Remington was arrested in a saloon, the papers stated that she was formerly a soldier with the 11th New York Infantry. That regiment, also known as the Fire Zouaves, was mainly composed of firemen from New York City, an unlikely fit for a woman soldier trying to blend in with her comrades.[27]

The flawed details of many articles might cast doubt on the veracity of all press reports regarding women soldiers, but other newspaper stories were amazingly accurate. Moreover, confirming references to women featured in both inaccurate and accurate newspaper articles are found in military and government records or the diaries and letters of their comrades. Regardless of accuracy, newspaper reports about women soldiers were quite numerous, spanning the entire length of the war and involving campaigns and battles both major and minor. Obviously, finding a woman serving in the ranks was not an uncommon phenomenon during the Civil War.

The fact that hundreds of newspaper articles were devoted to women soldiers attests to the public delight in tales of female cross-dressers. Wartime fiction in the form of novelettes, serialized stories, and ballads also publicly promoted the concept of women going to war in the guise of men. *The Lady Lieutenant; or, The Strange and Thrilling Adventures of Miss Madeline Moore*, published in Philadelphia in 1862, was a classic example of the Female Warrior genre. Although the author of this novelette assured the reader that "the foregoing narrative *may be relied on as strictly authentic*," with only the names of characters changed, the story was fiction. It was also a skillful blending of the accepted motif and the very real military actions of the 1861 West Virginia campaign only recently reported to the public. Her protestations of physical frailty notwithstanding, Madeline Moore adheres to the romantic ideal of being quite capable of holding her own on the field of battle, and typically, she also wins the man who originally caused her to seek a place in the military.[28]

Numerous fictitious wartime romances were published between 1861 and 1865. *Castine* appeared in the South at the end of the war. Published in Raleigh, North Carolina, as the "Southern Field and Fireside Novelette No. 2," the story of Castine has a somewhat darker theme but still corresponds to the familiar motif. In this book, the heroine joins the

Confederate army to avenge her sister, which she accomplishes by slaying the villain.[29]

The war years also saw the publication of the military memoirs of a bonafide woman soldier, although Sarah Emma Edmonds chose to tell her story in such a way that she never explicitly reveals that her patriotic adventures were undertaken while she was serving in the 2nd Michigan Infantry in male disguise. In 1864 the northern public was treated to *Nurse and Spy in the Union Army*, which became a best-seller. Even though Edmonds does not disclose in her book that she was Pvt. Franklin Thompson, she does recount adopting male disguise to pursue spying missions on unsuspecting Confederates and donning a Union uniform and acting as an orderly during the Battle of Fredericksburg. *Nurse and Spy* narrates Edmonds' experiences at First and Second Bull Run, in the Peninsula campaign and the Seven Days' Battles, and at Antietam. In all likelihood, Edmonds did not reveal her actual role as a soldier because she was a deserter from the Union cause she held so dear. The book does, however, report her finding a mortally wounded woman soldier after Antietam, and this episode shows her readers that the women who disguised themselves as men to serve as soldiers were in deadly earnest.

Edmonds wrote her book in Hartford, Connecticut, while recuperating from the bout of malaria that drove her from the army. Her inspirations were the popular adventure stories she read as a child as well as the prevailing sentimentalism of wartime Victorian literature. She also relied heavily on the journal she kept while serving as Pvt. Franklin Thompson. The result was a smashing success. Her book was reprinted twice, and more than 175,000 copies were sold. Edmonds donated the proceeds to the U.S. Sanitary and Christian Commissions for their work on behalf of Union soldiers.

Although Edmonds admitted in later life that her best-seller included both her own and others' experiences as well as some fictionalized stories, the basic truth underlying her narrative was painstakingly reconstructed by biographer Sylvia Dannett in the 1960 book *She Rode with the Generals*. Drawing from military records and correspondence, memories and keepsakes of Edmonds' friends and descendants, Dannett examined and documented the female soldier's early life, the war years, and her postwar life, including Edmonds' successful campaign to obtain a military pension.

But for the wartime audience, *Nurse and Spy* held the appeal of the familiar motif with the added thrill of knowing that the book was based on the actual exploits of a real woman, who re-created for her readers detailed scenes of hospitals, battlefields, and army camps. Although patriotic zeal rather than a lover impelled her into the army, Edmonds' memoirs, consciously or not, conform to the established model of a virtuous female adventurer, a distaff counterpart to male literary characters such as Odysseus. In penning her memoirs, Edmonds painted herself as a heroine in the best tradition of the Female Warrior Bold.[30]

Postwar readers were treated to a number of fictional and semifictional female soldiers as well as collections of true stories. Published in 1866, Frank Moore's *Women of the War* narrates the true stories of nurses, vivandières, and soldiers. Of the latter, Moore picked Emily as a highlight, undoubtedly because her story epitomized the virtue of self-sacrificing feminine heroism so irresistible to Victorian readers. Moore tried, unsuccessfully, to find former woman soldier Mary Owens, whose career had been positively reported in wartime newspapers. Seeking to interview her for his book, he tracked her to Coalmont, Pennsylvania, but found that she had left that town for another and had not left a forwarding address. Indeed, Moore's book garnered popular attention before it ever reached the printer because he publicly requested that information about the wartime activities of women be relayed to him. As a result, Moore received a letter from a Union veteran in February 1866 who pleaded with him to "not omit the name of Miss Edmonds of 'The Nurse and Spy' . . . one of the most illustrious of the heroines and no 'farce.'" Moore, however, chose to exclude Edmonds from his book.[31]

Linus P. Brockett and Mary Vaughan's *Women's Work in the Civil War* was published in 1867. Although they freely admitted that women fought in the ranks of Civil War armies, they departed from Frank Moore and failed to include individual stories of women soldiers in their compilation of women's war involvement, writing that "those who from whatever cause . . . donned the male attire and concealed their sex, are hardly entitled to a place in our record, since they did not seek to be known as women, but preferred to pass for men."[32]

Capt. David P. Conyngham, in his postwar collection of memories about Sherman's March to the Sea, relates a story told by a soldier who had the bad fortune to fall into the hands of a Confederate "Lady Major" after the Battle of Peachtree Creek. The woman officer is described as overtly sexual: "She wore a cap decked with feathers and gold lace, flowing pants, with a full kind of velvet coat coming just below her hips, and fastened with a rich crimson sash, and partly open at the bosom." As soon as she is out of sight of camp with her prisoner, the Lady Major proposes to hang him to avenge the death of the "the only man [she] ever loved." The Union prisoner escapes the noose, whereupon the bloodthirsty Lady Major draws a pistol, but the narrator seizes his chance and strikes her "with [his] heavy boot right in the face, spoiling her beauty, and giving the dentist a job." This northern veteran's picture of southern female militarism is clearly a tall tale, but to northern readers this apocryphal woman soldier symbolized the evil nature of the enemy, while conforming to the tried and true Female Warrior motif.[33]

In 1865, the same year that northern audiences were given Captain Conyngham's memories, they were treated to a biography of the celebrated actress turned Union spy Pauline Cushman. In an excellent example of the difficulty of determining the truth of some contemporary women soldier stories, the Cushman biography includes a letter allegedly written to the famous spy by former Union soldier Nellie A. K., who said she was turned out of her regiment after fighting at Antietam, Chancellorsville, Gettysburg, and Lookout Mountain. Nellie's letter to the famous spy begs her to take her along on her speaking tour. "I long for my old life of adventure," she wrote. Cushman's biographer did not include the letter to celebrate women soldiers, however, but rather as proof that "it is neither unladylike nor inelegant to serve one's country, or to overstep the ordinary rules of conventionalism in behalf of our glorious Union and its brave supporters." Whether the letter, like parts of Cushman's biography, was fabricated or artfully enhanced to advance Cushman's reputation and stage career is unknown.[34]

The postwar years also witnessed the publication of several novels in the best Female Warrior tradition. *Remy St. Remy; or, The Boy in Blue*, published in 1866, features a southern Unionist stranded in the North when the war breaks out, with her family captive behind enemy lines in the South. She joins the army and predictably embarks on many daring exploits, finding true love in the process. *Virginia Graham, the Spy of the Grand Army* and *Hilt to Hilt* were both published in 1868, and also feature cross-dressing female protagonists. These works were perhaps intended for audiences who craved more than Frank Moore's briefly outlined authentic stories and who missed reading about real-life adventurous women soldiers in the newspapers.

Those on the home front during the Civil War were treated not only to newspaper accounts of women in the ranks but also to stories about women soldiers in letters they received from loved ones on the front lines. In November 1863, for example, a Confederate soldier wrote to his sister, "We have some women in our army and I think I shall have to try to get a woman to put on pants and come for me." This private thought that women in uniform was a grand idea, if only because a female companion might ease his own loneliness.[35]

Like the press, male soldiers had conflicting opinions about the women in their midst. Their remarks about women soldiers in their letters home naturally revealed their own cultural and patriotic biases, often dependent upon the status of the woman in question. For example, a Union soldier at Hilton Head, South Carolina, immediately suspected the worst about a Confederate POW there, informing his wife that "she may be a noted caracter; perhaps the least said about caracter the better for her." Male soldiers sometimes suspected the worst about women soldiers even if those women fought for the same side as they. When two women were detected in the 2nd Maryland Cavalry (U.S.) in August 1862, a soldier in a New York regiment commented that they were "disreputable characters, I believe."[36]

On the other hand, women within a soldier's own command serving at the side of a husband were generally described with some admiration. In writing about the "heroine" of the 1st New York Cavalry, a woman who not only served with her husband "side by side in the ranks, and side by side in battle," but who also carried her beloved from the field when he was wounded, a fellow soldier praised her as a "patriotic young lady, a good soldier, and an industrious and persevering wife." Writing to his mother about a woman soldier who was found out when she gave birth, Soloman Newton related that she had "been in 3 or 4 fights," and that "she must have seen some hard times and heard some awful talk, for there was only one knew she was a woman." Newton added, "She must think a good deal of her man, dont you think so?" Her motivation for joining the military excused much in the opinion of this male soldier. Another soldier had nothing but praise for the same woman, and for reasons above and beyond anything so trivial as love or cultural norms of female behavior. He described her as "a young and good looking corporal, whose courtesy and military bearing . . . struck the officers very favorably and who was a real soldierly, thoroughly military fellow."[37]

Others on the home front knew about the presence of women soldiers in the Union and Confederate armies because these very women were their friends, sisters, and daughters. While some women soldiers used the army as a means of escaping their former lives, others served with the knowledge, if not with the acceptance and approval, of their loved ones back home. Sarah Edmonds, who made a new life for herself in the United States, kept in touch with at least one friend in Canada who knew she was serving in the army. He sent a letter to her early in 1862 expressing his disapproval and urging her to quit the army, but his letter failed to persuade her.[38]

Mary Ann Clark's mother believed that her daughter was "laboring under insanity." Her mother felt that Clark's bad marriage, coupled with the prewar death of two of her children, had driven Clark over the edge and that her service was a clear indication that her daughter was not in her right mind. When Melverina Peppercorn joined the Confederate army with her twin brother, her widowed mother reluctantly consented. But patriotism and pride soon took precedence in her mind, and when her daughter's service ended after only one battle, Mrs. Peppercorn was chagrined that Melverina had no more opportunities to fight.[39]

The family of Rosetta Wakeman knew full well about her army career, for she faithfully wrote to them throughout her service. Her letters indicate some family tensions but also reveal that Wakeman cared for her kin very deeply, as evidenced by her inquiries about the state of the farm and family and her generosity with her army paychecks, which she often sent home. Although the letters that Wakeman's family wrote to her presumably no longer exist, an impression emerges from Wakeman's writings that her parents loved and cared for their stubborn and independent firstborn, even if they did not fully understand her.[40]

Regardless of how women soldiers were viewed by their families, their comrades, or the reading public, it is clear that the presence of women serving their country in the ranks of the Union and Confederate armies as both enlisted soldiers and as officers was no secret. Their existence was widely publicized, accurately or not, in countless newspaper articles, nonfictional literature, and letters home from those at the front. Public interest in tales about women soldiers in turn generated a number of fictional novels during and after the war, as well as the wartime publication of the memoirs of Sarah Emma Edmonds.

Women soldiers who failed to claim patriotism or love as their excuse for joining the army took their chances on how the public perceived them, as these inducements were generally more acceptable to Victorian society. Pecuniary gain, desire for independence from family and home, and quest for adventure, all common motivations for many male soldiers, were far less permissible for women in a society that defined the ideal female realm as primarily home and family. Thus, women who talked about their military service tended to weave the story of their exploits to play to the cultural icon of the Female Warrior Bold. Women whose stories were told by others often saw their military history shaped in compliance with cultural expectations of female behavior. Women who claimed other motives for taking up arms risked disdain and condemnation, not necessarily from their regimental comrades, but certainly by the home front romantic idealists of the day.

9

WHEN JENNIE CAME MARCHING HOME
Women Soldiers in the Postwar Years

As one Confederate army after another finally capitulated, the bloodiest war in the history of the United States came to a close in the spring of 1865. Paroled southern soldiers returned home to find broken families, a devastated landscape, the very real threat of starvation, and martial law imposed by a victorious Federal government. For years thereafter, southern veterans rebuilt their shattered lives or headed west to start new ones, and the more fortunate returned to their prewar occupations. With the end of Reconstruction, former Confederate soldiers organized veterans associations, and as they aged into old men, they recalled with love and pride the cause for which they and their families had fought and suffered.

Most of the volunteer Union regiments were mustered out of the Federal service throughout the summer of 1865, although some remained on active duty until 1866. When their service ended, Union soldiers went home, too, usually receiving heroes' welcomes in their hometowns. White northern veterans benefitted enormously from their status as victors, and they found few obstacles to resuming their prewar lives as farmers, laborers, craftsmen, and professionals. Other Civil War veterans joined the regular army and went west to fight Native Americans. An organization of Union veterans, the Grand Army of the Republic (GAR), was formed, and chapters sprang up all over the country.

Like the men with whom they served, women soldiers also went home when the war was over, if they had a home to which they could return. In April 1865, Maria Lewis, a veteran of the 8th New York Cavalry, presented herself to northern abolitionists who were assisting freed slaves in Alexandria, Virginia. One of the philanthropists, a Quaker schoolteacher, noted in her diary, "We shall see that she has good place." The ultimate fate of Lewis, an African American woman who passed for a white man in the Union army, remains unknown.[1]

V. A. White, the unwed mother turned prostitute turned Union soldier, served with her regiment until it was mustered out of service. Arriving in Au Sable, Michigan, and still in possession of the profits from her days in a Nashville bordello, she bought a "nice home" on the shore of Lake Huron. White proudly wrote to an old friend in her hometown that she was finally "free and independent."[2]

Jenny Lockwood may have been free and independent after the war, but she was also poor and in bad health. Formerly a private in the 2nd Michigan Infantry, the same regiment that Sarah Edmonds served in, Lockwood stayed in Washington, D.C., after the war. She came to the attention of a local newspaper when she appeared at a police station seeking help. She informed them of her veteran status, and pleaded "that she was sick and without a home." A police officer delivered her to a local hospital.[3]

Women soldiers who served with their husbands usually did have homes to return to, and when the war was over they easily resumed their former lives. Elizabeth and John Finnern went back to Ohio and tried farming. They quickly gave up that pursuit and moved to Indiana, where John worked as a migrant laborer. Unfortunately, he was in bad shape for most of the postwar years, and by 1884 he was physically incapacitated and unable to make a living for himself and his wife. The childless Finnerns became a county charity case in Greensburg, as John's veteran's pension was not enough to keep them in food and shelter. Elizabeth died in 1907, two years after her husband, at the age of eighty-seven.[4]

Martha Lindley mustered out of her regiment in August 1864. She retrieved her two children from the care of her sister and then went home and awaited the return of her husband. The family reunited in July 1865 and eventually settled in Cleveland. Martha gave birth to two more children after the war. William Lindley died on July 3, 1899. Martha died on December 15, 1909, at the age of seventy-four.[5]

Elizabeth and Martin Niles began their life together on June 10, 1862, three months before joining the 14th Vermont Infantry. After the war, they resided in Raritan, New Jersey, and raised five children. After Martin's death from pneumonia in 1889, it came to light that the Nileses were never properly married but had entered a "cohabitation without ceremony." Elizabeth died on September 13, 1920, at the age of seventy-eight.[6]

When Ivory and Mary Brown went home in 1865, they worked a small farm that Mary owned in Brownfield, Maine, and lived comfortably until Ivory's health declined. Their marriage produced no children. As old age descended on them, they could no longer keep up their farm. Like the Finnerns in Indiana, the destitute couple survived on Ivory's pension and local charity. Ivory died of kidney disease in 1903. Mary survived him for more than thirty years. She lived meagerly in Portland during her widowhood and contended with serious health problems that she attributed to drinking bad water during the war. By 1932, Mary Brown was senile, claiming to have "lizards in her bloodstream." Portland authorities remanded her to a city hospital, where she remained for the rest of her life. On March 15, 1936, Mary Brown died at the age of ninety-eight.[7]

Elizabeth Finnern, Martha Lindley, Elizabeth Niles, and Mary Brown had more in common than just their status as Union veterans and faithful wives. After their army service, they returned to civilian life, resumed a traditional lifestyle, and did not publicly acknowledge their military service until quite late in their lives. None of the four women ever claimed a veteran's pension for themselves, preferring instead to share their husband's annuity. Even Elizabeth Finnern and Mary Brown, who were impoverished in their old age and dependent on charity for food and shelter, never sought for themselves any of the benefits offered by the federal government to Union veterans.

Because Elizabeth Finnern served as a battlefield nurse after her discovery as a soldier, she was also eligible for a nurse's pension. Apparently, she did not know this. When John Finnern applied for his pension, however, several of his comrades provided affidavits concerning his wartime injuries and as a matter of course mentioned the dutiful service of Elizabeth to the regiment. When Elizabeth passed away, her life and her service to her country were extolled in a lengthy obituary, with the facts of her service probably provided by her fellow veterans. That obituary was reprinted in the *National Tribune*, and thus after her death Elizabeth Finnern received widespread national recognition that she never sought during her lifetime.[8]

Even though Mary Brown never claimed her own pension, she did bring her service to the attention of the Pension Bureau in 1925, when she requested an increase in the monthly payments she received as the widow of a veteran. "I was with him in the war, and went to the hospital with him," she wrote. Her husband had mentioned his wife's service many years earlier when he initially applied for his payments, informing the Pension Bureau that he benefitted from "my wife remaining with me and taking care of me" after he was injured near Petersburg. Mary Brown came to the attention of her Portland neighbors when a local newspaper interviewed her in 1930, having been informed of Brown's veteran status by one of the city Samaritans who had taken an interest in her. Six years later, upon her death, another Portland newspaper offered a touching tribute to her on the obituary page.[9]

"The fact that she served throughout the war is known to but few of her friends and acquaintances," announced the Cleveland *Leader* in a lengthy article about Martha Lindley published in 1896. Lindley was too busy raising her children after the war to speak publicly about her martial experiences, but both she and her husband apparently regaled their children with war stories, and it was no secret in her family that she was as much a hero as her husband. Indeed, it was probably one of Lindley's offspring who brought her to public attention thirty years after she was discharged from the Union army. When she died, Lindley's grown children carefully saved their mother's uniform and pistol and lovingly passed them down to the next generation.[10]

It was obviously the grown sons of Elizabeth Niles who made sure that information about their mother's military service was included in her obituary. The story was picked up by a Washington, D.C., newspaper, which scrambled the facts. The press erroneously listed her age as ninety-two, and her regiment as the 4th New Jersey Infantry. The obituary was the first time that Niles's military service was publicly noted. When she applied for a widow's pension after her husband's death, she did not mention her own service. Fortunately for Niles, the Pension Bureau accepted her common-law marriage and approved monthly payments.[11]

Niles, Lindley, Brown, and Finnern were not the only women soldiers to resume traditional lives when the war was over. Even though Union soldiers Satronia Smith and Mary Owens and Confederate soldier Lucy

Gauss returned from the battlefields having lost the husbands with whom they went to war, none of these widows remained unmarried for long. Smith united with a fellow Iowa veteran named John Hunt and they went west. When she died at the age of ninety-eight in Sioux City, Nebraska, in July 1928, her status as a war veteran was announced in her obituary, which was subsequently reprinted in a Washington, D.C., newspaper.[12]

Mary Owens married Abraham Jenkins, and they lived in Massillon, Ohio, until her death in 1881. Buried in the village cemetery of West Brookfield, her grave was reverently decorated by members of the local chapter of the GAR for many years after her death. In 1937, the Sons of Union Veterans erected a headstone proclaiming her service to the Union cause. Just as her wartime experiences were chronicled in Civil War–era newspapers, the fame of Mary Owens continued long after her death. The District of Columbia press, long enamored of tales of women soldiers, published stories about her in 1896 and again in 1901.[13]

Lucy Gauss found herself not only widowed but also a single mother when her Confederate service ended. She married a southern man, Patrick Kenney, who claimed to have been coerced into serving on a Union gunboat during the war. They moved to Georgia, and Lucy gave birth to five children during the course of their marriage. Lucy Gauss Kenney never talked about her military service, not even to family and friends, until 1914. But then her story reached almost legendary proportions, not so much because she was a Confederate veteran, but because her descendants misread the handwriting on some family documents and their illiterate mother did not set the record straight. Thus, when Lucy Matilda Thompson Gauss Kenney died on June 22, 1925, her obituary proclaimed that she was 113 years old. Other posthumous reports incredulously exclaimed that she was born in 1812, married her first husband at the age of forty-nine, and gave birth to her last child at the age of sixty-eight. According to the 1900 census, however, Lucy Thompson was born in 1827, and therefore she was only ninety-seven when she died and only thirty-four when she married Bryant Gauss, and she gave birth to her last child at the age of fifty-three. Even with these corrected statistics, however, Lucy Gauss Kenney lived an extraordinary and long life.[14]

Sarah Edmonds also turned to a traditional female lifestyle after the war, which seemed surprising, given that she lived an unconventional life before the war, served as a soldier for nearly two years, and published her best-selling memoirs outlining her wartime exploits. Perhaps Edmonds

tired of the adventurous life. In any event, after *Nurse and Spy* was published, Edmonds obtained employment with the U.S. Christian Commission, a benevolent society that aided Union soldiers, and worked in
hospitals in West Virginia. In 1866, Edmonds visited relatives in New
Brunswick, where she met a carpenter, Linus H. Seelye. They married in
Cleveland on April 27, 1867. Their marriage produced two sons.

For the next twenty years, this former soldier never publicly talked
about her wartime career. Then in 1883 while living in Fort Scott, Kansas,
with her family, Edmonds went public with her story, and apparently did
so with a single goal in mind: to obtain a veteran's pension. She had two
serious obstacles to overcome, however. She needed to prove that she was
the same person as Franklin Thompson of the 2nd Michigan Infantry, and
she needed the charge of desertion against Private Thompson removed.
Edmonds guessed correctly that her pension campaign would be more
successful if she garnered popular as well as Union veteran support. On
May 26, 1883, "The Story of a Remarkable Life" appeared in the Detroit
Post and Tribune, recounting the life story of Sarah Emma Edmonds Seelye. This article was reprinted in a number of other newspapers over the
next two years. When it appeared in Edmonds' local paper, a reporter
there added that she was a good wife and mother, a fact of utmost impor-
tance in Victorian America.

Edmonds sought her pension because her family needed the income, in
part because of mounting doctor bills from her many health problems.
The young woman who selflessly gave away the proceeds of her best-selling book became a middle-aged invalid suffering from arthritis and rheu-
matism. Her health may have been broken, but the spirit, determination,
and shrewdness she displayed during her army days was still very much
intact. She went directly to Congress with a plea to remove the charge
of desertion against herself, knowing that the law forbade pensioning of
deserters. She wisely presented herself as a self-sacrificing caregiver in her
1884 congressional petition. "I had no other motive in enlisting than love
to God, and love for suffering humanity. I felt called to go and do what I
could for the defense of the right," her affidavit read. Edmonds further
vowed, "I went with no other ambition than to nurse the sick and care for
the wounded."

Former comrades of Franklin Thompson came forward with affidavits
of their own in support of her receiving a pension. They rallied around
their fellow veteran, testifying to the "good character" of the soldier while

in the service. General O. M. Poe personally wrote a letter to Congress on January 4, 1885, stating that he had spoken with Edmonds the previous fall at a regimental reunion and that there was no mistaking her as the same soldier he had known during the war. When the secretary of war voiced no objections to the "anomalous case . . . of a female soldier," Congress signed into law, on July 3, 1886, the Bill to Remove Charge of Desertion from the Record of Franklin Thompson, thus clearing the way for Edmonds to collect the enlistment bounty she never received during her service, back pay owed to her when she deserted, and most importantly, a monthly pension of twelve dollars. In accordance with congressional instructions, the secretary of war ordered that Franklin Thompson be "discharged to date April 19, 1863, . . . to complete his military record."

In granting Edmonds' petition, Congress noted that she performed "meritorious service," rendering "zealous and efficient aid" to "the cause of which she felt to be the highest and noblest that can actuate man or woman." Yet Congress was rather dismissive of Franklin Thompson's actual record as a soldier, mail carrier, and orderly, stating that by working for the Christian Commission she "rendered much more valuable aid to the cause nearest her heart than she could possibly have done as a soldier."

The military service of Sarah Edmonds may have been slighted by Congress, but her former comrades were in no way dismissive of her. Not only was she welcome at reunions of the 2nd Michigan Infantry, but she was also admitted as a member in good standing of the Fort Scott GAR. For the rest of her days, Edmonds proudly believed that she was the "*only woman* in the United States whom the Government ever pensioned as a *soldier*." Sarah Emma Edmonds Seelye died in Fort Scott on September 5, 1898. She was fifty-eight years old.[15]

Union veteran Frances Hook also took a traditional route when the war was over. She married and raised a daughter, Maggie, and must have told her child about her previous life in uniform. After her mother's death, Maggie Dickson wrote to the War Department seeking confirmation of the military service of Frances Hook. The daughter wrote that her mother served for a total of twenty-two months, adding that details of that service would be much appreciated. The letter was forwarded to the Adjutant General's Office (AGO), which was the custodian of the archives of the U.S. Army. AGO clerks conscientiously searched through the records in their holdings, and wrote back to Mrs. Dickson that a record of her mother's capture by Confederates and medical treatment in Union hospitals was located among the war records.[16]

Former women soldiers who acquired or continued acceptable roles as wives and mothers after the war consistently received favorable press and favorable treatment if and when their stories of military service became public. But not all of the former women soldiers wanted a traditional and acceptable lifestyle, and not all of the former women soldiers wanted public scrutiny, positive or otherwise. Jennie Hodgers, alias Albert D. J. Cashier, was a case in point. She mustered out with the rest of the 95th Illinois Infantry on August 27, 1865, having served a full three-year enlistment. Hodgers then decided to live the rest of her life under her male identity, but her reasons for choosing this route were never clearly delineated. By 1865, her male persona was so definitely established with all her friends and associates that she may have felt she had no choice but to continue the masquerade. Hodgers was also an illiterate Irish immigrant with no apparent family ties in the United States, and she needed to make a living for herself once the war was over. She undoubtedly recognized that she would find many more employment opportunities if the world continued to perceive her as a man.

Albert Cashier lived in four Illinois towns, working as a laborer and briefly owning a plant nursery with a comrade from the war, before she settled permanently in Saunemin, Illinois, in 1869. She then held a variety of jobs as a farmhand, handyman, day laborer, child sitter, janitor, and property caretaker for more than forty years. She even served for a time as the town lamplighter. One of her steady employers, the Chesbro family, became so fond of their handyman that they bought Cashier a house to live in, always set a place for Cashier at their dinner table, and reserved a space in their family cemetery plot as Cashier's final resting place.

In 1890, with the help of a local attorney, Cashier applied for and received a veteran's pension. In 1899, the fifty-five-year-old former soldier requested an increased allotment, as she was becoming disabled and found earning a living more difficult. On July 17, 1899, fifteen acquaintances and former employers signed a statement for the Pension Bureau declaring that Albert Cashier was enfeebled, destitute, and dependent on charity for "aid and support." Such was not exactly the case, but the statement showed that Cashier was highly regarded in her community and that people who knew the old soldier were more than willing to help when needed. The next year, Cashier's doctor informed the Pension Bureau that his patient was completely disabled and could perform only the lightest of manual labor.

No one, not even the physician, discovered that Albert Cashier was a woman until 1911. Even then, Cashier's sex did not become public knowledge for two more years. While doing odd jobs for Illinois state senator Ira Lish, Cashier's leg was fractured when the senator accidentally backed over her with his automobile. The town doctor was summoned, and in the course of setting the broken thigh discovered that Albert Cashier was a woman. The senator and the surgeon agreed to keep Cashier's secret, only telling the Chesbro sisters, who were summoned to help care for Cashier while her leg healed. The sisters also agreed to stay silent on the matter.

Cashier's health and physical capacities had been slowly declining as she aged, but the broken leg permanently and negatively affected her ability to further support herself. It never properly healed, and Cashier found herself an invalid at the age of sixty-six. Senator Lish, with the assistance of the Saunemin physician, arranged for Cashier's entrance into the Illinois Soldiers' and Sailors' Home in Quincy. As a disabled veteran of the Union army, Cashier qualified to live at the home, but it was certainly due to the influence of Senator Lish that the superintendent of the home agreed to take a woman soldier and keep her secret. The only other individuals at the home who were informed of Cashier's sex were the doctors and the nurses, for obvious reasons. They, too, were sworn to secrecy regarding the matter. Cashier's application for admission to the home showed no indication that she was any different from the other residents. Dated April 11, 1911, the document described Cashier as five feet two inches tall with blue eyes and light brown hair.

Cashier lived at the home for nearly three years, bedridden some of the time. As her physical health continually declined, so too did her mental health diminish. The superintendent placed Cashier under the care of a psychiatrist, Dr. Leroy Scott, who immediately took a keen interest in the female veteran. He talked with Cashier frequently, wanting to know all about her past and her reasons for living as she did. Even after Cashier left the home, Scott continued to piece together her life, interviewing all her old friends and employers and making written inquiries to various places in Ireland.

Dr. Scott's interest in Cashier, unfortunately, did little to improve her deteriorating mental condition. The chief physician of the home, Dr. D. M. Landon, noted in 1913 that Cashier was not only infirm but also senile. The other doctors at the home concurred that Cashier was too ill, mentally and physically, to be properly cared for at their facility. Acting on their assessment, the superintendent began proceedings to have Cashier declared insane by the State of Illinois, thereby paving the way to remove her from the Soldiers' Home and send her to a mental institution.

About the same time that officials at the home decided to send her away, the news that Albert D. J. Cashier was a woman reached the public. It is not known how, or by whom, the story was initially leaked, but by early 1914, the other residents of the home, the people of Saunemin, Cashier's fellow veterans, and, indeed, the rest of the country were reading about Cashier in the newspapers. Her former neighbors and employers were united in saying that they had never suspected Cashier was not a man, although they agreed that Cashier had always been regarded as a bit of an eccentric. When word reached the Pension Bureau, they appointed a special examiner to investigate the case, convinced that Cashier had defrauded the government for the past twenty-four years.

As news of Cashier's sex reached her friends and former comrades, she received frequent visitors at the home. Some went of their own volition, and others were sent at the behest of the Pension Bureau. Newspaper reporters also descended upon her. Cashier had no idea that her life story was available for public consumption, and the realization that everyone knew her lifelong secret made her feel vulnerable and afraid. In the midst of all the publicity, the officials at the home proceeded with their plan to have her judged insane.

At the February 1914 session of the Adams County Court, the Illinois State Bank of Quincy was appointed conservator of the estate of Albert Cashier. On March 27, 1914, the same court declared that Cashier was indeed insane and committed her to the Watertown State Hospital. The commitment papers noted that "he" was noisy, feeble, an insomniac, and suffering from complete loss of memory. Cashier was delivered to the hospital one day after the hearing. At the same time that Cashier was committed, seven other Civil War veterans and soldiers' home residents were also judged insane by the court and remanded to Watertown because they were "distracted." Cashier's sex was not mentioned in the court proceedings, as all eight of the veterans in question were referred to as male. Of course, given the recent publicity about Cashier, the court certainly knew the truth.

Not much is known about the year-and-a-half that Cashier spent in the asylum. In June 1914, officials there reported to the Pension Bureau that Cashier was "failing rapidly" and dressed in female attire. Indeed, when Cashier arrived at the facility, she was placed in the women's wing and forced to wear a dress despite her protests. This action on the part of hospital personnel greatly incensed Cashier's former comrades, who could hardly bear to witness the humiliation of one who had once been so fearless. Forcing Cashier to wear long skirts had tragic consequences. She was a frail seventy-year-old who did not know how to walk in such apparel, having worn pants her entire adult life and probably for a good part of her childhood as well. Cashier tripped, fell, and broke her hip. She never recovered from this injury, and spent the rest of her life mostly confined to her bed. Her days in the asylum could not have been happy ones. Nevertheless, in January 1915, Cashier was judged by an asylum doctor to be in fair physical condition and unchanged mental condition.

Her former comrades in the 95th Illinois Infantry rallied around Cashier during her incarceration, and even though they were powerless to change her circumstances or treatment, their support and visits were undoubtedly a comfort to Cashier in her lucid periods. Her most frequent visitor was her former commanding officer, Charles W. Ives. Another veteran, Robert Horan, was vocal in his criticism of Cashier's treatment, believing that the state committed her merely to save money. As far as Cashier's fellow veterans were concerned, her sex was a secondary issue. Once they recovered from the shock of learning she was a woman, and when they realized what was being done to her, they became very protective and solicitous. She was one of them, after all, and her sex did not change their attitude. As one scholar later aptly noted, "No mere matter of sexual identity could efface the valor and fellowship of their comrade Albert Cashier, who had stood in their ranks as a fighting member of the Union Army."

While Cashier was an inmate of the state hospital, and while her comrades and fellow veterans did their best to comfort her, the Pension Bureau continued its investigation into her case. The special examiner contacted former employers, residents of Saunemin, and many veterans of Cashier's regiment. The examiner especially wanted to know if the old soldiers of the 95th Illinois Infantry could positively identify the old woman in the asylum as being the same young person who enlisted in 1862. The universal response was yes. Those men deposed by the special examiner also consistently praised Cashier's performance as a soldier, and everyone swore that no one ever knew she was a woman during or after the war. The Pension Bureau was also interested in Cashier's mental health, supposing that she must have been insane her entire life. Her comrades disagreed. Eli Brainerd, who served in Cashier's company, said, "His mind seemed to be alright but his actions seemed to be a little funny. I suppose that was because he was a woman." Another compatriot declared, "His mind was alright and he was not simple in anyway." In fact, the only person deposed by the Pension Bureau who thought that Cashier might have been unstable prior to 1913 was one of the Chesbro sisters, who said, "He was always queer and some thought he was half witted."

Depositions were taken until December 1914, when the special examiner decided that Jennie Hodgers was indeed Pvt. Albert D. J. Cashier, that she had not defrauded the government, and that her pension checks would continue. This decision was passed along to a board of review, which declared on February 10, 1915, that "the evidence secured in this case shows beyond any possible doubt that the pensioner is the person who rendered the service. . . . Identity may be accepted." Cashier probably did not care whether or not her pension checks continued. As a ward of the state, she never received them directly anyway.

On October 10, 1915, Albert D. J. Cashier died of an unspecified infection at the Watertown State Hospital. The local chapter of the GAR to which Cashier belonged arranged her funeral. She was buried with full military honors, dressed in her uniform, with the U.S. flag draped over her coffin. Just as the Chesbro sisters wished, the Sunnyslope Cemetery in Saunemin became her final resting place. Cashier's obituary ran in newspapers across the country.

Cashier died intestate. After her burial expenses were paid, there was about $282 left in her estate, and the president of the bank, Mr. Singleton, dutifully tried to find a rightful heir to receive the money. He spent nine years trying to sort out Cashier's past, during which time several purported heirs came forward, but none of them could satisfactorily validate their claims. Cashier's estate finally reverted to the county treasurer. It was little wonder that Mr. Singleton could not find out much about Cashier's past. Many stories circulated about her life and motives, all of them were conflicting, and most of them had been told by Cashier herself.

She was always reticent about her life prior to the war and usually refused to talk about her family. The most popular story about Cashier was that she was born in Ireland in 1844, came to the United States as a shipboard stowaway, spent some time in the East, and then drifted to Belvedere, arriving before the war dressed as a man. When news of her sex became public, a number of her friends and fellow veterans, as well as the soldiers' home psychiatrist, pressed her for details. She told Charles Ives that she had a twin brother and that when they were growing up in Ireland their mother dressed them both in boy's clothing. She told the Chesbro sisters that she assumed male garb in order to enlist with a lover, who was mortally wounded early in the war. On his deathbed, she told them, he asked his beloved Jennie to stay true to him and never again wear a dress. She told the psychiatrist that she was illegitimate; was born in Clogherhead, Ireland; and as a child worked for her uncle, a sheepherder. She continued by narrating that her mother married a man named Cashier and the family emigrated to New York, where her stepfather dressed her as boy, dubbed her Albert, and found employment for both of them in a shoe factory. When her mother died, she headed west, retaining her identity of Albert Cashier.

Cashier's varied stories cannot be completely attributed to her senility because she had always been evasive on the subject of her personal history and had made a habit of telling conflicting stories about herself long before she entered the soldiers' home. When she enlisted in 1862, she said she was born in New York, but in 1907, she told the Pension Bureau that she was born in Belfast. Cashier clearly wanted to keep private her origins and her reasons for living as she did.

Part of her secret past obviously lay in Ireland. Before her death, Dr. Scott located a man he believed to be a relative of hers, Patrick Hodgers of Clogherhead, Ireland. Descendants of Patrick Hodgers believe they have solved at least part of the mystery of Jennie Hodgers. They discovered a record of her birth, on Christmas Day in 1843, in the parish at Clogherhead. Patrick was recorded as her brother, and there were two more siblings. The facts about how and when she left Ireland, however, are still not known.[17]

Cashier was not the only woman soldier to live as man after the Civil War. In the summer of 1896, a hermit farmer named Otto Schaffer died in Butler County, Kansas, when his cabin was struck by lightening during a severe storm. Neighbors found the body, and the county coroner discovered that Schaffer was a woman. Veterans of the local GAR post gave their deceased comrade a military funeral. Schaffer left considerable property, but no known relatives. Even though Schaffer's story ran in at least one national newspaper, her female identity and wartime regimental affiliation remain a mystery.[18]

If Otto Schaffer's cabin had not been hit by lightening, and if Albert Cashier had not been run over by a car, probably no one would ever have learned that these two veterans were women. It is entirely possible that Cashier and Schaffer were not anomalous cases. Perhaps other women soldiers also chose to live the rest of their lives as men. During the war, women soldiers "enjoyed a temporary passage into the male world, made acceptable only because of extraordinary historical circumstances," but those male privileges were revoked when the women resumed civilian life after the war. For unmarried working-class women returning home from the army, their only means of support were the same dreary jobs available to them before the war. If they continued to live as men, however, these army veterans could freely work in a number of occupations and draw much higher wages. Furthermore, they could do all manner of things as men that were either forbidden to women or seriously frowned upon. They could open bank accounts, travel anywhere unaccompanied, and exercise the right to vote. Albert Cashier took advantage of all these male privileges. Her neighbors in Saunemin recalled that she had voted in a number of elections in the postwar years.[19]

Recent scholarship suggests "that transvestism . . . [was] not so rare and that there must have been thousands of women wandering around America in the latter part of the nineteenth century . . . who were passing as men." In 1883, a female factory worker was caught, tried, and sentenced to six months in prison for the crime of impersonating a man. Her defense was simple economics. Her employer paid men nine dollars per week, but only paid women four. Women soldiers, having experienced the liberation of living as men, must have been painfully aware of their society's oppression of females when their superior status evaporated with a mere change of clothing. No wonder Cashier and Schaffer chose to remain in pants instead of taking up dresses when they laid aside their uniforms. Other female veterans may have done the same, continuing their private revolt against the constraints placed on them as women.[20]

Of course, female veterans did not have to continue their male masquerade in order to live nontraditionally, but pursuing such a course as a woman was far more difficult. The postwar life of Loreta Velazquez is a good example. When the war ended, she was living in New York, having extricated herself from her connections with the Confederate Secret Service. She joined her brother, also a Confederate veteran, and toured Europe with him and his family. Upon her return to the states, Velazquez traveled throughout the devastated South, where she met and allegedly married a former major in the Confederate army. In January 1867, she arrived in New Orleans and, using the name Mary DeCaulp, went to work as an agent for the Venezuelan Emigration Company. The New Orleans *Daily Picayune* hailed her arrival, adding, "It was very difficult for us to recognize in the rather graceful . . . lady in black . . . the rather shabby looking Lieut. Bufort of Confederate times." She then went to Venezuela with her husband to see if they might like to settle there with other southern expatriates. The husband died of "black fever" in Caracas, however, so Velazquez voyaged to Cuba to visit relatives. Returning again to the United States, she immediately went west in search of a new life and a new fortune. She married for a fourth time to a gentleman in the mining business and gave birth to a baby boy. Ten years after the close of the war, Velazquez resided in Texas, where she penned her memoirs.

Published in Richmond in 1876, *The Woman in Battle* was the most interesting and controversial of the postwar female soldier accounts presented to the public. Inspired by the ever-popular adventure novels, Velazquez wrote the book primarily as a means to support herself and her child. Having learned from her wartime experiences that the search for fame and prestige was ultimately unfulfilling, Velazquez wrote in her "prefatory notice" that she was not telling her story for praise, as she was "sufficiently philosophical to get along . . . without" it. It was a good thing she felt that way, for almost from the start, her narrative drew accusations of fraud from no less a figure than former Confederate Gen. Jubal A. Early.

Indeed, her experiences both during and after the war, as put forth in *The Woman in Battle*, were extraordinary. Her desire for constant action left the reader wondering how one person could possibly accomplish so much in so little time. After her editor's "prefatory notice," wherein Velazquez is described as a typical southern woman, endowed with such admirable qualities as self-reliance, self-approbation, honesty, and good manners, her rollicking tale of adventure begins.

Velazquez wrote that she was born into a wealthy Cuban family and was sent to New Orleans to complete her education. She married an American military officer, of whom her parents disapproved, and lived at a variety of forts with him. She gave birth to three children, but they all tragically died in their infancy. At the outbreak of the Civil War, Velazquez convinced her husband to resign his commission in the U.S. Army and offer his services to the South. As soon as he left home, she determined to join him and disguised herself as a man. She raised an overstrength cavalry company in Arkansas and then transported her men to Florida, where her husband was stationed. She left for New Orleans for supplies, her husband died in an accident, and her soon-to-be second husband took command of the regiment. Velazquez then headed to the front to drown her grief and avenge her husband's death. She fought in the Battles of Blackburn's Ford, First Manassas, and Ball's Bluff before moving west to join her original company, with whom she fought at Shiloh. After several arrests, Velazquez grew concerned that her secret was too widely known to continue soldiering, so she took up spying on behalf of the Confederacy, at one point becoming a double agent in the North. Her massive memoir also covers her postwar adventures in South America, California, and Utah.

Altogether, Velazquez's memoirs present a "startling chapter in the history of the war," as one advertising broadside for her book promised. And even though her account met with some skepticism at the time of publication and has been viewed by scholars as largely fiction, the veracity of much of her narrative is corroborated in Civil War–era newspapers, the testimony of fellow Confederates, and government documents. Granted, there are glaring historical inconsistencies in the book, and Velazquez did indeed cram a great deal of activity into very short periods of time. Clearly, as Sarah Edmonds had done twelve years earlier, Velazquez embroidered on the truth in order to tell a more exciting story. She probably also thought that the more fantastic the tale, the better the book would sell.

But unlike *Nurse and Spy*, Velazquez's book departed in significant ways from the Female Warrior motif so familiar to nineteenth-century audiences. She freely editorializes about and condemns her male comrades for their filthy mouths and uncouth behavior, and she chastises some women for being too forward in their attentions to her while she was disguised as a man. Although Velazquez quickly acquired and dispensed with husbands, these male love interests barely merit a page of attention in her six-hundred-page narrative, while she makes much of Lieutenant Buford's ability to attract the ladies. In these and several other areas, Velazquez failed to comply with the established motif and thus offended Victorian romantic sensibilities. Perhaps if she had cloaked her experiences in more acceptable themes, she and her book might have received a warmer critical reception, like the one enjoyed by Sarah Edmonds.

A boundless spirit of adventure permeates both *Nurse and Spy* and *The Woman in Battle,*/and both Edmonds and Velazquez claimed patriotism, rather than love, as their motives for joining the army. But Edmonds was a Yankee who presented her book to a Northern audience still in the throes of war, whereas the unreconstructed Velazquez delivered her memoirs to a mixed public, and her homage to the Lost Cause predictably did not play well in the North. Both books are equally bloodthirsty. Of doing battle and killing Union soldiers, Velazquez declares, "There is a positive enjoyment in the deadly perils of the occasion that nothing can equal." Edmonds gleefully describes dragging a southern civilian woman behind her horse, and boasts of shooting a Confederate officer in the face at point-blank range. Yet Edmonds is at pains to present herself as a traditional woman, despite performing all manner of masculine deeds. Edmonds frames the war, and her involvement in it, as a moral crusade, and quotes heavily from scripture throughout her narrative. Velazquez's book lacks such religious fervor and moral overtones and is written in a frank, straightforward style, offering no apologies and making no excuses. Edmonds was self-righteous and Velazquez was proud. Edmonds answered to God. Velazquez answered to no one.

Furthermore, Edmonds was a chaste heroine, in contrast to Velazquez and her multiple amours. Even though Velazquez wrote little about the men she married, her book nevertheless makes the point that she was not a virginal heroine. Velazquez probably mentions her various husbands only briefly because her love life was as unconventional as the rest of her life and because her first two husbands were probably not the southern patriots she wanted them to be. In her memoirs, Velazquez says that her first husband died in service to the Confederacy. At least two Civil War–era sources, however, state that Velazquez's first husband was a northerner in the Union army and that she divorced him.

Velazquez wrote that she met her second husband, Confederate Captain DeCaulp, while raising troops in Arkansas and later married him after they reunited in an Atlanta hospital, both suffering wounds. She further related that he was killed in battle shortly after their brief honeymoon. However, according to the military service record of Thomas DeCaulp of the 3rd Arkansas Cavalry, this officer deserted the Confederate army about the time Velazquez reported him dead. He took the oath of allegiance to the United States and further swore that he was a Unionist trapped in the South and forced to join the rebels. He went on to state that he was married to the daughter of a English rear admiral residing in Philadelphia. Thomas DeCaulp subsequently went to Baltimore under the alias William Irwin and was drafted into the Union army. He served under that alias in the 30th Wisconsin Infantry until February 1865, when he was discharged for chronic sciatica. Perhaps Velazquez really believed that DeCaulp had died, although his regiment promptly labeled him a deserter. A more plausible theory was put forth by another scholar of Velazquez, who concludes that Velazquez "found out that DeCaulp had gone North and abandoned her, and she was too embarrassed to report that, and so she wrote him out of her life and declared him 'dead.'"

As for the third husband of Loreta Velazquez, a Major Wasson who died in South America, it is quite probable that she never actually married such a man. When Velazquez went to work as a Venezuelan emigration agent in New Orleans, she used the surname DeCaulp, not Wasson. This third husband might have been entirely fictitious, or maybe their brief relationship was never sanctified. With regard to her last husband, the father of her son, nothing is known and she does not name him in her memoirs. Maybe he died, maybe he left her, or maybe she divorced him. What is known is that, by 1878, Velazquez was raising her son without the presence or support of a husband.

After the release of her book, the most outspoken critic of Loreta Velazquez was Jubal Early, who read *The Woman in Battle* in New Orleans in the winter of 1878 and concluded that it was false. A few months later in Richmond, he met another Confederate veteran who said he had once traveled on a train with Lieutenant Buford, reported that Velazquez was currently visiting Richmond, and asked Early if he had read her book yet. General Early proceeded to point out to the unnamed gentleman "several inconsistencies, absurdities, and impossibilities." Early then arranged "a brief interview" with Velazquez herself, and came away from their meeting "satisfied that she had not written the book . . . or that it had been very much changed . . . by her editor." The general also vowed that Velazquez was not of Spanish descent and then offered perhaps the ultimate insult, averring she probably did not even hail from the South.

The Woman in Battle offended Early on several levels. He was irate that a married woman used her maiden name. He questioned her personal morality because of her multiple marriages and contended that she was more likely a camp follower than an officer and a spy. Early dismissed much of the military history put forth in the book as well. He found it impossible that she traveled so widely, so frequently, and so quickly without military authority. He did not believe that a woman could raise and transport a battalion of men, again without military authority, and using only her personal wealth. Finally, he found her exploits as a Confederate secret agent "simply incredible." But General Early was outraged the most by Velazquez's description of some Confederate officers as profane, drunken brutes and her description of some Confederate women as rather fast and loose. He wholeheartedly believed that *The Woman in Battle* grievously injured "the character and fame of the Confederate armies, and of the people of the South, especially the women of the South."

Early was correct in noting chronological inconsistencies in *The Woman in Battle*, for in several places, Velazquez recorded events out of sequence. On the other hand, Early completely ignored the passages in the book that accurately recorded details such as the course of battles and the weather on a given day. His reservations about the wartime mobility of Lieutenant Buford were sound. How she managed to travel so freely over the southern railroads has never been adequately explained. Of course, many of Velazquez's unofficial movements were early in the war; in the last two years, her travel was undertaken while she was an agent of the Confederate government. Early dismissed the spy career of Velazquez mostly because she offended him on other matters and despite the fact that her narrative shows a definite understanding of Lafayette Baker's intelligence organization.

General Early, however, may have been on the mark when he stated that Velazquez was not "a cultivated Spanish lady." She may have been Laura J. Williams, an Arkansas native whose story was published in 1864 and whose wartime exploits were virtually identical to those described in *The Woman in Battle*. Velazquez definitely had ties to Arkansas. She raised and equipped her battalion there, her second husband served in an Arkansas regiment, and in her imbroglio with General Early she was championed by one of the congressional representatives from that state. Then again, Laura J. Williams may simply have been an anglicized version of Velazquez's name put forth for public consumption during the war years. Velazquez's involvement with Venezuelan colonization, as well as the fact that in 1878 she landed a job as a newspaper correspondent in South America, lend credence to her claim of Spanish heritage. At the very least,

Velazquez must have spoken Spanish, which was not a common second language among the educated classes in nineteenth-century North America.

In any event, General Early was vocal in his condemnation of Velazquez, and he was perplexed that other former Confederates did not join him in his criticism. It troubled him that Velazquez enjoyed "the apparent endorsement of some forty or fifty Southern members of Congress." Additionally, *The Woman in Battle* received endorsements from several Confederate officers. Brig. Gen. George Anderson vouched from Atlanta that "Madame L. J. Velazquez is the person known during the late war . . . as Lieut. Harry T. Buford, C.S.A." and Dr. J. F. Hammond, who had been an assistant surgeon at the Empire Hotel Hospital in Atlanta, avowed, "Her conduct was that of a brave soldier, whose life was at the disposal of home and country. Her work is founded on fact."

Loreta Velazquez was not content to let others defend her, though. When friends in Richmond informed her that Early was publicly attacking her book, she wrote to him personally, sending the letter in care of the Honorable W. F. Slemmons, House of Representatives. Stating that her letter was "prompted by a high sense of honor," Velazquez explained to Early that the incorrect dates in her manuscript were the result of writing from memory, as she had lost her wartime journal, and that discrepancies in names were intentional, as she had not wished to publicly mortify some specific individuals or their families. She then pleaded with Early to make his criticisms directly to her, rather than to the public, conceding that she penned her memoirs "on account of pecuniary embarrassments," and admitting that "my book and correspondence with the Press is my entire support of myself and little son." Her health was failing, she added, and she worried about how she would provide for her child and see to his education. Her letter continued, "I have had trials enough to have driven almost any proud spiritual woman to madness . . . but I have struggled and born my lot . . . and with Gods protection I have lived above it all, and all I now ask from you . . . is justice to my *child*. I live for him."

Perhaps if Velazquez had played to romantic and chivalric sensibilities in her book, as she did in her letter to Early, the controversy might have been avoided. If the adventures put forth in her memoirs had been written by a man, such a controversy definitely would never have arisen. No one would have questioned a man's ability to perform military duty, raise a company, fight in battle, and act as a secret agent. And no one would have looked so askance at his personal morality for having numerous wives.

Velazquez icily ended her letter to Early "with the most profound regard for you as a gentleman of culture and a patriot." At the time she wrote to him, in May 1878, she was living with her child in Rio de Janeiro, Brazil, and working as a newspaper correspondent. Velazquez then seemingly disappeared from the historical record. Where, when, and how she died, and what happened to her son, have yet to be discerned.[21]

The details of the postwar lives of most of the women who served as soldiers during the Civil War are simply not known. Apparently, most of these women returned to civilian life and did not talk about their wartime experiences, at least not in a public forum. As a group they did not seek the benefits that society provided to Civil War veterans. The U.S. government provided pensions to veterans of the Union army, and many of the former states of the Confederacy offered pensions to southern veterans. Why women soldiers did not claim these benefits is a matter of conjecture. Perhaps they did not think the government entities would honor their service since they were women. Maybe they felt unable to prove that they had rendered such service because they used aliases during the war. As an unfortunate result of their reticence about their war days and their reluctance to seek the compensation due to them, there is virtually no written record of their postwar lives.[22]

Women soldiers' male compatriots often wondered what happened to them. In August 1895, a veteran wrote to the *National Tribune* stating that when he was a prisoner of war in Atlanta, he made the acquaintance of "a girl of medium stature by the alias Frank Miller" but lost track of her when she was exchanged. If Frances Hook was reading the publication that summer, she declined to write a letter telling her comrades about her postwar life. In November 1898, a former Confederate soldier wrote to *Confederate Veteran* stating that he had been a POW at Point Lookout when Jane Perkins arrived. "Who can tell further about her?" he asked the other readers of the magazine. Perkins did not come forward. In December 1923, *Confederate Veteran* received a letter from a retired judge, asking if anyone knew the whereabouts of Loreta Velazquez or, if she was no longer living, any of her heirs. This inquiry also went unanswered.[23]

The male veterans of the Civil War, both Union and Confederate, did more than wonder about their long-lost female comrades-in-arms. They actively supported women veterans in times of need, as illustrated by the cases of Sarah Edmonds and Albert Cashier. They sent female comrades to their final resting places with full military honors, as evidenced by the funerals of Mary Owens Jenkins, Elizabeth Finnern, and, of course, Albert Cashier. And they never seemed to tire of telling war stories about female soldiers. Well into the twentieth century, veterans' publications routinely supplied stories and anecdotes of encounters with women in uniform. As regiment after regiment published their individual histories, stories of women soldiers were included as a matter of course. As one regimental historian explained, the war was so compelling that even women "were inspired with a desire to share the rougher dangers of the field, and donning male attire were discovered . . . carrying a musket."[24]

Not every former woman soldier was showered with praise by the male veterans, however. In 1895 and 1896, *Confederate Veteran* ran short articles about Malinda Blalock, who served two weeks with the 26th North Carolina Infantry. Both articles recorded "the great amusement of the army" when she revealed her sex and went home. Nearly two years later, when the subject of Blalock once again arose in that magazine, a former Confederate attested that Blalock "did drilling, doing guard and picket duty when she could not frame excuses for avoiding it. It is said she was adept at excuse making." Such derision might well have stemmed from the fact that in the postwar years, Malinda and her husband reached almost legendary status in the mountainous region of their home state, but their fame had nothing to do with supporting the Lost Cause.[25]

When the Blalocks returned home from the southern army in 1862, their pro-Confederate neighbors viewed their lack of enthusiasm for the rebellion dimly, so Malinda and Keith fled into nearby Tennessee and for two years were pro-Union bushwhackers in the Tennessee and North Carolina mountains. On June 1, 1864, Keith enlisted in the 10th Michigan Cavalry under his given name of William and served for the rest of the war as a scout. Malinda dressed as a man and was hired as an unenlisted "independent scout" for the same regiment. When the war was over, they settled in Avery County, North Carolina, and raised four sons. Malinda Blalock died in 1903 at the age of sixty-one. Her husband outlived her by ten years.[26]

A woman named Kate W. Howe, who claimed soldier status, received mixed reviews from the Union veteran community in the postwar years. In 1885, she traveled around the country as an entertainer, claiming to be the granddaughter of the venerable Gen. Winfield Scott. She said that during the Civil War she was a drummer boy and scout in the 27th Massachusetts Infantry, serving under the alias Tom Smith. Howe further claimed to have been wounded and discovered at the Battle of Lookout Mountain, and to be a bona fide pensioner of the U.S. government. The GAR post of San Antonio, Texas, however, believed her to be a fraud who was claiming to be a veteran in order to garner a larger audience. They also vowed that Howe was not donating her profits to the Women's Relief Corps of the GAR even though promotional materials for her show stated that she was. The GAR post in Los Angeles complained that Howe told her audiences she was a member of that organization, but in fact she was not. On the other hand, the GAR post of Montello, Wisconsin, proudly endorsed Howe, proclaiming that her "grand entertainment" was a smashing success and that they appreciated the money she donated to their charity fund.[27]

Was Kate Howe a fraud, capitalizing on the public knowledge of women soldiers in the Civil War and the general goodwill of the male veteran community? War Department records do not document any soldier named Tom Smith as serving in the 27th Massachusetts Infantry, and no extant pension file for Kate Howe can be found. However, the second volume of the *History of Woman Suffrage*, published in 1887, recounts a story found in Civil War–era newspapers of a woman named Tom Smith, a teamster from Illinois who was a scout during the Battle of Lookout Mountain. Even so, Howe's wartime activities, if any, cannot be reliably documented.[28]

It is difficult to discern whether many postwar stories of women soldiers are fact or fiction or a blend of both. As the old soldiers of the Civil War reminisced about their female compatriots, some of their stories took on the rosy glow of Victorian romanticism. An example is the legend of the "Hero of Pickett's Old Brigade," retold in at least two Confederate magazines. A husband and wife, thought to be father and son by their comrades, went into battle for the final time on the third day of Gettysburg. During the famous charge, "a flag-bearer in the Confederate ranks is shot. A fair, sweet-faced young soldier raises the old standard," bearing it forward. The young soldier was none other than the wife, who was subsequently pierced by a sword and fell by the side of her husband. "Both surrender life in this wonderful charge," the story says.[29]

Another equally romantic tale again involves a southern husband and wife in General Johnston's army at Bentonville. Charlie and Frank Stan-

hope were brothers in the 10th Georgia Infantry, as the regiment's surgeon tells the story. The night before the battle, Charlie appealed to the
surgeon to keep Frank away from the fight, as he had a horrible presenti-
ment of doom. The surgeon, of course, could do nothing, as the Confederate ranks were so thin. The following day, Charlie Stanhope was
brought to the surgeon's tent with a mortal wound, and when Frank
learned of his brother's fate, he fainted. The surgeon loosened Frank's collar to give him air and learned the truth, that Frank was a young woman,
and the wife of the dead Charlie Stanhope.[30]

Both of these stories were written by veterans and are more than plausible, given the fairly large number of women who followed their husbands
into the army. At Gettysburg a burial party did find a woman soldier dead
on the field of Pickett's Charge. And a woman soldier whose husband was
killed in action did fight at Bentonville, but the 10th Georgia Infantry was
not present at the battle. These two postwar tales are most likely senti-
mentalized versions of true wartime events.

The numerous stories of women soldiers told by veterans after the war
point to a continued fascination with the distaff members of the Union
and Confederate armies. One regiment even invented a woman soldier, or
rather picked one of their members to assume the role of a woman pretending to be a man. On May 25, 1899, the *National Tribune* ran an article
written by a veteran of the 15th Battery, Indiana Light Artillery, stating
that one of its members, William H. C. Riley, was a woman. The article
praised Riley's prowess on the battlefield—"as a cannoneer he was a
model"—and noted that in camp Riley was retiring and tidy and liked to
look at himself in the mirror he carried in his knapsack. The article further
stated that no one knew that Riley was a woman until after the war, when
a former comrade learned the secret and passed it along to the other veterans of the battery. The article did not describe how Riley's femininity was
allegedly discovered but did state that Riley had died after the war by her
own hand.[31]

How one of Riley's comrades came to the conclusion that he was a
woman is not known, but it appears to have been a mistaken assumption.
Not only did Private Riley marry after the war, but he also fathered a child.
His pension application file included affidavits from men who had known
him since childhood. On May 26, 1885, William Riley poisoned his
daughter and then committed suicide by slashing his own throat. A county
coroner examined his body. What is most interesting about the sad Riley

case was the willingness of his comrades to believe that he was a woman, despite all evidence to the contrary. Perhaps it was due to his short stature and his manner of keeping to himself, traits shared by many of the real women soldiers. The Riley case also illustrates how the perception of a soldier's sex did not change the perception of the individual's service. Riley's comrades praised him as a soldier both before and after they believed he was a woman.[32]

The stories about women soldiers as told by their male compatriots fell into three categories: strictly factual, true stories romantically embellished to comply with Victorian sensibilities, and complete fiction. Of course the stories that male veterans told about themselves and the exploits of their regiments also fell into the same three categories. In the postwar years, the veterans of the Civil War showed a remarkable dedication to keeping alive the memories of all those who fought in the war, and just as they showed remarkable tolerance and respect for women soldiers during the war, they continued to honor them long after the conflict.

The veterans were not alone in their acknowledgments. Just as the literate public devoured stories of female warriors during the war, they continued to read about these women long afterward in books, magazines, and newspapers. The stories of Sarah Edmonds and Albert Cashier graced newspapers across the country. Loreta Velazquez created a sensation with the publication of her memoirs. Obituary columns carried death notices of former women soldiers. Until World War I, national newspapers periodically brought up the subject of distaff warriors in human interest stories, which were oftentimes nothing more than rehashings of columns printed during the war. Additionally, the literary market was flooded in the postwar years with memoirs and regimental histories penned by those who witnessed or participated in the war. These volumes frequently mentioned women soldiers. The reading public was obviously interested in the stories of all participants of the Civil War, male and female.

News stories about women soldiers ranged from anecdotal to apocryphal. Some of the postwar reports were accurate, and others were implausible. The most outlandish account appeared in 1898 in the Charles Town (West Virginia) *Farmer's Advocate*. According to the article, Mary Walters enlisted in a Michigan regiment to be with her husband, although he had no knowledge of her actions. She stayed in the service until he failed to return from a scouting expedition, whereupon she "applied for her discharge and returned to her Michigan home." She never believed, however,

that her husband was dead, and in fact she had recurring dreams in which
she saw where he lived. Her dreams eventually led her to Natural Bridge,
Virginia, where she found her husband working on a farm. He had suffered a head injury on that fateful scouting trip and was robbed of his
memory. When his wife appeared before him after a separation of thirty
years, all of his memories rushed back and he recognized her. The reunited couple returned to Michigan, according to this undoubtedly apocryphal account.[33]

Another suspicious story was that of Mountain Charley, whose real
name was supposedly Elsa Jane Guerin, although Gen. George West
vowed that her given name was Charlotte. Actually, there were several different versions of the Mountain Charley story; some of them read like romance novels and others sound very much like true stories. Mountain
Charley first appeared in 1861, in an autobiography outlining her adventures dressed as a man in California and Colorado. After the war, two very
different stories about the wartime exploits of Mountain Charley appeared
in western newspapers. In one adventure series, Mountain Charley joins a
Wisconsin regiment, fights throughout the war, then goes to Wyoming,
where she runs a gambling house, and by 1879 lands in prison. In the second Mountain Charley story, she enlists in the Iowa cavalry and is promoted to lieutenant. By 1885, she has been married for eighteen years and
is the mother of four children. The shadowy and mysterious Mountain
Charley may well have been a complete literary fabrication, but it is just
as likely that her story was a composite of the experiences of several
women settlers. Like most legends, the stories of Mountain Charley probably contain a kernel or two of truth.[34]

When stories of women soldiers were not available, the public and the
press invented them. A civilian female inmate who died at Alton Military
Prison was posthumously promoted into the soldier ranks in 1909, when
a newspaper article about a proposed monument at the prison site chronicled the sad story of "Barbara Duravan" [sic], a woman so "strong in the
belief of the Southern cause" that she served as a private in the Army of
Northern Virginia. In reality, Barbara Ann Dunavan was a poor and illiterate Tennessee woman who was court-martialed for smuggling revolvers to
the Confederate army. Convicted of the charge, she was sent to Alton,
where she died of smallpox.[35]

Not every postwar account of women soldiers was inaccurate, however.
A 1901 feature in the Washington *Post* nicely summarized the military ca-

reers of a handful of women soldiers, and fairly and admiringly explained the phenomenon:

> Physical examinations for enlistment during the civil war did not amount to much . . . and this was particularly the case when the war had been in progress for a couple of years. The wonder does not, therefore, seem so great that a considerable number of women actually soldiered as uniformed men during the civil war . . . , their sex in most cases . . . only revealed when they were wounded in action. There were doubtless many more women who enlisted in the armies on both sides as men than the records show—women who, having escaped wounds and detection, were mustered out at the close of their enlistments, or at the conclusion of the war, without their actual sex becoming known to their officers or comrades. . . . [T]he fact remains that very few of them were discovered to be women through their poor acting of their soldierly roles.[36]

Accounts of the deeds of women soldiers were standard fare in both books and newspapers from the beginning of the Civil War until the beginning of World War I. Sporadic stories were published after 1914, but most of these were in veterans publications. By and large, the general public lost interest in the Civil War as the world events that culminated in the Great War took center stage in both national and local reporting. By the 1930s, women soldiers had all but disappeared from the print media. But in February 1934 the discovery of a Civil War grave adjacent to Shiloh National Military Park was excitedly reported by the press. Mancil Milligan, who owned land on the outskirts of the battlefield, was digging in his flower bed on February 8 when his hoe struck bone. He notified authorities, and R. H. Bailey, the superintendent of the park, along with Dr. F. H. H. Roberts, an archeologist from the Smithsonian Institution who happened to be at Shiloh that winter digging Native American burial mounds, arrived on the scene. The subsequent excavation in Milligan's yard revealed "nine human skeletons, pieces of uniform cloth, two pocket knives, several buttons, a comb, and at least two minie balls."[37]

What the archeologist and the superintendent discovered that day was an overlooked and unrecorded mass grave from the Battle of Shiloh. Judging from the buttons, they concluded that the soldiers were Union. Finding a Civil War mass grave seventy years after the war was enough to secure a place in the papers, but what made headlines was the determination that one of the dead soldiers was female. It was probably Dr. Roberts who reported the sex of the nine casualties. Superintendent Bailey would not have been able to tell the difference between male and female pelvic bones—the most common way to determine a skeleton's sex—but the archeologist did. Given the proximity of the female skeleton to one of the minié balls, the presumption was that she was shot to death during the battle. The remains were reinterred at Shiloh National Cemetery, and Bailey ordered a military headstone to mark the new resting place of the nine unknown soldiers. In the meantime, the papers trumpeted yet another heroine of the Civil War.[38]

All the postwar publicity surrounding women soldiers finally prompted a few women to come forth and talk about their service, but interestingly, most of those women who went public told tales that were unverifiable. In 1895, Emma Kinsey's husband said that his wife held an honorable discharge as the lieutenant colonel of the 45th New York Infantry. Mr. Kinsey neglected to give his wife's alias during the war, so the veterans of the local GAR post who tried to look into the matter were stymied in their search for documentation. In 1912, Mrs. Peter Johnson of Worcester, Massachusetts, claimed to have served in the 53rd Massachusetts Infantry as Samuel Hill, alongside her brother Tom Murphy. The muster rolls of that regiment, however, did not list either name. Anna Hundley Glud of Oakland, California, told her wartime story shortly before her death, claiming to have been a ten-year-old drummer boy who went to war with her widower father in 1862. She said she suffered a mild wound at Gettysburg and served a three-year enlistment. Mrs. Glud, however, was sketchy on such details as her regimental affiliation and alias. Kinsey, Johnson, and Glud might have been real veterans whose memories were failing by the time they told their stories, or they may not have been former soldiers at all but merely trying to draw attention to themselves by claiming to be.[39]

The various stories and claims put forth by and about women soldiers prompted a number of citizens to write to the U.S. War Department seeking verification of either the veteran status of a particular individual or generic documentation about women soldiers as a group. The War Department did not share the public's enthusiasm for the subject, however, and in fact held no regard whatsoever for women soldiers, Union or Confederate. Despite recorded evidence to the contrary, the Adjutant General's Office in the early twentieth century actively denied that women played a military role, however small, in the Civil War.

For example, on October 21, 1909, Ida Tarbell of the *American Magazine* wrote to General F. C. Ainsworth, the adjutant general: "I am anxious to know whether your department has any record of the number of women who enlisted and served in the Civil War, or has it any record of any women who were in the service?" She received a swift reply from the Records and Pension Office, a division of the AGO, over Ainsworth's signature. The response read in part: "I have the honor to inform you that no official record has been found in the War Department showing specifically that any woman was ever enlisted in the military service of the United States as a member of any organization of the Regular or Volunteer Army at any time during the period of the civil war. It is possible, however, that there may have been a few instances of women having served as soldiers for a short time without their sex having been detected, but no record of such cases is known to exist in the official files."[40]

This response was patently untrue, but it was sent to anyone who requested general information about women soldiers. Letters of inquiry were routed to the AGO since that office maintained the War Department archives. The AGO took good care of the extant records created during the Civil War, and the AGO clerks were well versed in the contents of their holdings. By 1909, the AGO had also compiled military service records for the volunteer soldiers of the Civil War, both Union and Confederate, through painstaking copying of names and remarks from official Federal documents and captured Confederate records. Since the AGO clerks created service records for both men and women, Ainsworth's assertion cannot be viewed as an honest mistake made by an organization that did not realize what documents were in its possession.

Ainsworth's reasons for denying the participation of women soldiers during the Civil War are not known, but he was quoted in an 1895 newspaper article about Sarah Edmonds as saying that he believed very few of the stories of women as soldiers. Apparently, Ainsworth's personal opinion became the official response of the AGO. Ainsworth could not very well deny Edmonds' service, however, since her service had been endorsed by his superior, the secretary of war, a decade earlier.[41]

Ainsworth may have dismissed women soldiers, but the AGO clerks who worked for him labored under no such delusions. When they received any inquiry for information about a specific woman, such as the letter from the daughter of Frances Hook, they dutifully searched their records and wrote an honest response. Two of the AGO clerks, Mr. Edmondson and Mr. Frech, even kept personal reference files, wherein they noted War Department records concerning women soldiers and included newspaper clippings and obituaries about the women, some of them dated as late as 1929. The quiet collecting of information by these two men belied the official denial routinely issued by their boss.[42]

One of these clerks consented to a newspaper interview in 1901, but declined to have his name printed, perhaps fearing reprisal. As the Washington *Post* reported, "A Washington man who has been in the War Department for more than forty years, and who during the civil war kept a record of all the cases that came to his notice wherein women were discovered under arms in both services, Federal and Confederate, gave the writer hereof access to his 'women soldiers' data the other day, and the matter is both peculiar and interesting."[43]

Because the notion of women soldiers was indeed peculiar and interesting, the periodic denials issued by the AGO did not squelch public enthusiasm for the subject. In fact, as long as the generation that fought the Civil War lived, the memory that some of the soldiers were women lived also, even though most women veterans were reluctant or unable to tell their life stories themselves. In so many cases, their war histories were told by others—comrades, family members, and newspaper reporters. Sometimes their stories were told truthfully, and other times the narratives took on the qualities of legend or popular romance. But in whatever style or form the women soldier tales were told, the fact remains that they were related often and consistently found an interested audience. Eventually, the generation that lived through the Civil War inevitably passed away. And the memory of Civil War soldier women died with them.

10

BEYOND HEROES AND HARLOTS
The Changing Historical Perspective

Since the final shots of the Civil War were fired, two very distinct and divergent interpretations of the experiences of women soldiers have emerged. The first was that women who heeded the call to arms were a romantic and heroic archetype. This view predominated in most published stories about women soldiers until the early twentieth century and the onslaught of World War I. The second interpretation was that women who masqueraded as men and enlisted in the armies were crazy, sexually loose, lesbians, or all of the above. This theory emerged in texts on women in the Civil War in the 1930s and came to dominate the historical interpretation of women soldiers so thoroughly that any mention of them virtually disappeared from Civil War studies by the late 1960s. Only since the early 1990s has the subject of women soldiers received renewed and serious scholarly attention.

Long articles extolling the legacy of women soldiers appeared in magazines and newspapers as early as 1865. The *United States Service Magazine* took an admiring view of women who entered the army and explained, prefatory to detailing the histories of several such women, that

> when we reflect on . . . thousands upon thousands of women who have lost
> every means of support through the ravages of the enemy, who have seen their
> lovers and perhaps every male relative enter the army, or who have been fired

by a burning zeal to serve their country . . . it does not seem wonderful that
occasionally a vigorous and healthy damsel should have ventured to don the
uniform and shoulder a musket. Those who generalize on the impropriety and
unladylikeness of such conduct, are unquestionably in the right, according to
the practical parlor standard of life; but they know very little of the vast variety
of phases which humanity assumes, or of the strange and wonderful moulds into
which it is forced by Nature and circumstances.[1]

In 1866, Frank Moore set the tone for the next four decades in interpret-
ing women soldiers. As he wrote in his seminal history of the important
war work of women: "Other wars have furnished here and there a name,
which the world delights to repeat in terms of affection or admiration, of
some woman who has broken through the rigidity of custom, and been
conspicuous, either among armed men, like the Maid of Saragossa, or in
the hospitals, like the heroine of Scutari. But our war has furnished hundreds as intrepid as the one, and as philanthropically devoted as the
other."[2]

The venerable trio of Susan B. Anthony, Elizabeth Cady Stanton, and
Matilda Gage made special mention of women soldiers in their work *History of Woman Suffrage*. They protested that army regulations were used
by the government as an excuse to deny postwar recognition of women
soldiers, even though "hundreds of women marched steadily up to the
mouth of a hundred cannon pouring out fire and smoke, shot and shell,
mowing down the advancing hosts like grass; men, horses, and colors
going down in confusion, disappearing in clouds of smoke; the only sound,
the screaming of shells, the crackling of musketry, the thunder of artillery.
. . . [T]hrough all this women were sustained by the enthusiasm born of
love of country and liberty."[3]

Few collections of war stories published in the latter half of the nineteenth century lacked references to women warriors. The largest volume
of this type was *The Pictorial Book of Anecdotes and Incidents of the War of
the Rebellion*. Based largely on contemporary news reports, the collection
specifically addressed "female soldiers" and promised "a choice and dis-
criminating exhibition of Woman's Career in the Scenes and Events of the
War!" Despite the sensational tone of the volume, the majority of the
women soldier stories included therein were accurately summarized from
the original newspaper accounts.[4]

As late as 1911, when Ethel Hurn published the highly regarded *Wis-*

consin Women in the War between the States, women soldiers were described in a straightforward manner and usually with admiration. Distaff soldiers also figured in the numerous published memoirs of both male soldiers and female nurses. Seldom did these veterans and nurses mention a woman soldier in anything other than respectful tones unless the woman served the enemy, in which case she, like her male comrades, was subject to a patriot's contempt for his or her foes. Of course, these recollections of personal encounters with women who abandoned their female identities in order to pursue military careers were all published within living memory of the war.

But by the time that Francis Simkins' and James Patton's study of women of the Confederacy was first published in 1936, attitudes had changed drastically, and women soldiers were no longer culturally accepted without question or condemnation. "Although their services were not impressive, a few women are reputed to have assumed the attire of men, joined military organizations, and participated in battles," they wrote. Before turning to stories of the wives of public figures and women who took on nurturing wartime occupations such as nursing, the authors mentioned a handful of women soldiers and then summarily dismissed their military experiences. "It should not be assumed," they editorialized, "that these Confederate Amazons were taken seriously. They were regarded as eccentrics, and if not always morally loose, they were so considered by the public." Simkins and Patton did not, however, cite any Civil War–era sources to bolster this assertion.[5]

Other writers raised questions about women soldiers that betray their own perceptions as clouded by modern conceptions of military life. One twentieth-century historian puzzled at great length over the problem of disguise. "Most of the accounts of the women *travesti en soldat* assert that their sex was not known to their masculine comrades-in-arms," Agatha Young wrote, "but that the men with whom she lived, slept, ate and washed in the lack of privacy of an army should not be aware of her sex is beyond credibility." Young also made much of contemporary descriptions of the discovery of a woman in the ranks as "demoralizing" to her comrades, inferring that women soldiers were immoral or amoral individuals. Actually, this term was frequently used by Civil War scribes to depict disheartened troops who had taken heavy losses during a battle—morale, of course, being something quite apart from morality. Indeed, it is quite understandable that messmates might become confused or upset when they suddenly learned that one of their own, whom they thought was a man, was actually a woman.[6]

At the close of the Civil War centennial, the view presented of women who shouldered a musket was very dim. "Many a romantic girl dreamed of being a second Joan of Arc, but those who actually entered the ranks by posing as men were usually viewed by contemporaries as mentally unbalanced or immoral," wrote Mary Elizabeth Massey in the now-classic *Bonnet Brigades*. Of all the twentieth-century historians who considered women soldiers, Massey was the most negative. Unfortunately, her views of women soldiers have been widely accepted because her work, republished in the 1990s as *Women in the Civil War*, remains the most exhaustive survey of women's participation at large. Massey proclaimed that newspaper stories about women in the ranks "evidence their determination, pathetically illustrate the effects of their unconventional behavior, and raise doubts about the individual." Furthermore, Massey recorded instances of two of the women who were not discovered until they delivered babies and took this as proof that "many and probably most of the women soldiers were prostitutes or concubines," while failing to mention that a primary motivation for many women to join the military service was to stay by the side of their husbands.[7]

In his classic studies of the common soldier of the Civil War, the venerable Bell Irvin Wiley correctly pointed out that many women soldiers went to war with their husbands, but he was quick to add that "the motive of some who laid aside skirts for uniforms was immoral." Based on a small number of cases, Wiley decided that "probably the majority of women who entered the ranks in male disguise were respectable characters, motivated by patriotism or the desire to be near husbands or sweethearts," but believed that there were also women who "were persons of easy virtue who enrolled as soldiers to further their lewd enterprises." Wiley also alleged that "usually their sex was soon detected and they were sent home," although most of the women soldiers cited in his works served for long periods of time without discovery.[8]

In all fairness to Simkins and Patton, Wiley, Massey, and Young, at least these scholars mentioned women soldiers. The majority of works published from the 1930s to the 1980s make no such references. With the notable exceptions of Sarah Edmonds and Albert Cashier, whose lives and service were so overwhelmingly documented and publicized that it was impossible to ignore them, the rest of the women soldiers of the Civil War were consigned to the oddities category or, more frequently, completely overlooked. For example, in James I. Robertson's *Soldiers Blue and Gray*, a 1980s study of Civil War soldiers that celebrates the diversity of the Civil War armies, whose "composition ran the full gauntlet of humankind," mention of women soldiers is reserved solely for the discussion of prostitutes who followed the armies. These omissions of and misconceptions about women soldiers, whether calculated or not, resulted in a historical oblivion regarding females as patriotic and armed combatants during the nation's most-studied military conflict.[9]

Modern writers do occasionally mention Loreta Velazquez but only in the context of heaping scorn upon her unconventional life and hyperbolic memoirs. General Early's criticism of Velazquez largely informed the treatment of her at the hands of twentieth-century historians, who generally accepted his assertions of her inauthenticity without question. Mary Massey, no friend to women soldiers, called *The Woman in Battle* "the most fantastic of all accounts which claimed to be factual" and waved off its "sensational exaggerations." Simkins and Patton, who also disdained women soldiers, declared, "The only person impressed with the valor and worth of Loreta Janeta Velazquez was that woman herself." Obviously, none of these writers was aware that in 1888, former Confederate Gen. James Longstreet wrote, "There was a woman in the ranks with us who . . . was [a] Lieutenant, and called her name Buford." Longstreet thought that the adventures of Velazquez were "remarkable." Granted, General Longstreet met Velazquez in New Orleans after the war and did not know her during her service. Then again, neither did General Early, her most vocal contemporary critic.[10]

In an era when women soldiers as a group were overlooked or ridiculed, it was perhaps not surprising that military and social historians did not verify whether Velazquez was truly the fraud they believed her to be. Even feminist historians coolly received the exploits of Loreta Velazquez. As late as 1996, one scholar posited that Velazquez's ready disregard of conventional gender roles and spurning of Victorian standards of appropriate behavior for women were probably not at all true, "not the actual realization of power for women during wartime," but merely a literary device for dramatizing "the war's catalytic role in creating the *fantasy* of such power."[11]

One scholar has found Civil War women soldiers worth noting, not because he views them as compelling or interesting in their own right but because they support a modern political agenda. Randy Shilts in *Conduct Unbecoming* cites two distaff soldiers as proof that lesbians historically have stepped forward to serve their country in times of need.[12]

One notable exception to the general misunderstanding and condemnation of female soldiers by twentieth-century historians is found in Sylvia Dannett, the biographer of Sarah Edmonds. In addition to her groundbreaking 1960 study of Edmonds' life and times, Dannett produced other examinations of Civil War women that cast female soldiers in a more realistic light. But even Dannett drew flawed conclusions, such as her assertion that the "patriotic deception" of women disguising themselves as men and enlisting "occurred almost entirely during the confusion and haste of initial recruiting."[13]

On the whole, what readers can glean about Civil War women soldiers from the few twentieth-century historians who addressed them is that they were crazy, whores, or homosexuals. The historical evidence, however, does not support these conclusions, and while there were a small number of women soldiers who fit in some of these categories, they were not numerous enough to justify such sweeping and negative generalizations.

In all of the contemporary and postwar newspaper accounts of women soldiers, only three have been identified that imply the soldiers in question were psychologically unsound. Toward the end of the war the Richmond *Whig* reported that Mollie Bean of the 47th North Carolina Infantry was "manifestly crazy," although another article described Bean only as being a suspicious character, meaning she was accused of being a spy. A year earlier in the North, the Brooklyn *Daily Times* reported that the late Emily was a monomaniac who believed that she had been "called by Providence to lead our armies to certain victory in this great civil contest." A District of Columbia newspaper described Confederate Ida Ellison as "violent and suicidal." Except for these few instances, judgments in contemporary accounts about the sanity of Civil War female soldiers were reserved.[14]

In fact, only three women soldiers acted in ways that raise questions about the state of their mental health. Early in the war, a woman followed her husband into the 19th Illinois Infantry, but her sex was quickly detected and she was sent away from camp. She attempted suicide that evening by jumping into the Chicago River. Similarly, "a rather romantic young lady" from New Jersey followed her sweetheart into the "Garibaldi Guards" but was soon discovered and sent home to her parents. She was so despondent upon her return that she tried to commit suicide with arsenic. A woman soldier called Charlie actually succeeded in killing herself when faced with expulsion from her regiment.[15]

A larger group of women soldiers appear to have been prostitutes at one time or another. Two Union soldiers and one Union officer were court-martialed for assisting women to enlist in regiments, women that the court documents described as indecent or as prostitutes. In two of the trials, the women in question did not appear during the proceedings to defend themselves or their reputations. The court-martial of Capt. Jerome Taft of the 59th New York Infantry charged that, among other things, he had induced Harriet Merrill not only to enlist but to become his mistress. Although Merrill lived in a house of "ill fame" prior to enlistment, no proof was offered during the trial that Merrill had engaged in sexual activity with Taft or anyone else in the regiment. Taft was acquitted of keeping Merrill as his mistress and was also exonerated of persuading her to sign up for military duty. The evidence indicated that Merrill enlisted in order to leave a life of prostitution rather than to pursue one.[16]

Such was definitely the case of V.A. White, who had "tired and worried of that life." Posing as "Little Pete," she used the Union army to escape life in a Nashville brothel. When Marian McKenzie was discovered after serving in a Kentucky regiment, a provost marshal recorded that she was a former prostitute. He did not, however, assert that she prostituted herself while in the army.[17]

Another woman who might have been a former prostitute joined an Illinois regiment in late 1862 in the company of a lieutenant. Described as a previous "occupant of the Brick," Kate blended in well among the men in her regiment, and performed drill, picket, and other duties of a soldier. Despite a comrade's observation that "there is a few in our Company that would like to have such rips as her in camp," it nevertheless seemed that the military, and a specific lieutenant, provided refuge from a hard past life. Frances Jamieson originally served as a soldier, then found a series of patriotic employments as a spy, scout, nurse, and detective. A final wartime reference to "Miss Frank Abel," however, showed her working as both a detective and a prostitute in Virginia.[18]

Three women soldiers, after being discovered and arrested, were denounced by their commanding officers as indecent. Mary and Mollie Bell, jailed in Richmond after serving for two years, were accused of "iniquity" by their captain, although it seems unlikely that they could have served in soldier garb undiscovered for two years while simultaneously plying their wares among their comrades. When Nellie Williams was arrested while drunk in St. Louis, her captain showed up the following day and stated that he had never enlisted her and that she was merely a local prostitute. He offered no explanation, though, for how she had procured the full uniform of the 2nd Iowa Infantry that she was wearing when arrested. In these cases, the officers seem to have dealt with the public embarrassment of finding they had enrolled women by denouncing them as nefarious types.[19]

Only two more instances can be found in which women soldiers were alleged by their contemporaries to be less than honorable. When a Confederate POW gave birth at Johnson's Island, a local newspaper believed she must have joined the army "for profit," but did not hazard a guess as to how this woman rose into the officer ranks. Finally, while the 20th Army Corps passed by the town of Milledgeville, Georgia, on its March to the Sea, the state penitentiary was burned down by the inmates. A local historian reported that one of the female convicts donned a uniform and joined the 33rd Indiana Infantry, where she plied "an ancient trade." This last story is the most explicit reference found to a prostitute working while in the ranks.[20]

The accumulated record shows that six women soldiers used the military to escape prostitution; four were the targets of unsubstantiated accusations; one engaged in prostitution after she left the service; and only one actually sold herself while enlisted. Obviously, there is little to support the generalizations made by several historians that females who served in Civil War armies did so primarily for purposes of selling their bodies to male comrades. And the notion that women dressed as men in order to prostitute themselves is counterintuitive. Prostitution did, indeed, flourish during the war. At least eighty-five bordellos existed in Washington, D.C.; there were three separate parts of Richmond designated as centers for prostitution and other vices; and in Nashville and Memphis prostitution was legal.[21] With such a plethora of opportunity, why would any woman so inclined join the army and endure the severe hardships of soldier life?

Only one scholar has explicitly stated that a pair of Civil War soldier women were "the first apparent lesbians documented to have served in the U.S. military." However, modern audiences often assume that female warriors in the Civil War were lesbians, even though most gender and sexuality studies indicate that nineteenth century cross-dressing women were motivated by economic and social realities, not by sexual orientation. Nevertheless, Randy Shilts labeled Ella Reno and Sarah Bradbury as lesbians because General Sheridan wrote in his memoirs that an "intimacy had sprung up between" the two women while they were serving together in the army.[22]

There is evidence of women soldiers being able to recognize and acknowledge one another more easily than the men around them, and in several instances, women were discovered while in each other's company. After one of her detections, Frank Martin told a reporter that she had "discovered a great many females in the army," and that she was "intimately acquainted with a young lady who is a Lieutenant." Martin's use of the term "intimately acquainted" might lead some to question her meaning and infer she was a lesbian.[23] Like the modern misinterpretation of contemporary assertions that women soldiers "demoralized" the troops around them, any explanation of women's sexual relationships based on the language of Victorian reports says more about the cultural divide between nineteenth- and twentieth-century Americans than it accurately implies about the women in question. And the fact that many young women who wished to "go for a soldier" sought the company of like-minded female friends should not surprise. Nor should it enable the historian to classify these women's relationships with one another definitively, any more than does the usage of the word "intimate," a typical Victorian term meaning "the best of friends."

The record with regard to the sexual orientation of the martial women of the Civil War is inconclusive except for that large group who followed husbands or male sweethearts into the ranks. Just like the accusation that many of these women were prostitutes, any inference that women soldiers were lesbians is counterintuitive. Why would a lesbian join the army, where she would be surrounded by men? And why should the sexual preference of women soldiers matter anyway? While love did compel a number of women into the service, their sex lives hardly mattered when it came to the performance of their military duty. Any focus on the sexuality of women soldiers is nothing more than a smokescreen that obscures consideration of their military record.

Obviously, something occurred in American society between the time of the Civil War and the time that modern historians began to write about women soldiers, something that caused them to draw conclusions that were not supported by the facts. In their own time, women soldiers had their detractors, but they had more champions by far, not to mention a great deal of public support and interest. The most obvious difference between pre-

and post–World War I interpretations is that most nineteenth- and early twentieth-century writers either remembered the war themselves or had access to veterans and others who experienced the conflict firsthand.

But social and psychological views about women also played a role in the changing perception of women soldiers. The concept of separate spheres of influence for men and for women was so entrenched in nineteenth-century society that wartime exceptions to the rule were no threat to the accepted cultural norms of gender behavior. In addition, the long-standing popularity of the real and fictional Female Warriors Bold, particularly among the lower and working classes, created an atmosphere in which it was not so astonishing to encounter an actual example. Women who professed undying patriotism as motivation for enlisting, or who followed their beloved husbands into the army, earned the admiration of Victorian romantics who readily endorsed any woman who followed either impulse.

Ironically, the broadening of women's legal and economic status at the beginning of the twentieth century changed this fairly liberal attitude toward women who pursued nontraditional military roles. During World War I, the American military establishment finally created official capacities, other than nurse and laundress, for women to occupy in the various branches. America's entry into the war also led to more women entering the civilian work force, because young men were shipped off to Europe by the tens of thousands. (Dramatic expansions of opportunities for women in both military service and civilian employment occurred again, on a much larger scale, during World War II.) Although progress had been made with regard to women's rights since the Civil War, the sudden expansion of women's legal and economic power during the First World War fired a more robust movement to obtain the vote. With suffrage secured for all U.S. women in 1920, after seventy-two years of protest and agitation, the stage was set for the inevitable cultural backlash.

It came in the form of the 1920s popularization in America of the concepts advanced by European sexologists, in particular Sigmund Freud with his theories about independent women generally being insane and most likely lesbians. As historian Lillian Faderman points out, "When women's increasing freedom began to threaten to change the world—or at least parts of Europe and America—many who had vested interests in the old order were happy to believe the medical views of lesbians as neurotic and confused and to believe that women who wanted independence usually were lesbians." From this point forward, women who insisted on challenging the cultural boundaries of gender were suspected and accused of sexual and mental abnormality, and such accusations became effective means of controlling any female behavior perceived as a threat to societal norms. "Women who did not wish to stay in their place were depicted as masculine . . . . The link between feminism and 'sexual abnormality' was made" at this juncture, Faderman argues.[24]

No wonder, then, that twentieth-century historians examining the part that women took in supporting the Civil War in the North and the South looked askance at those women who donned britches, cut their hair short, and engaged in the one activity that was still legally banned to American women at the close of the twentieth century: armed infantry combat. One can hardly think of a more destabilizing and demoralizing figure than that of a trained woman soldier, willing and able to use the weapons at her disposal, in a society where the status quo struggled with a constantly changing and ever-expanding definition of female rights and roles in the legal, social, and economic realms.

Furthermore, the improved legal and economic landscape for women in the mid-twentieth century obscured the dismal state of opportunities for women in the mid-nineteenth century. Historians failed to grasp that working-class women masqueraded as men not because they were abnormal but merely as a means to an end. Transvestism was a way to find increased employment options and, as an added bonus, increased personal freedom.

At the close of the twentieth century, however, a new interest in women warriors sprang up both in popular culture and in the academic realm. Social as well as military historians began taking a fresh look at the subject. As early as 1967, British writer John Laffin chastised historians when he wrote of women soldiers, both European and American:

> Ignorance about them is perhaps understandable for little has been written about them. . . . Perhaps one reason is that the chroniclers of war have nearly all been men and as males they have not wanted to give too much emphasis to the very fact that women are capable of fighting. They resent the intrusion of women into what clearly should be the one impregnable male bastion. The score or so women whose exploits are known in detail have been regarded as freaks. The mildest assessment they can expect is to be labeled 'queer,' an opinion that tends to detract from their gallantry.[25]

Laffin was largely a voice in the wilderness until 1989, when two works examining the roots and ultimate course of the female soldier phenomenon in western culture and society appeared. In *Warrior Women and Popular Balladry: 1650–1850,* Dianne Dugaw explored the literary tradition of the Female Warrior Bold, explaining its important influence in popular culture. Historian Julie Wheelwright focused on the military and social experiences of real women cross-dressers, military and civilian, in *Amazons and Military Maids: Women Who Dressed as Men in Pursuit of Life, Liberty, and Happiness.* Since then, the topic of cultural constructions of male and femaleness in literature and history has become a common academic theme, which was brought to the study of Civil War history with the publication of *Divided Houses: Gender and the Civil War* in 1992. And in the context of gender studies, numerous books and articles dealing with cross-dressing and transvestism appeared in the 1990s.[26]

In 1998, historian Linda Grant DePauw brought forth *Battle Cries and Lullabies: Women in War from Prehistory to the Present.* Several works examining the lives of women who disguised themselves to fight, or who otherwise tackled nontraditional roles specifically in the American Civil War, appeared in the 1990s, beginning with Wendy King's *Clad in Uniform,* followed by Richard Hall's *Patriots in Disguise.* In 1994, the only collection of letters known to exist that were written by a Civil War woman soldier, those of Sarah Rosetta Wakeman, was published. In 1999, Elizabeth Leonard contributed to the growing record of women's military service with *All the Daring of the Soldier.*[27]

The field of traditional Civil War history also began taking note of distaff soldiers. Numerous military studies of Civil War battles, campaigns, personages, and armies published since 1990 have included the participation of relevant women combatants. As scholars and society continue probing cultural notions of gender and identity, the reemerging evidence that women historically and successfully engaged in combat has met with less intellectual resistance and has taken on new cultural significance.

At the dawn of the twenty-first century, no longer are the cross-dressing women soldiers of the Civil War the entertaining and romantic anomaly that they were considered to be in their own time. Neither are they perceived as the deviants that Freudian influence and analysis suggested to twentieth-century Americans. The rising interest in these martial women signals a positive movement into an era beyond the dichotomy of hero or harlot, an era in which women soldiers are no longer sensationalized as romantic heroines nor disdainfully viewed as aberrant exceptions, but an era in which their military service may be finally and honestly assessed.

"I Love My Country"

A Summation of Women's Military Service

Women who served as soldiers during the Civil War did so in deadly earnest. They were effective in combat and performed their full share of military duties, both routine and special. Women soldiers bore all of the same hardships and dire consequences of soldiering as their male comrades. They suffered wounds, disease, and internment as prisoners of war, and they died for their country, too. Women's motivations for entering the ranks of the blue or the gray largely equated with those of their male compatriots. In order to soldier, however, women had to change their gender identity, and when they did so, they gained a great measure of legal, economic, and personal freedom previously unavailable to them. While some elements of Victorian society took a dim view of martial women and their unconventional wartime contributions, there were many more enthusiasts for distaff soldiers and their accomplishments, both throughout the war and in the subsequent living memory of the conflict. Indeed, popular interest in the women soldiers of the Civil War continued unabated until only a dwindling number of veterans remained alive to remember their female comrades.

Approximately three million soldiers served throughout the Civil War. While no one will ever know exactly how many of these soldiers were women, extant documentation suggests they only numbered in the hundreds. Clearly, the service of women did not affect the outcome of battles and campaigns, and the service of women did not alter the course of the war. Their individual contributions and exploits are fascinating but are not the primary reasons for their historical significance. Women soldiers of the Civil War merit recognition because they were there and because they were not supposed to be. They deserve remembrance because their actions made them uncommon and revolutionary, possessed of a valor at odds with Victorian and, in some respects, even modern views of women's proper role. Quite simply, the women in the ranks of the Union and Confederate armies refused to stay in their socially mandated place, even though it meant resorting to subterfuge to achieve their goal of being soldiers. They faced down not only the guns of the adversary but the sexual prejudices of their society.

The significance of Civil War soldier women, however, reaches beyond their actual lives and times and touches on one of the most controversial questions about women and society in the twenty-first century: that of women in combat. It is instructive, therefore, to paint a more comprehensive picture of women's military service by examining their careers. Such an examination yields important and interesting information about the service of women soldiers as a group.[1]

Seventy percent fought for the Union and 30 percent fought for the Confederacy. A large part of this discrepancy in the numbers of women who aligned with the North and the South can be attributed to the overall difference in population between the Union and the Confederacy and the military enlistment figures between the two sides during the war. Federal armies enjoyed a two-to-one advantage over Confederate armies in enlisted and commissioned personnel. Another reason for the larger number of women documented as serving in Union regiments is the far better preservation of army records for U.S. troops. An untold number of Confederate records were lost at the end of the war.

Casualties and casualty rates are an important indication of the nature and extent of women's participation in combat, which is arguably the real measure of any soldier's contribution to his or her nation's war effort. Fifteen percent of women soldiers sustained battle wounds, with many of them incurring more than one combat injury. Wounds were also the most common cause of a woman's discovery in the ranks.

Eleven percent of women soldiers died while in the military. Of these, for every three killed on the field of battle or succumbing to wounds, one died of disease. These figures represent an inverse ratio to that of male

Civil War soldiers, among whom twice as many died of disease as from wounds sustained in combat. This difference is explained by the relative lack of attention diseased soldiers received from army doctors compared with wounded soldiers. Medical science of the time had no cure or effective treatment for most contagious diseases, so sick soldiers received relatively little attention from physicians, unlike wounded soldiers, who were attended to and operated on by field surgeons. It is not, therefore, surprising that wounded women were often discovered and their existence recorded. Women soldiers who died of disease were much more likely to take their secret to the grave.[2]

Eighteen percent of women soldiers were captured by the enemy, while 16 percent of male soldiers suffered this fate. Capture and imprisonment virtually ensured that a woman disguised as a man was discovered.[3]

Women warriors clearly suffered all of the grievous repercussions of military service, which is reflected in their combined casualty rate of more than 44 percent. This exceeds the average of about 30 percent for male soldiers. The disparity could be explained by assuming that women exhibited lesser skills and abilities on the battlefield. More plausibly, the apparent higher casualty rate reflects the fact that the sex of wounded, killed, and imprisoned women soldiers was more likely to be discovered because they were subjected to a higher level of scrutiny by burial parties, surgeons, and prison guards than they would otherwise have encountered in the normal course of duty. Therefore, women who became casualties were more likely to leave some record of their presence in the military service. Those women who evaded death, wounds, and imprisonment more easily escaped detection and may never have revealed the fact of their army service in a way that can be documented by historians. Indeed, this entire study of women soldiers is heavily skewed toward those whose secret was made public either during or after the war.[4]

Any argument that the higher casualty rates for women is evidence of their relative incapacity for the rough business of soldiering also wanes in light of the promotion rate of 14 percent for female soldiers over the course of the war. This promotion rate is higher than the 10 percent cited for men who served in the Civil War.[5]

The average length of service for women soldiers was sixteen months, including those who enlisted in both nine-month and three-year regiments. This is a striking figure considering that this study is weighted toward those women who were discovered and ejected from the ranks long before their enlistments were up. Seventy-two percent of women soldiers were discovered as casualties or by accident, 17 percent eventually served openly as women, and almost 10 percent were never discovered while in the service. Among those who were not discovered, the average length of service was a little more than two years.

Taken as a group, women were successful soldiers. If their aim was the same as the majority of the three million men who enlisted—to contribute to the war effort to the best of their ability—then women soldiers accomplished their goal. In their experiences as soldiers, women differed little from their male comrades, especially those men who enthusiastically volunteered as opposed to being drafted. Women soldiers asked for no special consideration due to their sex, if only because by doing so they risked immediate dismissal from the ranks. In point of fact, most women were successful and capable soldiers precisely because their sex was unknown to their officers. With gender prejudices and stereotyping removed from consideration of their performance as soldiers, women were given and accomplished the same assignments in camp and on the battlefield, they suffered the same consequences of military life, and they were promoted at slightly higher rates than the men surrounding them. Although they numbered only several hundred out of several million soldiers, women who heeded the call to defend their country were overwhelmingly effective in their martial roles.

Yet the very existence of nineteenth-century women soldiers, and their demonstrated competence as combatants, challenge long-held cultural assumptions about gender roles. Arguably, the reason that women soldiers from this period of American history have been, until recently, ignored or vilified by modern historians is that the specter of women actively engaged in combat during our nation's most costly conflict violates the seemingly immutable cultural boundaries between male and female conduct. More than a century after the fact, women's historical presence on the bloody fields of America's Civil War is a violation of the cultural norm that holds, among other things, that women are not and should not be violent. Beliefs persist that a woman's place is neither in executing orders nor giving them on the battlefield, despite growing historical evidence that women served ably and willingly as combatants from the Revolution through the Civil War. From a historical perspective, the women warriors of the Civil War were not just ahead of their time. They were ahead of our time.[6]

Examination of the record of female Civil War soldiers in their own time shows that the biggest difference between female and male soldiers was that the boys in blue and gray had every right and responsibility to serve their countries, whereas the girls who volunteered found it necessary to masquerade as men in order to render what they felt was their patriotic duty. Women soldiers felt obliged to put their lives on the line for their country, even though their governments denied them the full rights and advantages of citizenship merely on the basis of their sex. When asked why she enlisted as a soldier, Margaret Catherine Murphy explained simply, "I love my country." The link between pretending to be a man in order to fulfill perceived patriotic obligations was made clear by another woman soldier, who described wearing male attire as taking "citizen's dress."[7]

Despite women soldiers' desire to shoulder this most dangerous obligation of citizenship, the fact remained that in nineteenth-century America, although "freeborn women had the appearance of citizenship," they "lacked the basic rights to be real citizens." White men held jobs that paid more simply because men occupied them; they were free to attend schools and colleges or apprentice themselves to gain marketable skills; they voted in local and state elections; they served on juries and were judged in turn by their peers if they were accused; they signed contracts and conducted business with few restrictions; and they ran for and served in public office. These rights came with certain responsibilities, including the obligation to perform military duty in time of war. As veterans, men who served during the Civil War were held in high esteem in their communities and were granted special privileges, such as military pensions.[8]

Victorian women, on the other hand, found limited or poorly paid occupational opportunities; endured restricted access to higher education and skilled apprenticeships; suffered legal oblivion if married; were judged solely by male juries if brought before the courts; were taxed without the benefit of the vote; and for the most part, were barred from holding public office. Although women enjoyed the ostensible protection of the state in times of war and crisis, women were not expected to defend their country, and when they did nevertheless and were found out, they learned that they were not necessarily a welcome addition to the military. Women who returned home from the Civil War as veterans reaped few of the societal rewards for having rendered such service.

Most of the disparities between the rights and responsibilities of citizenship for men and for women have been addressed in the years since the

Civil War ended, thus obscuring yet another, and perhaps the most poignant, significance of Civil War women soldiers. They went to extraordinary lengths to defend their beloved country, even though their governments and their societies viewed them as second-class citizens and held them in lower regard than their fathers, husbands, and brothers.[9]

Appendix

The Female Warrior Bold

Two Civil War–era novels, *The Lady Lieutenant* and *Castine*, were classic examples of the Female Warrior genre of fiction. By the beginning of the Civil War, this genre had celebrated the model of the martial heroine for two hundred years. The characters of Madeline Moore and Castine were developed for an audience in the throes of an actual war, but the style of the novels and the spirit of their adventures, not to mention their patriotic and emotional motivations, echoed the hundreds of Female Warrior novels that had preceded them well before the Civil War. Thus an examination of these works not only illustrates the tastes of Victorian audiences but also illuminates the style and typical substance of the broader Female Warrior motif.

In *The Lady Lieutenant*, Miss Madeline Moore is an orphaned but nevertheless wealthy young woman when the war breaks out, who lives with a despised spinster aunt in Kentucky. When President Lincoln calls for recruits, the heroine's beau, Frank Ashton, announces his intention to enlist with a local company that is forming despite their border-state governor's refusal to raise troops for either side. Not wishing to be left behind, Moore outfits herself as a man, using a false mustache and whiskers to better disguise herself, and joins her beloved's company as it leaves Kentucky via river boat, bound for western Virginia to join General McClellan's 1861 campaign against the Confederates. In true Female Warrior style, the protagonist introduces herself as Albert Harville to her sweetheart, who fails to recognize her. She, on the other hand, relates that "It was only by a great effort at self-control that I was prevented from throwing myself into his arms and avowing my deception." Claiming to be related to Miss Moore, "Albert Harville" becomes Frank Ashton's closest confident and a lieutenant in Captain Ashton's company.

Disembarking at Wheeling, the Kentucky regiment soon merges with McClellan's command and sets off to join battle with the rebel army at the town of St. George. Although "Albert" expresses nothing but apprehension while waiting for the orders to advance, she explains that "somehow, the moment the action began," her fear disappeared. The lady lieutenant immediately suffers a superficial head wound in her first battle and is separated from her company and Captain Ashton. Attempting to flee from bands of rebels roaming through the town, she is captured by a resident and dragged into his home as his contribution to the southern war effort. The secessionist's wife takes pity on Albert, who is "apparently a mere youth" (her "whiskers and moustache had fallen off during the fight"), and treats the lieutenant's wound. The two repair to the roof of the house to watch the remainder of the battle as the Union forces claim victory in the town square. Here the secessionist's wife is killed by a Confederate sniper who was aiming for the Union officer, Albert Harville, standing at her side. Her husband faults Lieutenant Harville for his wife's death, and in the ensuring scuffle, our heroine kills her captor and escapes. Thus passes the lady lieutenant's first experience of battle.

Soon after, Captain Frank Ashton obtains orders to take dispatches to Washington, D.C., and asks Lieutenant Harville to accompany him. While there the two learn that the "Grand Army" is to make a move toward Richmond, and "No sooner did Frank learn the truth of this report than he determined to volunteer in this expedition." They manage to join a New York regiment as first and second lieutenants and soon set off with the Union army for its first fateful clash with southern troops at Bull Run.

Here, the author gives a creditable description of what the battle might have looked like from an officer's viewpoint. The lady lieutenant also describes unhorsing and dispatching a rebel trooper with her revolver during a terrifying cavalry charge on her regiment. Mounting her foe's horse, she begins to take flight from the battlefield ("Just at that time I thought of little else than self preservation," she relates) and is attacked and wounded in the neck by two dragoons, who also kill her horse. Despite all of the foregoing action, in which the heroine functions quite well in battle and bests two men in close physical confrontations, in this situation the lady lieutenant decides to remain out of the rest of the fight, not because she is wounded, but because she "dared not venture again into the heat of the conflict," considering herself "too weak to cope successfully with the stern warriors of the opposite sex," and feeling certain that to do so would cost her life.

As the battle wanes, with considerable ingenuity Madeline Moore secures another mount and follows the army on its retreat to Centreville. There she finds Frank Ashton severely wounded. His "is a case requiring great care and careful nursing; and the latter alone can save you," the doctor tells him. "Then he shall be saved," cries the lady lieutenant, and she makes arrangements to take apartments and nurse her sweetheart back to full health, still in disguise as Albert Harville. Ultimately, Frank Ashton admits to his friend Albert that he wishes only two things: "rewarding you for the untiring watchfulness and care you have bestowed upon me, and [to] marry Madeline Moore," whereupon Miss Moore reveals her true identity, and the lovers are reunited.

Castine opens on the field of Manassas in July 1862. There Sergeant Walter Larksly, "a youth of about nineteen summers, delicate in frame and effeminate in features," reveals to Captain Waterfield that he is bent on avenging the death of his sister Jennie at the hands of a rejected suitor, "a lord of wealth and fashion, with black glossy hair and sparkling black eyes." Jennie had preferred another man, "with light hair and blue eyes." The two part and prepare to give battle at Second Manassas.

During the battle Sergeant Larksly performs with valor and rallies his command to take an artillery position. Here the Sergeant finds his man in the form of Yankee Captain Richard Lester, who is in command. Swearing revenge for Jennie's death, the young Larksly demands the truth from Lester and reveals, " 'I am Jennie's sister—I am a woman in soldier's attire. . . . Yes, I am Castine.' " Captain Lester maintains that he has not killed Jennie but rather has married her and that she resides in New York. Captain Waterfield, who has overheard this conversation, intervenes to save the life of Richard Lester and declares himself to be the suitor that Jennie favored over Lester. No sooner have the sergeant and Captain Waterfield turned Lester over to be shipped off to Libby Prison than they are both captured and sent to a POW camp in Washington, D.C.

There they escape by asking a fellow POW, an Irishman, to bribe his way out on a pass to purchase clothing for two gentlemen and a lady. Sergeant Larksly reassumes the identity of Castine, the Irishman and Captain Waterfield become gentlemen about town, and the three of them are allowed to pass out of the prison, for they look "like anything else than . . . 'rebel prisoner[s].'" The narrator notes that "It was well for [them] that men are so easily deceived by the external appearance of their fellow men."

The trio—Captain Waterfield, Castine, and Patrick the Irishman—make their way to New York to find Jennie at the address that Lester has given them. During the night of their arrival, a fire breaks out in the city, and the three set off from their hotel to observe. When they reach the street, they learn that not only is it the same street mentioned by Captain Lester, but the house that is burning is his and no one has yet made their escape. Captain Waterfield boldly rescues Jennie, and all being reunited, they return to the hotel. All four travel to Richmond to allow Jennie to see her husband, Captain Lester, who is imprisoned at Libby. Although Jennie and Captain Waterfield briefly acknowledge their feelings for one another, Jennie chastely reminds the officer that she is now married to another. But when Jennie visits Lester in Libby Prison, his jealous nature overwhelms him and he attempts to kill her, striking her with a sword. Castine intervenes, grabs the sword, "and with a well aimed blow . . . she dipped its point in the mean, hot blood of Capt. Lester's heart, saying: 'And that is *kinder* still—I bless the world with one villain less.'" The novelette closes on a scene a year later, with Jennie recovered from her wound and married to Captain Waterfield, Patrick back with his command, and Castine in residence with the Waterfields.

BIBLIOGRAPHY

MANUSCRIPT COLLECTIONS AND GOVERNMENT RECORDS

Alderman Library, University of Virginia, Charlottesville
Correspondence of James L. Dunn

Alexandria (Virginia) Library, Lloyd House
Diary of Julia Wilbur (microfilm)

Allen County (Ohio) Historical Society, Lima
Diary of John Ashton

Bancroft Library, University of California at Berkeley
"The Drummer Boy: Mrs. Anna Hundley Glud of Kentucky"

Bentley Historical Library (Michigan Historical Collections), University of Michigan, Ann Arbor
Diary of Jerome Robbins
Papers of Nina L. Ness (Judson L. Austin Letters)
Papers of Thomas Reed

Colorado Historical Society, Denver
Mountain Charley Manuscript Collection

Connecticut Historical Society, Hartford
Letters of Joseph Orin Cross

Connecticut Valley Historical Society, Springfield, Massachusetts
Diary of Francis Beckwith

Delaware State Archives, Hall of Records, Dover
Diary of Spencer Hitch (Small Manuscripts, Hitch Papers)

Galveston and Texas History Center, Rosenberg Library
Letters of Robert Hodges, Manuscript Collection, H. W. Darst Papers

Illinois Veterans Home, Quincy, Ill.
Case file of Albert D. J. Cashier

Indiana State Archives, Indianapolis
Letters of E. W. H. Beck

Kansas State Historical Society, Topeka
Correspondence of Frederick L. Haywood

Kentucky Historical Society, Frankfort
Mary Ann Clark Collection

Library of Congress, Manuscript Division, Washington, D.C.
Correspondence of Daniel Reed Larned
Journal of Gilbert Thompson, 1861–1865
Papers of Caleb H. Carlton

Library of the University of North Carolina at Chapel Hill
Southern Historical Collection, Tucker Papers

Museum of the Confederacy, Eleanor S. Brockenbrough Library, Richmond, Virginia
The Confederate States Roll of Honour, Volume 237
Diary of Thomas L. Pinckney
Southern Women Collection

National Archives and Records Administration, Washington, D.C.

Record Group (RG) 15, Records of the Veterans Administration
  Pension Application Files
RG 29, Records of the Bureau of the Census
  U.S. Census Records
RG 94, Records of the Adjutant General's Office (AGO)
  AGO Document File Record Cards
  Administrative Precedent File ("Frech File")
  Carded Medical Records, Mexican and Civil Wars
  Compiled Military Service Records
  Carded Service Records of Hospital Attendants, Matrons, and Nurses
  Enlisted Branch Document File
  Hospital Registers, Civil War
  Muster Rolls, Regular Army
  Reference File: Old Records Division ("Edmondson File")
  Records and Pension Office (R&P) Document File
  R&P Record Cards
RG 109, War Department Collection of Confederate Records
  Chapter 1, Volume 56, Register of Letters Received, Adjutant and Inspector
    General's Office, April–July 1863
  Chapter 2, Volume 186, Letters Sent, Commander of the Troops at Atlanta,
    July 1863–May 1864
  Chapter 9, Volume 90, Applications for Appointments in Military Service,
    Confederate States
  Chapter 9, Volume 23, Register of Claims of Deceased Officers and Soldiers
  Compiled Military Service Records
RG 110, Records of the Provost Marshal General's Bureau (Civil War)
  Entry 36 (correspondence, reports, appointments, and other records relating to
    individual scouts, guides, spies, and detectives)
  Entry 95 (Secret Service accounts)
RG 153, Records of the Office of the Judge Advocate General (Army)
  Court-Martial Case Files
RG 393, Records of U.S. Army Continental Commands
  Part 1, Entry 916 (Department of the Cumberland and Division and Depart-
    ment of the Tennessee, telegrams sent)
  Part 1, Entry 2517 (Military Division of the Mississippi, letters sent by the Pro-
    vost Marshal General, 1864–1865)
  Part 1, Entry 5812 (Army of Virginia, two or more name citizen file)
  Part 4, Entry 2072 (Carroll Prison guard reports, volume 329)
Microfilm Publications
  M233, *Register of Enlistments in the U.S. Army, 1798–1914*

M345, *Union Provost Marshal's File of Papers Relating to Individual Civilians*
M416, *Union Provost Marshal's File of Papers Relating to Two or More Civilians*
M437, *Letters Received by the Confederate Secretary of War, 1861–1865*
M598, *Selected Records of the War Department Relating to Confederate Prisoners of War, 1861–1865*
M797, *Case Files of Investigations by Levi C. Turner and Lafayette C. Baker, 1861–1866*

National Park Service

Chalmette National Cemetery, Louisiana
Burial Register

City Point National Historic Site, Petersburg National Battlefield Park, Virginia
"The Diary of General Marsena R. Patrick, Provost Marshal of the Army of the Potomac" (unpublished transcription by Donald C. Pfanz)
Letter of Jackson Crossley, May 29, 1864

Fredericksburg and Spotsylvania National Military Park, Virginia
Letter of N. H. Hunt, April 27, 1863
Letter of Samuel S. Partridge, April 10, 1863

Shiloh National Military Park, Tennessee
Papers of Superintendent R. H. Bailey

New York State Library, Albany
Diary of Uberto A. Burnham

Ohio Historical Society, Columbus
Diary of Nelson Purdum, Volume 938
Graves Registration File
Muster Rolls, 21st Ohio Infantry

Point Lookout POW Organization, Virginia Beach, Virginia
Diary of Sgt. J. Jones

Private Collections
Lee Coutts, Cedarburg, Wisc.: Discharge Papers of Jennie Gregg
Frank and Velma Crawford, Caledonia, Ill.: Letters to Albert D. J. Cashier
Mike Donovan, Boulder, Colo.: Letters of John Q. Wilds
Joe Jones, Mentone, Ala.: Letters of M. F. Amos

Thomas and Beverly Lowry, Woodbridge, Va.: Letter of V. A. White
Ron Maness, Richmond, Va.: Letters of Altus Jewel
Benedict Maryniak, Buffalo, N.Y.: Letters of Adrian Root
Charles Morrison, Vienna, Va.: Letters of William B. Norris

South Carolina Historical Society, Charleston

Capt. Thomas L. Pinckney Reminiscences

Special Collections and Archives, Rutgers University, New Brunswick, New Jersey

Letters of Washington Roebling

Special Collections Library, Duke University, Durham, North Carolina

Broadside Collection
Diary of Henry Besancon
Papers of Huldah A. F. Briant
Papers of Gen. James Longstreet
Papers of Frank Moore
Papers of Gen. Joseph Wheeler

University of Iowa Libraries, Iowa City

Letters of Miles H. Beatty

U.S. Army Military History Institute, Carlisle Barracks, Carlisle, Pennsylvania

Diaries and Letters of Abiel Teple LaForge
Papers of John Harrod
"Recollections of the Civil War by a High Private in the Front Ranks"

Virginia Historical Society, Richmond

Diary of Amanda Virginia Edmonds
Diary of Mary E. Terry
Letter of Capt. Alonzo D. Pratt, Provost Marshal, Military District of Harper's
    Ferry, to Lt. Col. John Wooley, Provost Marshal, Middle Department, Sep-
    tember 12, 1864

Wisconsin State Historical Society Archives, Madison

Diary of Alfred Galpin II (Alfred Galpin Family Papers, 1861–1970)
Wisconsin History Commission Papers, Ethel A. Hurn Collection

NEWSPAPERS

Arkansas Democrat (Little Rock), 1925
Army and Navy Register, 1882
Augusta (Georgia) *Daily Chronicle and Sentinel*, 1863
Austin *Southern Intelligencer*, 1866
Baltimore *American and Commercial Advertiser*, 1863
Brooklyn *Daily Times*, 1864
Cairo (Illinois) *City Weekly Gazette*, 1862
Charles Town (West Virginia) *Farmer's Advocate*, 1898
Charleston (South Carolina) *Mercury*, 1863
Charlotte *Western Democrat*, 1865
Chelsea (Massachusetts) *Telegraph and Pioneer*, 1864
Chicago *Evening Journal*, 1865
Chicago *Tribune*, 1865
Cincinnati *Daily Commercial*, 1861–1863
Cincinnati *Daily Enquirer*, 1864
Cincinnati *Daily Gazette*, 1863
Cleveland *Leader*, 1896
Coffee County *Progress* (Douglas, Georgia), 1925
Colorado *Transcript* (Golden), 1885
Covington (Kentucky) *Journal*, 1862
Detroit *Advertiser and Tribune*, 1863–1864
Detroit *Free Press*, 1861–1864
Detroit *Post and Tribune*, 1883
Dollar Weekly *Bulletin* (Maysville, Kentucky), 1862
Dollar Weekly *Times* (Cincinnati), 1864
Evening Star (Washington, D.C.), 1865–1866, 1896
Fayetteville (North Carolina) *Observer*, 1927
Fincher's Trades' Review, 1863–1864
Florence (South Carolina) *Morning News*, 1959
Fort Scott (Kansas) *Weekly Monitor*, 1884
Frank Leslie's Illustrated Newspaper, 1863–1864
Grant County Witness (Platteville, Wisconsin), 1864–1865
Greensburg (Indiana) *News*, 1907
Indianapolis *Daily Sentinal*, 1861–1864
Indianapolis *Journal*, 1863
Kansas City *Star*, 1929
Logansport (Indiana) *Journal*, 1863
Lynchburg *Daily Virginian*, 1863
Lynchburg *Virginian*, 1864

Memphis *Bulletin*, 1862
Missouri Democrat (St. Louis), 1861–1864
Monongahela (Pennsylvania) *Republican*, 1865
National Tribune (Washington, D.C.), 1882–1935
New Albany (Indiana) *Daily Ledger*, 1862
New Orleans *Daily Picayune*, 1863, 1867
New York *Daily Tribune*, 1861–1864
New York *Herald*, 1861–1864
New York *Sun*, 1901
New York *Times*, 1864, 1934, 2000
Owensboro (Kentucky) *Monitor*, 1862
Pittsburgh *Evening Chronicle*, 1861
Pittsburgh *Gazette*, 1861
Portland (Maine) *Herald*, 1936
Portland (Maine) *Sunday Telegram*, 1930
Princeton (Indiana) *Clarion*, 1863
Richmond *Daily Examiner*, 1863–1864
Richmond *Whig*, 1863–1865
Roxbury (Massachusetts) *City Gazette*, 1863
Saint Paul *Pioneer*, 1863–1865
Sandusky (Ohio) *Commercial Register*, 1864
Southern Federal Union (Milledgeville, Georgia), 1862
Sturgis (South Dakota) *Weekly Record*, 1885
Sunday Star Magazine (Washington, D.C.), 1906
Washington *Daily Morning Chronicle*, 1864–1865
Washington *Post*, 1901, 1928
Washington *Times*, 1895, 1920
Wheeling (West Virginia) *Daily Intelligencer*, 1862–1863
Wisconsin State Journal (Madison), 1865
Worcester (Massachusetts) *Aegis and Transcript*, 1863–1864

BOOKS

Adams, George Worthington. *Doctors in Blue: The Medical History of the Union Army in the Civil War*. New York: Henry Schuman, 1952.

Baer, Elizabeth R., ed. *Shadows on My Heart: The Civil War Diary of Lucy Rebecca Buck of Virginia*. Athens: University of Georgia Press, 1997.

Bellesiles, Michael A., ed. *Lethal Imagination: Violence and Brutality in American History*. New York: New York University Press, 1999.

Bergeron, Arthur W., Jr., and Lawrence L. Hewitt. *Miles' Legion: A History and Roster*. Baton Rouge: Elliott's Bookshop Press, 1983.

Blakey, Arch Fredric. *General John H. Winder, C.S.A.* Gainesville: University of Florida Press, 1990.

Borcke, Heros von. *Memoirs of the Confederate War for Independence.* 1865–66. Reprint, Philadelphia: Lippincott & Co., 1867.

Bowen, J. R. *Regimental History of the First New York Dragoons.* Lyons, Mich.: published by the author, 1900.

Brockett, Linus P., and Mary Vaughan. *Women's Work in the Civil War.* Philadelphia: Zeigler, McCurdy & Co., 1867.

Brown, William Fiske, ed. *Rock County Wisconsin.* Vol. 1. Chicago: C. F. Cooper & Co., 1908.

Bullough, Vern L., and Bonnie Bullough. *Cross Dressing, Sex, and Gender.* Philadelphia: University of Pennsylvania Press, 1993.

Burgess, Lauren Cook, ed. *An Uncommon Soldier: The Civil War Letters of Sarah Rosetta Wakeman, Alias Pvt. Lyons Wakeman, 153rd Regiment, New York State Volunteers, 1862–1864.* Pasadena, Md.: Minerva Center, 1994.

Burlingame, Michael. *The Inner World of Abraham Lincoln.* Urbana: University of Illinois Press, 1994.

Campbell, Edward D. C., Jr., and Kym S. Rice, eds. *A Woman's War: Southern Women, Civil War, and the Confederate Legacy.* Richmond: Museum of the Confederacy; Charlottesville: University Press of Virginia, 1996.

Cavada, F. F. *Libby Life: Experiences of a Prisoner of War in Richmond, Virginia, 1863–1864.* Lanham, Md.: University Press of America, 1985.

Cheek, Philip, and Mair Pointon. *History of the Sauk County Riflemen.* Gaithersburg, Md.: Butternut, 1984.

Clinton, Catherine, and Nina Silber, eds. *Divided Houses: Gender and the Civil War.* New York: Oxford University Press, 1992.

Coco, Gregory A. *On the Bloodstained Field.* Hollidaysburg, Pa.: The Wheatfield Press, 1987.

Cohen, Daniel A., ed. *The Female Marine and Related Works: Narratives of Cross-Dressing and Urban Vice in America's Early Republic.* Amherst: University of Massachusetts Press, 1997.

Conyngham, David. *Sherman's March through the South.* New York: Sheldon & Co., 1865.

Craft, David. *History of the One Hundred Forty-First Regiment, Pennsylvania Volunteers, 1862–1865.* Towanda, Pa.: Reporter-Journal Printing, 1885.

Creelman, Samuel. *Collections of a Coffee Cooler.* Pittsburgh: Pittsburgh Photoengraving, 1890.

Creighton, Margaret S., and Lisa Norling, eds. *Iron Men, Wooden Women: Gender and Seafaring in the Atlantic World, 1700–1920.* Baltimore: Johns Hopkins University Press, 1996.

Cronin, David E., ed. *The Evolution of a Life Described in the Memoirs of Major Seth Eyland.* New York: S. W. Green's Son, 1884.

C.S. War Department. *Regulations for the Army of the Confederate States, 1863*. Richmond: J. W. Randolph, 1863.

Cuffel, Charles A. *History of Durell's Battery in the Civil War*. Philadelphia: Craig Finley & Co., 1903.

Cunningham, H. H. *Doctors in Gray: The Confederate Medical Service*. Baton Rouge: Louisiana State University Press, 1993.

Curtis, O. B. *History of the Twenty-Fourth Michigan of the Iron Brigade*. Detroit: Winn & Hammond, 1891.

Daniel, Larry J. *Soldiering in the Army of Tennessee*. Chapel Hill: University of North Carolina Press, 1991.

Dannett, Sylvia G. L., *She Rode with the Generals*. New York: Thomas Nelson & Sons, 1960.

Dannett, Sylvia G. L., and Katherine M. Jones. *Our Women of the Sixties*. Washington: U.S. Civil War Centennial Commission, 1963.

Davis, Burke. *Sherman's March*. New York: Random House, 1980.

Davis, Jack C., ed. *Dear Wife: The Civil War Letters of a Private Soldier*. Louisville: Sulgrave, 1991.

Dawson, Sarah Morgan. *A Confederate Girl's Diary*. James I. Robertson Jr., ed. Bloomington: Indiana University Press, 1960.

de Erauso, Catalina. *Lieutenant Nun: Memoir of a Basque Transvestite in the New World*. Michele and Gabriel Stepto, trans. Boston: Beacon, 1996.

DeFontaine, Feliz G. *Marginalia: Gleanings from an Army Notebook*. Columbia, S.C.: F. G. DeFontaine & Co., 1864.

Dekker, Rudolf, and Lotte van der Pol. *The Tradition of Female Transvestism in Early Modern Europe*. London: Macmillan, 1989.

DePauw, Linda Grant. *Battle Cries and Lullabies: Women in War from Prehistory to the Present*. Norman: University of Oklahoma Press, 1998.

Devons, Richard Miller. *The Pictorial Book of Anecdotes and Incidents of the War of the Rebellion*. Hartford: Hartford Publishing, 1867.

Drickamer, Lee C., and Karen D. Drickamer, eds. *Fort Lyon to Harper's Ferry—On the Border of North and South with "Rambling Jour": The Civil War Letters and Newspaper Dispatches of Charles H. Moulton*. Shippensburg, Pa.: White Mane, 1987.

Dugaw, Dianne. *Dangerous Examples: Warrior Women and Popular Balladry, 1650–1850*. Cambridge: Cambridge University Press, 1989.

Dyer, Frederick H. *A Compendium of the War of the Rebellion*. Dayton: Morningside Bookshop, 1978.

Edgeville, Edward. *Castine*. Raleigh: William B. Smith & Co., 1865.

Edmonds, S. Emma E. *Nurse and Spy in the Union Army*. Hartford: W. S. Williams & Co., 1865.

Eggleston, George C. *Southern Soldier Stories*. 1898. Reprint, Fairfax, Va.: SCS Publications, 1998.

Evans, Sara M. *Born for Liberty: A History of Women in America*. New York: Macmillan, 1989.

Faderman, Lillian. *Odd Girls and Twilight Lovers: A History of Lesbian Life in Twentieth Century America*. New York: Columbia University Press, 1991.

———. *Surpassing the Love of Men: Romantic Friendship and Love between Women from the Renaissance to the Present*. New York: Quill William Morrow, 1981.

Faust, Patricia L., ed. *Historical Times Illustrated Encyclopedia of the Civil War*. 1986. Reprint, New York: HarperPerennial, 1991.

Fellman, Michael. *Inside War: The Guerrilla Conflict in Missouri during the American Civil War*. New York: Oxford University Press, 1989.

Fishel, Edwin C. *The Secret War for the Union: The Untold Story of Military Intelligence in the Civil War*. Boston: Houghton-Mifflin, 1996.

Fox, William F. *Regimental Losses in the American Civil War, 1861–1865*. Albany: Albany Publishing, 1889.

Frank, Joseph Allan. *With Ballot and Bayonet: The Political Socialization of American Civil War Soldiers*. Athens: University of Georgia Press, 1998.

Franklin, Wayne. *American Voices, American Lives: A Documentary Reader*. New York: W. W. Norton & Co., 1997.

Fremantle, Arthur J. L. *Three Months in the Southern States: April–June 1863*. Lincoln: University of Nebraska Press, 1991.

Frost, Griffin. *Camp and Prison Journal*. Iowa City: Camp Pope Bookshop, 1994.

Garber, Marjorie. *Vested Interests: Cross-Dressing and Cultural Anxiety*. New York: Routledge Press, 1992.

Gardner, Ira B. *Recollections of a Boy Member of Co. I, Fourteenth Maine Volunteers, 1861–1865*. Lewiston, Maine: Lewiston Journal, 1902.

Ginsberg, Elaine K., ed. *Passing and the Fictions of Identity*. Durham: Duke University Press, 1996.

Gower, Herschel, ed. *The Beersheba Springs Diaries of L. Virginia French, 1863–1864*. Nashville: East Tennessee Historical Society, 1986.

Guerin, E. J. *Mountain Charley: An Autobiography*. Fred M. Mazzulla and William Kostka, eds. Norman: University of Oklahoma Press, 1968.

Hale, Laura Virginia. *Four Valiant Years in the Lower Shenandoah Valley, 1861–1865*. Strasburg, Va.: Shenandoah Publishing House, 1968.

Hall, James E. *The Diary of a Confederate Soldier*. Ruth Woods Dayton, ed. Lewisburg, W.Va.: n.p., 1961.

Hall, Richard. *Patriots in Disguise: Women Warriors of the Civil War*. New York: Paragon House, 1993.

Haviland, Laura S. *A Woman's Life-Work*. Chicago: C. V. Waite & Co., 1887.

Henry, Robert Selph. *Nathan Bedford Forrest: First with the Most*. New York: Konecky & Konecky, 1992.

Herbert, Melissa S. *Camouflage Isn't Only for Combat: Gender, Sexuality, and Women in the Military*. New York: New York University Press, 1998.

Hess, Earl J. *The Union Soldier in Battle: Enduring the Ordeal of Combat.* Lawrence: University of Kansas Press, 1997.

Hoar, Jay S. *The South's Last Boys in Gray.* Bowling Green: Bowling Green State University Popular Press, 1986.

Holland, Mary A. Gardner, ed. *Our Army Nurses.* Boston: B. Wilkins & Co., 1895.

Holstein, Anna Morris. *Three Years in Field Hospitals of the Army of the Potomac.* Philadelphia: J. B. Lippincott & Co., 1867.

Holzer, Harold, ed. *Dear Mr. Lincoln: Letters to the President.* New York: Addison-Wesley, 1993.

Hughes, Nathaniel C., Jr. *Bentonville: The Final Battle of Sherman and Johnston.* Chapel Hill: University of North Carolina Press, 1996.

Hurn, Ethel. *Wisconsin Women in the War between the States.* Madison: Wisconsin History Commission, 1911.

Isenberg, Nancy. *Sex and Citizenship in Antebellum America.* Chapel Hill: University of North Carolina Press, 1998.

Jackson, Alto L., ed. *So Mourns the Dove: Letters of a Confederate Infantryman and His Family.* New York: Exposition, 1965.

Jackson, H. W. R. *The Southern Women of the Second American Revolution.* Atlanta: Intelligencer Steam-Power Press, 1863.

Jordan, Ervin L., Jr. *Black Confederates and Afro-Yankees in Civil War Virginia.* Charlottesville: University Press of Virginia, 1995.

Katz, Jonathan. *Gay American History: Lesbians and Gay Men in the U.S.A.* New York: Thomas Y. Crowell, 1976.

Keiley, A. M. *In Vinculis; or, The Prisoner of War.* New York: Blelock & Co., 1866.

Keller, Allan. *Morgan's Raid.* Indianapolis: Bobbs-Merrill, 1961.

Kennett, Lee. *Marching through Georgia.* New York: HarperCollins, 1995.

Kerber, Linda K. *No Constitutional Right to Be Ladies: Women and the Obligations of Citizenship.* New York: Hill & Wang, 1998.

Kerber, Linda K., Alice Kessler-Harris, and Kathryn Kish Sklar, eds. *U.S. History as Women's History: New Feminist Essays.* Chapel Hill: University of North Carolina Press, 1995.

Kerksis, Sydney C., Lee A. Wallace Jr., and Margie R. Bearss, eds. *The Atlanta Papers.* Dayton: Morningside Bookshop, 1980.

King, Wendy A. *Clad in Uniform: Women Soldiers of the Civil War.* Collingwood, N.J.: C.W. Historicals, 1992.

Laffin, John. *Women in Battle.* London: Abelard-Schuman, 1967.

Leon, Louis. *Diary of a Tar Heel Confederate Soldier.* Charlotte, N.C.: Stone Publishing, 1913.

Leonard, Elizabeth D. *All the Daring of the Soldier: Women of the Civil War Armies.* New York: W. W. Norton & Co., 1999.

Linderman, Gerald F. *Embattled Courage.* New York: Free Press, 1987.

Livermore, Mary A. *My Story of the War.* Hartford: A. D. Worthington & Co., 1888.

Livermore, Thomas L. *Numbers and Losses in the Civil War in America.* Carlisle, Pa.: John Kallman, 1996.

Long, Clarence D. *Wages and Earnings in the United States, 1860–1890.* Princeton: Princeton University Press, 1960.

Long, E. B., and Barbara Long. *The Civil War Day by Day: An Almanac, 1861–1865.* New York: Da Capo, 1985.

Lowry, Thomas P. *The Story the Soldiers Wouldn't Tell: Sex in the Civil War.* Mechanicsburg, Pa.: Stackpole Books, 1994.

Lumpkin, Martha Neville, ed. *"Dear Darling Louilie": Letters of Cordelia Lewis Scales to Louilie W. Irby during and after the War between the States.* Boulder, Colo.: n.p., 1955.

Meriwether, Elizabeth Avery. *Recollections of 92 Years: 1824–1916.* Nashville: Tennessee Historical Commission, 1958.

Martin, Edgar W. *The Standard of Living in 1860.* Chicago: University of Chicago Press, 1942.

Marvel, William. *Burnside.* Chapel Hill: University of North Carolina Press, 1991.

Massey, Mary Elizabeth. *Women in the Civil War.* Lincoln: University of Nebraska Press, 1994.

McPherson, James M. *Battle Cry of Freedom.* New York: Oxford University Press, 1988.

———. *For Cause and Comrades: Why Men Fought in the Civil War.* New York: Oxford University Press, 1997.

Miller, William J. *The Training of an Army: Camp Curtin and the North's Civil War.* Shippensburg, Pa.: White Mane, 1990.

Minnesota Board of Commissioners. *Minnesota in the Civil and Indian Wars, 1861–1865.* Vol. 1. St. Paul: Pioneer, 1891.

Moore, Frank, ed. *The Rebellion Record: A Diary of American Events, with Documents, Narratives, Illustrative Incidents, Poetry, Etc.* Vols. 4 and 8. New York: D. Van Nostrand, 1871.

———. *Women of the War.* Hartford: S. S. Scranton & Co., 1866.

Moore, Madeline. *The Lady Lieutenant.* Philadelphia: Barclay & Co., 1862.

Oates, Stephen B. *A Woman of Valor: Clara Barton and the Civil War.* New York: Free Press, 1994.

Palmer, Abraham J. *The History of the Forty-Eighth Regiment New York State Volunteers.* New York: Charles T. Dillingham, 1885.

Penny, Virginia. *The Employment of Women: A Cyclopedia of Women's Work.* Boston: Walker, Wise, & Co., 1863.

Phillips, Harlan B., ed. "An Immigrant Goes to War: The Civil War Correspondence of Herman and Adeline Weiss." *History 4: A Meridien Periodical.* New York: Word Publishing, 1961.

Pryor, Elizabeth Brown. *Clara Barton, Professional Angel.* Philadelphia: University of Pennsylvania Press, 1987.

Ransom, John L. *Andersonville Diary, Escape, and List of Dead . . . .* Auburn, N.Y.: John L. Ransom, 1881.

Reardon, Carol. *Pickett's Charge in History and Memory.* Chapel Hill: University of North Carolina Press, 1997.

Richardson, Albert D. *The Secret Service, the Field, the Dungeon, and the Escape.* Hartford: American Publishing, 1865.

Rigdon, Raymond M., ed. *Letters to Amanda.* Nashville: Champion Resources, 1992.

Robertson, James I., Jr. *Soldiers Blue and Gray.* Columbia: University of South Carolina Press, 1988.

Robertson, John. *Michigan in the War.* Lansing: W. S. George & Co., State Printers & Binders, 1882.

Robertson, Mary D., ed. *Lucy Breckinridge of Grove Hill: The Journal of a Virginia Girl, 1862–1864.* Columbia: University of South Carolina Press, 1994.

Ross, FitzGerald. *Cities and Camps of the Confederate States.* Richard B. Harwell, ed. Urbana: University of Illinois Press, 1958.

Rowe, David Watson. *A Sketch of the 126th Regiment Pennsylvania Volunteers.* Chambersburg, Pa.: Cook & Hays, 1869.

Sarmiento, F. L. *Life of Pauline Cushman.* Philadelphia: John E. Potter, 1865.

Scharf, J. Thomas. *History of Baltimore City and County.* Vol. 1. Baltimore: Regional Publishing, 1971.

Schmidt, Lewis G. *A Civil War History of the 47th Regiment Pennsylvania Veteran Volunteers.* Allentown, Pa.: Lewis G. Schmidt, 1986.

Sears, Stephen. *To the Gates of Richmond: The Peninsula Campaign.* New York: Ticknor & Fields, 1992.

Seeley, Charlotte Palmer, comp. *American Women and the U.S. Armed Forces: A Guide to the Records of Military Agencies in the National Archives Relating to American Women.* Revised by Virginia Cardwell Purdy and Robert Gruber. Washington: National Archives and Records Administration, 1992.

Senour, Rev. F. (Faunt Le Roy). *Morgan and His Captors.* Cincinnati: C. F. Vent & Co., 1865.

Sheridan, Philip Henry. *Personal Memoirs of Philip Henry Sheridan, General, United States Army.* New and enl. ed. Vol 1. 1902. Reprint, New York: D. Appleton & Co., 1904.

Shilts, Randy. *Conduct Unbecoming: Lesbians and Gays in the U.S. Military, Vietnam to the Persian Gulf.* New York: St. Martin's, 1993.

Simkins, Francis Butler, and James Welch Patton. *The Women of the Confederacy.* Richmond: Garrett & Massie, 1936.

Smith, Barbara A., ed. *The Civil War Letters of Col. Elijah H. C. Cavins, 14th Indiana.* Owensboro, Ky.: Cook-McDowell, 1981.

Speer, Lonnie R. *Portals to Hell: Military Prisons of the Civil War*. Mechanicsburg, Pa.: Stackpole Books, 1997.

Speer, Morgan, and Greg Nichalson, eds. *For Our Beloved Country: American War Diaries from the Revolution to the Persian Gulf*. New York: Atlantic Monthly Press, 1994.

Stanton, Elizabeth Cady, Susan B. Anthony, and Matilda Joslyn Gage, eds. *History of Woman Suffrage*, Vol. 2. Rochester: Charles Mann, 1887.

Stanyan, John M. *A History of the Eighth Regiment of New Hampshire Volunteers*. Concord, N.H.: Ira C. Evans, 1892.

Stevens, Peter F. *Rebels in Blue: The Story of Keith and Malinda Blalock*. Dallas: Taylor, 2000.

Styple, William B., ed. *Writing and Fighting the Civil War: Soldier Correspondence to the New York "Sunday Mercury."* Kearny, N.J.: Belle Grove, 2000.

Temple, Wayne C., ed. *The Civil War Letters of Henry C. Bear: A Soldier in the 116th Illinois Volunteer Infantry*. Harrogate, Tenn.: Lincoln Memorial University Press, 1961.

Thomson, Orville. *Narrative of the Service of the Seventh Indiana Infantry in the War for the Union*. n.p: published by the author, n.d.

Trotter, William R. *Bushwhackers! The Civil War in North Carolina: The Mountains*. Winston-Salem: J. F. Blair, 1988.

Tucker, Glenn. *High Tide at Gettysburg*. New York: Bobbs-Merrill, 1958.

U.S. Congress. *Report of the Committee of the Senate upon the Relations between Labor and Capital, and Testimony Taken by the Committee*, Vol. 2, *Testimony*. Washington: Government Printing Office, 1885.

U.S. War Department. *Revised Regulations for the Army of the United States, 1861*. Philadelphia: J. G. L. Brown, 1861.

U.S. War Department. *The War of the Rebellion: The Official Records of the Union and Confederate Armies*, Series I, Vol. 27, Part 1; Series II, Vol. 5; Series II, Vol. 7; Series II, Volume 8; and Series III, Vol. 1, Part 1. Washington: War Department, 1889–1901.

Velazquez, Loreta Janeta. *The Woman in Battle*. Richmond: Dustin, Gilman & Co., 1876.

Ward, George W. *History of the Second Pennsylvania Veteran Heavy Artillery*. Philadelphia: George W. Ward, 1904.

Wheelock, Julia S. *The Boys in White: The Experience of a Hospital Agent*. New York: Lange & Hillman, 1870.

Wheelwright, Julie. *Amazons and Military Maids: Women Who Dressed as Men in the Pursuit of Life, Liberty, and Happiness*. London: Pandora, 1989.

Wiley, Bell I. *Confederate Women*. Westport, Conn.: Greenwood , 1975.

———. *The Life of Billy Yank: The Common Soldier of the Union*. New York: Bobbs-Merrill, 1951.

————. *The Life of Johnny Reb: The Common Soldier of the Confederacy.* New York: Bobbs-Merrill, 1943.

Wittenmyer, Annie. *Under the Guns: A Woman's Reminiscences of the Civil War.* Boston: E. B. Stillings & Co., 1895.

Young, Agatha. *The Women and the Crisis.* New York: McDowell, Obolensky, 1959.

PERIODICALS

Anderson, Fanny J., ed. "The Shelly Papers." *Indiana Magazine of History* 65, no. 2 (1948).

Blanton, DeAnne. "Women Soldiers of the Civil War." *Prologue* 25, no. 1 (1993).

Brooks, Fred. "Shiloh Mystery Woman." *Civil War Times Illustrated* 17, no. 5 (1978).

Clausius, Gerhard P. "The Little Soldier of the 95th: Albert D.J. Cashier." *Journal of the Illinois State Historical Society* 51, no. 4 (1958).

Confederate Veteran 1, no. 6 (1893); 3, no. 4 (1895); 4, no. 9 (1896); 6, no. 6 (1898); 7, no. 11 (1898); 15, no. 5 (1907); 23, no. 10 (1915); and 31, no. 12 (1923).

Davis, Rodney O. "Private Albert Cashier As Regarded by His/Her Comrades." *Journal of the Illinois State Historical Society* 72, no. 2 (1989).

"Dietary Amenorrhoea." *British Medical Journal* (February 11, 1978).

Hass, Paul H., ed. "A Volunteer Nurse in the Civil War: The Diary of Harriet Douglas Whetten." *Wisconsin Magazine of History* 68, no. 3 (1965).

"The Hero of Pickett's Division," *Confederate War Journal* 2, no. 3 (1894).

Hoffert, Sylvia D. "Heroine or Hoaxer?" *Civil War Times Illustrated* 38, no. 4 (1999).

King, G. Wayne. "Death Camp at Florence." *Civil War Times Illustrated* 12, no. 9 (1974).

Larson, C. Kay. "Bonnie Yank and Ginny Reb." *Minerva: Quarterly Report on Women and the Military* 8, no. 1 (1990).

————. "Bonny Yank and Ginny Reb Revisited." *Minerva: Quarterly Report on Women and the Military* 10, no. 2 (1992).

Leisch, Juanita. "The Look of the Ladies." *Military Images* 21, no. 6 (2000).

"Letters to a Mother from a Union Volunteer." *Yankee* (June 1961).

Mast, Greg. "'Sam' Blaylock, 26th North Carolina Troops." *Military Images* 11, no. 1 (1989).

Mellon, Knox, Jr., ed. "Letters of James Greenalch." *Michigan History* 44, no. 2 (1960).

Olson, Beatriz R. "Exercise-Induced Amenorrhea." *American Family Physician* (Feb. 1989).

Peña, Chris, ed. "F. S. Twitchell's Letter Describing a Female Guerrilla." *Louisiana History* 39 (Winter 1998).

Petterchak, Janice. "A Conversation on History." *Dispatch* 4, no. 13 (1991).

Robertson, James I., Jr., ed. "An Indiana Soldier in Love and War." *Indiana Magazine of History* 59, no. 3 (1963).

Tolis, G., and E. Diamanti. "Distress Amenorrhea." *Annals of the New York Academy of Science* (1996).

Welter, Barbara. "The Cult of True Womanhood: 1820–1860." *American Quarterly* 18, no. 2 (1966).

"Women in the War." *United States Service Magazine* 3, no. 3 (1865).

Theses and Dissertations

Lannon, Mary Catherine. "Albert D. J. Cashier and the Ninety-Fifth Illinois Infantry (1844–1915)." Master's thesis, Illinois State University, 1969.

Schultz, Jane Ellen. "Women at the Front: Gender and Genre in Literature of the American Civil War." Ph.D. diss., University of Michigan, 1988.

Notes

Abbreviations

ALUVA	Alderman Library, University of Virginia
ALLH	Alexandria Library, Lloyd House
ACOHS	Allen County (Ohio) Historical Society
BLUCB	Bancroft Library, University of California, Berkeley
BHLUM	Bentley Historical Library, University of Michigan
CHS	Colorado Historical Society
CMSR	Compiled Military Service Records
CtHS	Connecticut Historical Society
CVHS	Connecticut Valley Historical Society
DSA	Delaware State Archives, Hall of Records
EB	Enlisted Branch
G&THC	Galveston and Texas History Center
IVH	Illinois Veterans Home, Quincy
ISL	Indiana State Library
KSHS	Kansas State Historical Society
KHS	Kentucky Historical Society
LC	Library of Congress
LUNCCH	Library of the University of North Carolina, Chapel Hill
MOC	Museum of the Confederacy
NPS	National Park Service
NYSL	New York State Library
OHS	Ohio Historical Society
OR	*The War of the Rebellion: The Official Records of the Union and Confederate Armies*

PLPOWO   Point Lookout POW Organization
RG   Record Group
SCHS   South Carolina Historical Society
SCARU   Special Collections and Archives, Rutgers University
SCLDU   Special Collections Library, Duke University
UIL   University of Iowa Libraries
USAMHI   U.S. Army Military History Institute
VHS   Virginia Historical Society
WSHSA   Wisconsin State Historical Society Archives

INTRODUCTION. "Entrenched in Secrecy": *Women Soldiers of the Civil War*

1. Bell I. Wiley, *The Life of Johnny Reb: The Common Soldier of the Confederacy* (Baton Rouge: Louisiana State University Press, 1951), and *The Life of Billy Yank: The Common Soldier of the Union* (Baton Rouge: Louisiana State University Press, 1943); Gerald F. Linderman, *Embattled Courage* (New York: Free Press, 1987); James M. McPherson, *For Cause and Comrades: Why Men Fought in the Civil War* (New York: Oxford University Press, 1997); Earl J. Hess, *The Union Soldier in Battle: Enduring the Ordeal of Combat* (Lawrence: University Press of Kansas, 1997); Joseph Allan Frank, *With Ballot and Bayonet: The Political Socialization of American Civil War Soldiers* (Athens: University of Georgia Press, 1998).

2. Among male Union soldiers, nearly half were farmers and another tenth were common laborers, while a large number of immigrants served the southern cause and the Confederacy's agrarian economy dictated that the majority of Rebels were farmers. See *Wiley, Johnny Reb*, 322–24 and *Billy Yank*, 304.

3. Loreta Velazquez may have been a pen name rather than the author's real name, although she claimed that Velazquez was her maiden name. In any event, she used a number of aliases during and after the war. Further complicating matters, she married four times, resulting in multiple surname changes. For the sake of clarity, we refer to her as Velazquez throughout this narrative.

4. Vern L. Bullough and Bonnie Bullough, *Cross Dressing, Sex, and Gender* (Philadelphia: University of Pennsylvania Press, 1993), 153–57; Barbara Welter, "The Cult of True Womanhood: 1820–1860," *American Quarterly* 18, no. 2 (1966): 151–74. For an in-depth discussion of women's lives and Victorian ideology prior to the Civil War, see Sara M. Evans, *Born for Liberty: A History of Women in America* (New York: Macmillan, 1989).

5. Wayne Franklin, ed., *American Voices, American Lives: A Documentary Reader* (New York: W. W. Norton & Co., 1997), 427–30.

6. Virginia Penny, *The Employment of Women: A Cyclopedia of Women's Work* (Boston: Walker, Wise & Co., 1863), 426; Clarence D. Long, *Wages and Earnings in the United States, 1860–1890* (Princeton: Princeton University Press, 1960), 105–7; Edgar W. Martin, *The Standard of Living in 1860* (Chicago: University Of Chicago Press, 1942), 413.

7. Dianne Dugaw, "Female Sailors Bold," in *Iron Men, Wooden Women: Gender and Seafaring in the Atlantic World, 1700–1920*, ed. Margaret S. Creighton and Lisa Norling (Baltimore: Johns Hopkins University Press, 1996), 35, 37. See also Daniel A. Cohen, ed., *The Female Marine and Related Works: Narratives of Cross-Dressing and Urban Vice in America's Early Republic* (Amherst: University of Massachusetts Press, 1997); Julie Wheelwright, *Ama-*

zons and Military Maids: Women Who Dressed as Men in the Pursuit of Life, Liberty, and Happiness (London: Pandora, 1989); Rudolf Dekker and Lotte van de Pol, *The Tradition of Female Transvestism in Early Modern Europe* (London: Macmillan, 1989); Dianne Dugaw, *Dangerous Examples: Warrior Women and Popular Balladry, 1650–1850* (Cambridge: Cambridge University Press, 1989).

8. Catalina de Erauso, *Lieutenant Nun: Memoir of a Basque Transvestite in the New World,* trans. Michele and Gabriel Stepto (Boston: Beacon, 1996); Wheelwright, *Amazons and Military Maids,* 8, 17, 133–36, 145.

9. Mary A. Livermore, *My Story of the War* (Hartford: A. D. Worthington, 1888), 119–20.

Chapter 1. "They Fought like Demons": *A Military History of Women in Combat*

1. M. F. Amos to his wife, 4 Sep. 1861, private collection of Joe Jones, Mentone, Ala.; "A Woman Soldier," Washington *Daily Morning Chronicle,* 26 Aug. 1864; Laura S. Haviland, *A Woman's Life-Work* (Chicago: C. V. Waite, 1887), 262; Julia S. Wheelock, *The Boys in White: The Experience of a Hospital Agent* (New York: Lange & Hillman, 1870), 114–15.

2. AGO, EB file 3132 C 1884, RG 94, National Archives; Long, *Day by Day,* 99.

3. "Mrs. Mary De Caulp," New Orleans *Daily Picayune,* 5 Jan. 1867; Loreta Janeta Velazquez, *The Woman in Battle* (Richmond: Dustin, Gilman, 1876), 95–117; Feliz G. DeFontaine, *Marginalia: Gleanings from an Army Notebook* (Columbia, S.C.: F. G. DeFontaine, 1864), 65–66; Long, *Day by Day,* 129.

4. Velazquez, *Woman in Battle,* 117, 155.

5. Long, *Day by Day,* 107; AGO, CMSR, 1st Kansas Infantry, Luther, Alfred J., RG 94, National Archives; AGO, Carded Medical Records, Mexican and Civil Wars, 1st Kansas, Luther, RG 94, National Archives; "A Woman May Have Fought for Kansas in the Civil War," Kansas City *Star,* 24 May 1929.

6. Long, *Day by Day,* 162; "A Scotch Woman . . . ," Covington (Kentucky) *Journal,* 31 May 1862; AGO, CMSR, 17th Ohio Infantry, Deming, Frank, RG 94, National Archives; Frederick H. Dyer, *A Compendium of the War of the Rebellion* (Dayton: Morningside Bookshop, 1978), 1504.

7. "A Female Warrior," *Fincher's Trades' Review,* 21 Nov. 1863; Velazquez, *Woman in Battle,* 154–220; DeFontaine, *Marginalia,* 65–66; "Mrs. Mary De Caulp," New Orleans *Daily Picayune,* 5 Jan. 1867.

8. "Female Soldiers: Two Women Discovered in the Union Uniform," New York *Times,* 26 Aug. 1864; "A Patriotic Woman," Washington *Daily Morning Chronicle,* 26 Aug. 1864; Fred Brooks, "Shiloh Mystery Woman," *Civil War Times Illustrated* 17, no. 5 (1978), 29; Frank Moore, ed., *The Rebellion Record: A Diary of American Events, with Documents, Narratives, Illustrative Incidents, Poetry, Etc.* (New York: Van Nostrand, 1871), 8:37–38; Examination of Mary Ann Pitman by Col. J. P. Sanderson, Provost Marshal General, Dept. of Missouri, 20 June 1864, *OR,* Ser. 2, Vol. 7, pp. 345–55.

9. Col. John Q. Wilds, 24th Iowa Infantry, to his wife, 13 Dec. 1862, personal collection of Mike Donovan, Boulder, Colo.; Long, *Day by Day,* 258; DeFontaine, *Marginalia,* 133; H. W. R. Jackson, *The Southern Women of the Second American Revolution* (Atlanta: Intelli-

gencer Steam-Power Press, 1863), 7–8; Robert Hodges, 24th Texas Cavalry, CSA, to his father, 7 Aug. 1863, Letters of Robert Hodges, Manuscript Collection (MS 95–0016), H. W. Darst Papers, G&THC.

10. "A Broken Link: A Story of the Battle of Perryville," Monongahela (Pennsylvania) *Republican*, 12 Jan. 1865; Arthur J. L. Fremantle, *Three Months in the Southern States: April–June 1863* (Lincoln: University of Nebraska Press, 1991), 172–73; Sgt. Hiram Holt to his wife, quoted in Larry J. Daniel, *Soldiering in the Army of Tennessee: A Portrait of Life in a Confederate Army* (Chapel Hill: University of North Carolina Press, 1991), 153–54.

11. "Women in the War," *United States Service Magazine* 3, no. 3 (1865), 274; "Eventful History of a Soldier Woman," Princeton (Indiana) *Clarion*, 10 Oct. 1863; "An Amazon," St. Paul *Pioneer*, 26 May 1863; "Epitome . . . ," *Frank Leslie's Illustrated Newspaper*, 19 Dec. 1863; "Female Warrior," *Fincher's Trades' Review*, 21 Nov. 1863; James Greenalch to his wife, 20 April 1863, in "Letters of James Greenalch," ed. Knox Mellon Jr., *Michigan History* 44, no. 2 (1960), 205; "From the 75th Regiment . . . ," Logansport (Indiana) *Journal*, 9 May 1863.

12. *Union Provost Marshal's File of Papers Relating to Individual Civilians*, file for Fitzallen, Henry, M345, National Archives; AGO, CMSR, 23rd Kentucky Infantry, Fitzallen, Henry, RG 94, National Archives; Long, *Day by Day*, 1079–80.

13. Long, *Day by Day*, 1044–45; AGO, muster rolls, 6th U.S. Cavalry, Co. D, 1861–1865, RG 94, National Archives.

14. AGO, CMSR, 2nd Michigan Infantry, Thompson, Franklin, RG 94, National Archives; AGO, EB file 3132 C 1884, RG 94, National Archives; S. Emma E. Edmonds, *Nurse and Spy in the Union Army: Comprising the Adventures and Experiences of a Woman in Hospitals, Camps, and Battle-Fields* (Hartford: W. S. Williams, 1865), 141.

15. Long, *Day by Day*, 230–35, 1044; AGO, EB file 3132 C 1884, RG 94, National Archives.

16. E. S., letter, 28 Aug. 1862, in *Writing and Fighting the Civil War: Soldier Correspondence to the New York "Sunday Mercury,"* ed. William B. Styple (Kearny, N.J.: Belle Grove, 2000), 119; Altus Jewel, 77th New York Infantry, to his family, 10 Apr. 1863, private collection of Ron Maness, Richmond, Va.; Jay S. Hoar, *The South's Last Boys in Gray* (Bowling Green: Bowling Green State University Popular Press, 1986), 10–12; War Department Collection of Confederate Records, CMSR, 18th North Carolina Infantry, Gauss, Bryant, RG 109, National Archives.

17. Americus V. Taylor, Guy's Battery, Virginia, Entry 180, in *The Confederate States Roll of Honour* (Confederate Memorial Literary Society), Vol. 237, MOC.

18. Long, *Day by Day*, 257–58; "Female Soldiers," *Frank Leslie's Illustrated Newspaper*, 17 Dec. 1864; AGO, EB file 3132 C 1884, RG 94, National Archives.

19. Long, *Day by Day*, 267; Thomas L. Livermore, *Numbers and Losses in the Civil War in America* (Carlisle, Pa.: John Kallman, 1996), 92–93; Edmonds, *Nurse and Spy*, 290.

20. "Remarkable Incident of the War," Princeton (Indiana) *Clarion*, 14 Nov. 1863; Stephen B. Oates, *A Woman of Valor: Clara Barton and the Civil War* (New York: Free Press, 1994), 91–93; Altus Jewel to his family, 10 Apr. 1863, Maness Collection; Mark Nickerson, "Recollections of the Civil War by a High Private in the Front Ranks," memoir, USAMHI.

21. "A Woman in Regimentals," Detroit *Advertiser and Tribune*, 27 Aug. 1863; Lauren Cook Burgess, "Women in Combat: A New Front to an Old War," *Minerva's Bulletin Board* 5, no. 1 (1992), 2; "Another Female Soldier," St. Paul *Pioneer*, 19 Feb. 1865.

22. Long, *Day by Day*, 296; Rev. F. (Faunt Le Roy) Senour, *Morgan and His Captors* (Cincinnati: C. F. Vent & Co., 1865), 110; AGO, EB file 3132 C 1884, RG 94, National Archives; Edmonds, *Nurse and Spy*, 309, 311.

23. Samuel S. Partridge, 13th New York Infantry, to his brother, 10 Apr. 1863, Fredericksburg and Spotsylvania National Military Park, NPS; Barbara A. Smith, ed., *The Civil War Letters of Col. Elijah H. C. Cavins, 14th Indiana* (Owensboro, Ky.: Cook-McDowell, 1981), 132.

24. Long, *Day by Day*, 344–48; Livermore, *Numbers and Losses*, 98–99; Bradney Griffin, 1st New York Mounted Rifles, to his father, Dec. 1863, quoted in "The Myriad Ways in Which War Has Been Hell," New York *Times*, 12 Nov. 2000; J. Thomas Scharf, *History of Baltimore City and County* (Baltimore: Regional Publishing, 1971), 1:142.

25. "Many Women Served on Both Sides in Civil War," *National Tribune*, 17 Jan. 1935; "A Brave Bird and a Brave Girl," Washington *Daily Morning Chronicle*, 9 July 1864; Long, *Day by Day*, 378; Livermore, *Numbers and Losses*, 102–3; Gregory A. Coco, *On the Bloodstained Field* (Hollidaysburg, Pa.: Wheatfield, 1987), 40; Thomas Reed, 5th Michigan Infantry, to his parents, 20 Aug. 1863, Papers of Thomas Reed, BHLUM.

26. Glenn Tucker, *High Tide at Gettysburg* (New York: Bobbs-Merrill, 1958), 379; Long, *Day by Day*, 377.

27. Carol Reardon, *Pickett's Charge in History and Memory* (Chapel Hill: University of North Carolina Press, 1997), 28; burial report of Brig. Gen. William Hays, 17 July 1863, OR, Ser. 1, Vol. 27, Part 1, p. 378.

28. Long, *Day by Day*, 354, 378, 1112; Veterans Administration, pension application file C 2,573,248, Cashier, Albert D. J., RG 15, National Archives; *Selected Records of the War Department Relating to Confederate Prisoners of War, 1861–1865*, registers of prisoners at Gratiot and Myrtle Street Prisons (St. Louis) and Camp Morton (Indiana), M598, National Archives.

29. Long, *Day by Day*, 376–79, 391; Senour, *Morgan*, 110; Allan Keller, *Morgan's Raid* (Indianapolis: Bobbs-Merrill, 1961), 35.

30. Long, *Day by Day*, 411–12; Dyer, *Compendium*, 1224; Ira B. Gardner, *Recollections of a Boy Member of Co. I, Fourteenth Maine Volunteers, 1861–1865* (Lewiston, Maine: Lewiston Journal, 1902), 24.

31. Long, *Day by Day*, 437; "A Female Soldier . . . ," Indianapolis *Daily Sentinel*, 20 Aug. 1864; "Romantic History and Terrible Death of a Brooklyn Girl," Brooklyn *Daily Times*, 19 Feb. 1864.

32. Long, *Day by Day*, 446; Dyer, *Compendium*, 1369; Bradney Griffin to his father, Dec. 1863, quoted in "War Has Been Hell," New York *Times*, 12 Nov. 2000.

33. Dyer, *Compendium*, 1086–87; Long, *Day by Day*, 474, 1061–62.

34. Rosetta Wakeman to her family, 29 Mar. 1863, 27 Mar. 1864, and 14 Apr. 1864, in *An Uncommon Soldier: The Civil War Letters of Sarah Rosetta Wakeman, Alias Pvt. Lyons Wakeman*, ed. Lauren Cook Burgess (Pasadena, Md.: Minerva Center, 1994), 25, 67, 71.

35. Burgess, *Uncommon Soldier*, 77–82.

36. Long, *Day by Day*, 495, 849–50.

37. Long, *Day by Day*, 501–2, 529; "A Woman Soldier," *National Tribune*, 13 May 1886; "While a Working Party . . . ," Austin *Southern Intelligencer*, 21 June 1866; Sgt. Robert Ardry to his father, 3 June 1864, quoted in *A Woman's War: Southern Women, the Civil War, and the Confederate Legacy*, ed. Edward D. C. Campbell and Kym S. Rice (Richmond: Museum of the Confederacy; Charlottesville: University Press of Virginia, 1996), 92–93.

38. Long, *Day by Day*, 542; James L. Dunn to his wife, 22 July 1864, Correspondence of James L. Dunn (accession 8301), ALUVA; Judson Austin to his wife, 21 July 1864, Papers of Nina L. Ness (Judson L. Austin Letters), BHLUM.

39. Long, *Day by Day*, 579; John Ashton diary, 118th Ohio Infantry, 9 Oct. 1864, ACOHS; William Ludlow, "Atlanta Paper No. 3: The Battle of Allatoona, October 5, 1864 (Read April 2, 1891)," in *The Atlanta Papers*, ed. Sydney C. Kerksis, Lee A. Wallace Jr., and Margie R. Bearss (Dayton: Morningside Bookshop, 1980), 782.

40. Dyer, *Compendium*, 1086–87; Long, *Day by Day*, 610–15.

41. Veterans Administration, pension application file C 2,573,248, RG 15, National Archives; Rodney O. Davis, "Private Albert Cashier as Regarded by His/Her Comrades," *Journal of the Illinois State Historical Society* 72, no. 2 (1989): 108–12.

42. Dyer, *Compendium*, 1086–87; Long, *Day by Day*, 1018.

43. Dyer, *Compendium*, 1224; Long, *Day by Day*, 493, 503, 861.

44. Dyer, *Compendium*, 1224; Gardner, *Fourteenth Maine Volunteers*, 24; Long, *Day by Day*, 506, 549, 1080–81; James I. Robertson Jr., *Soldiers Blue and Gray* (Columbia: University of South Carolina Press, 1988), 119–20; "Pants versus Petticoats," Richmond *Daily Examiner*, 31 Oct. 1864.

45. Long, *Day by Day*, 492; Livermore, *Numbers and Losses*, 110–11.

46. Long, *Day by Day*, 494; Mary A. Gardner Holland, ed., *Our Army Nurses* (Boston: B. Wilkins, 1895), 341.

47. Long, *Day by Day*, 507–9; Henry Besancon diary, 104th New York Infantry, 26 May 1864, SCLDU; Jackson Crossley to "Sam," 29 May 1864, City Point National Historic Site, Petersburg National Battlefield Park, NPS; James E. Hall, *The Diary of a Confederate Soldier*, ed. Ruth Woods Dayton (Lewisburg, W.Va.: n.p., 1961), 106; *Confederate Prisoners of War*, general registers of prisoners at Point Lookout, Md., M598, National Archives.

48. Long, *Day by Day*, 514; Washington Roebling to his fiancée, 7 June 1864, SCARU; Anna Morris Holstein, *Three Years in Field Hospitals of the Army of the Potomac* (Philadelphia: J. B. Lippincott, 1867), 72.

49. Long, *Day by Day*, 522–28, 530, 547–48; "Body of a White Female Soldier Found in the Crater at Petersburg," Washington *Evening Star*, 7 Sep. 1866.

50. Long, *Day by Day*, 626, 636, 657, 1046; Veterans Administration, pension application file XC 2,651,527, Brown, Ivory, RG-15, National Archives; Dyer, *Compendium*, 1016; Sgt. Joseph O. Cross, 29th Connecticut Infantry (Colored), to his wife, 2 Mar. 1865 (MS 74274), CtHS.

51. Long, *Day by Day*, 631, 682, 1083; Nathaniel C. Hughes Jr., *Bentonville: The Final Battle of Sherman and Johnston* (Chapel Hill: University of North Carolina Press, 1996), 272; "Bentonville, Last Battle of the War Between the States," Fayetteville (North Carolina) *Observer*, 19 Mar. 1927.

52. Long, *Day by Day*, 663, 665–70; postwar editorial note (unnumbered page following 272), journal of Gilbert Thompson, 1861–1865, LC.

CHAPTER 2. "To Dress and Go as a Soldier": *Means and Motivations*

1. Martha Neville Lumpkin, ed., *"Dear Darling Louilie": Letters of Cordelia Lewis Scales to Louilie W. Irby during and after the War between the States* (Boulder, Colo.: n.p., 1955), 13; Mary D. Robertson, ed., *Lucy Breckinridge of Grove Hill: Journal of A Virginia Girl, 1862–1864* (Columbia: University of South Carolina Press, 1994), 140–41; Sarah Morgan Dawson, *A Confederate Girl's Diary*, ed. James I. Robertson (Bloomington: Indiana University Press, 1960), 25.

2. Anne M. Bond to General Lee, 25 Feb. 1862, Southern Women Collection, MOC; *Letters Received by the Confederate Secretary of War, 1861–1865*, file 692 B 1864, M437, National Archives.

3. "A Lady Drafted," New Orleans *Daily Picayune*, 3 Sep. 1863; Moore, *Rebellion Record*, 4:70; "Spunky Girl," (St. Louis) *Missouri Democrat*, 21 June 1861; Harold Holzer, ed., *Dear Mr. Lincoln: Letters to the President* (New York: Addison-Wesley, 1993), 270–71.

4. "Many Women Served," *National Tribune*, 17 Jan. 1935.

5. *OR*, Ser. 3, Vol. 1, Part 1, pp. 384–85, 721–22; George Worthington Adams, *Doctors in Blue: The Medical History of the Union Army in the Civil War* (New York: Henry Schuman, 1952), 13; Keller, *Morgan's Raid*, 35; Wiley, *Billy Yank*, 23.

6. Newspaper clipping from the [Mr. and Mrs. Richard] Halsted scrapbook, quoted in Sylvia Dannett, *She Rode with the Generals* (New York: Thomas Nelson & Sons, 1960), 52; Veterans Administration, pension application file C 2,573,248, RG 15, National Archives; AGO, CMSR, 95th Illinois Infantry, Cashier, Albert D. J., RG 94, National Archives; Orville Thomson, *Narrative of the Service of the Seventh Indiana Infantry in the War for the Union* (n.p: published by the author, n.d.), 42.

7. "Another Pennsylvania Amazon," Pittsburgh *Evening Chronicle*, 9 Oct. 1861; "Romance of the War," Detroit *Advertiser and Tribune*, 18 Nov. 1864; Judge Advocate General (Army), court-martial case file II 704, RG 153, National Archives; Lee Kennett, *Marching through Georgia* (New York: HarperCollins, 1995), 45.

8. David Craft, *History of the One Hundred Forty-First Regiment, Pennsylvania Volunteers, 1862–1865* (Towanda, Pa.: Reporter-Journal Printing, 1885), 101; Oates, *Woman of Valor*, 91–93.

9. Henry Schelling to "Friend William," 21 Nov. 1863, quoted in Thomas P. Lowry, *The Story the Soldiers Wouldn't Tell: Sex in the Civil War* (Mechanicsburg, Pa.: Stackpole Books, 1994), 35.

10. "Who Was She?" *National Tribune*, 10 July 1902.

11. "A Female Volunteer—Bound to Be a Soldier Boy," (Cincinnati) *Dollar Weekly Times*, 11 Aug. 1864.

12. For a comprehensive understanding of why men marched off to the Civil War, see Bell Wiley's classic studies *Billy Yank* and *Johnny Reb* and James McPherson's *For Cause and Comrades*. Although Wiley and McPherson do not specifically write about women soldiers, their conclusions about the motivations of the common soldier are as valid for female combatants as they are for males.

13. Ludlow, "Atlanta Paper No. 3," in Kerksis et. al., *Atlanta Papers*, 782.

14. Diaries and Letters of Abel Teple LaForge, MS transcription, 24 Feb. 1864, USAMHI; AGO, CMSR, 81st Ohio Infantry, Finnan, John, RG 94, National Archives; Veterans Administration, pension application file WC 620,476, Finnern, John, RG 15, National Archives; AGO, CMSR, 1st Maine Infantry [3 mos.], Brown, Ivory, RG 94, National Archives; AGO, CMSR, 31st Maine Infantry, Brown, Ivory, RG 94, National Archives; "Mrs. Mary A. Brown, 98, Who Fought in Civil War with Husband, Dies," Portland (Maine) *Herald*, 16 Mar. 1936.

15. William Boldt, great-grandson of Martha Parks Lindley, oral history recorded by DeAnne Blanton, July 1994–February 1995; AGO, muster rolls, 6th U.S. Cavalry, Co. D, 1861–1865, RG 94, National Archives; *Register of Enlistments in the U.S. Army, 1798–1914*,

entry for Smith, James, M233, National Archives; "Romance of an Ohio Woman Who Fought by Her Husband's Side as a Dare-devil Cavalry Man," Cleveland *Leader*, 7 Oct. 1896.

16. Confederate Records, CMSR, 18th North Carolina Infantry, Gauss, Bryant, RG 109, National Archives; Confederate Records, Chapter 10, Vol. 23, Register of Claims of Deceased Officers and Soldiers of North Carolina Organizations Filed in the Second Auditor's Office, 1861–1865, 53, RG 109, National Archives; Bureau of the Census, 1900 Census, Kenney household, Pierce County, Ga., RG 29, National Archives; "Democrat Employee's Mother was Soldier in Civil War," (Little Rock) *Arkansas Democrat*, 21 July 1925.

17. "Woman Who Fought in Civil War beside Hubby Dies, Aged Ninety-Two," Washington *Times*, 4 Oct. 1920; AGO, CMSR, 14th Vermont Infantry, Niles, Martin, RG 94, National Archives; "A Female Soldier," Detroit *Advertiser and Tribune*, 26 Feb. 1863; Gardner, *Fourteenth Maine Volunteers*, 24; "Romantic Story," Logansport (Indiana) *Journal*, 2 May 1863; *Personal Memoirs of Philip Henry Sheridan, General, United States Army*, new and enl. ed. (New York: D. Appleton, 1904), 1:255; "An Iowa Girl Discovered in Soldier's Costume," New York *Daily Tribune*, 1 Sep. 1861.

18. "Military . . . ," *Frank Leslie's Illustrated Newspaper*, 7 Mar. 1863; "Served by Her Lover's Side," Washington *Evening Star*, 7 July 1896; "Women Soldiering as Men," New York *Sun*, 10 Feb. 1901; "Broken Link," Monongahela (Pennsylvania) *Republican*, 12 Jan. 1865.

19. Mary Livermore, *My Story*, 114; "Attempt at Suicide by a Young Lady in Jersey City," New York *Herald*, 14 Oct. 1861.

20. "Women as Warriors" Washington *Sunday Star Magazine*, 8 Apr. 1906; Moore, *Rebellion Record*, 8:54–55; Oates, *Woman of Valor*, 91–93; Elizabeth Brown Pryor, *Clara Barton, Professional Angel* (Philadelphia: University of Pennsylvania Press, 1987), 99; Caleb H. Carlton, 89th Ohio Infantry, to his wife, 27 Aug. and 15 Sep. 1863, Caleb H. Carlton Papers [Family Correspondence], LC.

21. Bureau of the Census, 1860 Census, Haney household, town of Ellenboro, Grant County, Wis., RG 29, National Archives; "Another Female Soldier," St. Paul *Pioneer*, 19 Feb. 1865.

22. "Women Soldiering as Men," New York *Sun*, 10 Feb. 1901; "A Gallant Female Soldier—Romantic History," *Fincher's Trades' Review*, 26 Mar. 1864; "Many Women Served," *National Tribune*, 17 Jan. 1935; Bureau of the Census, 1860 Census, Wallace household, Lake Mills, Jefferson County, Wis., RG 29, National Archives; Ethel Hurn, *Wisconsin Women in the War between the States* (Madison: Wisconsin History Commission, 1911), 103; Hall, *Diary of a Confederate Soldier*, 106.

23. Elizabeth Cady Stanton, Susan B. Anthony, and Matilda Joslyn Gage, eds., *History of Woman Suffrage* (Rochester: Charles Mann, 1887), 2:19; U.S. Army Continental Commands, part 1, entry 5812 (Army of Virginia, two or more name citizen file), file for Margaret Catherine Murphy, RG 393, National Archives.

24. Confederate Records, CMSR, 26th North Carolina Infantry, Blalock, Mrs. S. M., RG 109, National Archives; AGO, Record and Pension Office (R&P) document file, 158003 and 1507832, filed with 184934, RG 94, National Archives; AGO, R&P record card 1507832, filed with 184934 Y1, RG 94, National Archives; Wiley, *Johnny Reb*, 334; Greg Mast, "'Sam' Blaylock, 26th North Carolina Troops," *Military Images* 11, no. 1 (1989): 10; William R. Trotter, *Bushwhackers! The Civil War in North Carolina: The Mountains* (Winston-Salem: J. F. Blair, 1988), 147–55.

25. "Another Pennsylvania Amazon," Pittsburgh *Evening Chronicle*, 9 Oct. 1861; AGO, CMSR, 126th Pennsylvania Infantry, Mayne, Frank, RG 94, National Archives; David Watson Rowe, *A Sketch of the 126th Regiment Pennsylvania Volunteers* (Chambersburg, Pa.: Cook & Hays, 1869), 10–11; "Eventful History of a Soldier Woman," *Fincher's Trades' Review*, 10 Oct. 1863.

26. AGO, CMSR, 31st Maine Infantry, Brown, Ivory, RG 94, National Archives; Veterans Administration, pension application file XC 2,651,527, Brown, Ivory, RG 15, National Archives; Elizabeth Avery Meriwether, *Recollections of 92 Years: 1824–1916* (Nashville: Tennessee Historical Commission, 1958), 160–61.

27. "Bentonville," Fayetteville (North Carolina) *Observer*, 19 Mar. 1927.

28. "A Feminine Soldier," (St. Louis) *Missouri Democrat*, 4 May 1863.

29. E. A. W. Burbage to Mrs. Kate Huffman, 27 Dec. 1862, Mary Ann Clark Collection, KHS.

30. E. A. W. Burbage to Mrs. Kate Huffman, 27 Dec. 1862, and Mary Ann Clark to Mrs. Huffman and Tucker, undated, Mary Ann Clark Collection, KHS.

31. "Women Soldiering as Men," New York *Sun*, 10 Feb. 1901; Mary Elizabeth Massey, *Women in the Civil War* (Lincoln: University of Nebraska Press, 1994), 80; "Soldier Girl, Second Minnesota," Roxbury (Massachusetts) *City Gazette*, 14 May 1863; Senour, *Morgan*, 110; Keller, *Morgan's Raid*, 35; "Johnny: Another Girl Who Was Discovered Wearing the Blue," *National Tribune*, 25 Sep. 1884.

32. "Romantic History," Brooklyn *Daily Times*, 19 Feb. 1864; Frank Moore, *Women of the War* (Hartford: S. S. Scranton, 1866), 529–31; Michael A. Bellesiles, ed., *Lethal Imagination: Violence and Brutality in American History* (New York: New York University Press, 1999), 193.

33. Maj. Joseph Darr Jr. to Col. W. Hoffman, commissary general of prisoners, 24 Dec. 1862, *OR*, Ser. 2, Vol. 5, pp. 121–22; AGO, CMSR, 23rd Kentucky Infantry, Fitzallen, Henry, RG 94, National Archives; "A Female Soldier in Custody—An Eventful Career," Wheeling (West Virginia) *Daily Intelligencer*, 25 Dec. 1862; Judge Advocate General (Army), court-martial case file II 704, RG 153, National Archives.

34. V. A. White to Mrs. Jane Trail, 6 Feb. 1866, private collection of Thomas and Beverly Lowry, Woodbridge, Va.

35. Rosetta Wakeman to her family, 24 Nov. 1862, in Burgess, *Uncommon Soldier*, 18; AGO, CMSR, 153rd New York Infantry, Wakeman, Lyons, RG 94, National Archives; Burgess, *Uncommon Soldier*, 8–10.

36. "Iowa Girl," New York *Daily Tribune*, 1 Sep. 1861.

37. E. A. W. Burbage to Mrs. Kate Huffman, 27 Dec. 1862, Mary Ann Clark Collection, KHS; "A Confederate Romance—History of Mrs. Anna Clark," Cairo (Illinois) *City Weekly Gazette*, 25 Dec. 1862; "Women Soldiering as Men," New York *Sun*, 10 Feb. 1901; "Female Soldier: A Romantic History," Worcester (Massachusetts) *Aegis and Transcript*, 9 May 1863; "A Female Volunteer," Owensboro (Kentucky) *Monitor*, 20 Aug. 1862; "Female Recruits," Detroit *Free Press*, 3 June 1864.

38. Dannett, *She Rode with the Generals*, 19; "Female Volunteer," (Cincinnati) *Dollar Weekly Times*, 11 Aug. 1864; Bureau of the Census, 1860 Census, entry for Adams household, town of Danville, Pittsylvania County, Va., RG 29, National Archives.

39. "Lizzie Compton, the Soldier Girl," Washington *Daily Morning Chronicle*, 24 Feb.

1864; Meriwether, *Recollections of 92 Years*, 102–5; Confederate Records, Chapter 10, Vol. 23, Register of Claims of Deceased Officers and Soldiers of North Carolina Organizations Filed in the Second Auditor's Office, 1861–1865, 53, RG 109, National Archives; Veterans Administration, pension application file WC 620,475, RG 15, National Archives; *Register of Enlistments*, entry for Smith, James, M233, National Archives.

40. Rosetta Wakeman to her parents, 5 Aug. 1863, in Burgess, *Uncommon Soldier*, 42; William J. Miller, *The Training of an Army: Camp Curtin and the North's Civil War* (Shippensburg, Pa.: White Mane, 1990), 60–61; "Female Soldiers," New York *Times*, 26 Aug. 1864; Hurn, *Wisconsin Women*, 103; Mr. Culver to Ethel Hurn, undated, Wisconsin History Commission Papers, Ethel A. Hurn Collection, WSHSA.

41. Velazquez, *Woman in Battle*, 154; "A Romantic Girl," (St. Louis) *Missouri Democrat*, 22 Aug. 1861; Edmonds, *Nurse and Spy*, 121; Davis, "Private Albert Cashier," 108–12.

42. Burgess, *Uncommon Soldier*, 1; AGO, CMSR, 153rd New York Infantry, Wakeman, Lyons, RG 94, National Archives; "Female Soldiers," *Army and Navy Register*, 11 Feb. 1882.

43. Livermore, *My Story*, 493; Veterans Administration, pension application file C 2,573,248, RG 15, National Archives; Dannett, *She Rode with the Generals*, 11–35; "A Remarkable Career," Fort Scott (Kansas) *Weekly Monitor*, 17 Jan. 1884.

44. "Romance of an Ohio Woman," Cleveland *Leader*, 7 Oct. 1896. For an extensive discussion of the largely pre-twentieth-century phenomenon of women passing as men, see Wheelwright, *Amazons and Military Maids*.

45. AGO, CMSR, 1st Kentucky Infantry, Thompson, John, RG 94, National Archives; "A Female Spy," Detroit *Free Press*, 2 Aug. 1861.

46. Mary Ann Clark to Mrs. Huffman and Tucker, undated, Mary Ann Clark Collection, KHS; Robert Hodges Jr. to his father, 7 Aug. 1863, Letters of Robert Hodges, G&THC; Velazquez, *Woman in Battle*, 13; Examination of Mary Ann Pitman by Col. J. P. Sanderson, Provost Marshal General, Dept. of the Missouri, 20 June 1864, *OR*, Ser. 2, Vol. 7, pp. 345–55; *Papers Relating to Individual Civilians*, file for Pitman, Mary A., M345, National Archives.

47. Edmonds, *Nurse and Spy*, 19; "The Story of a Remarkable Life," Detroit *Post and Tribune*, 26 May 1883.

48. "Maine's Only Woman to Shoulder a Musket in the Civil War . . . ," Portland (Maine) *Sunday Telegram*, 14 Sep. 1930; "A Female Teamster," (St. Louis) *Missouri Democrat*, 25 Feb. 1864; Craft, *One Hundred Forty-First Regiment*, 102.

49. "A Young Lady Eager to be a Soldier," (St. Louis) *Missouri Democrat*, 3 Dec. 1863.

50. George C. Eggleston, *Southern Soldier Stories* (1898; reprint, Fairfax, Va.: SCS Publications, 1998), 75–81.

51. "Another Feminine Volunteer," Pittsburgh *Gazette*, 21 Sep. 1861; "A Female Volunteer," (Milledgeville, Georgia) *Southern Federal Union*, 19 Aug. 1862; "Female Volunteer," (Cincinnati) *Dollar Weekly Times*, 11 Aug. 1864.

52. Dannett, *She Rode with the Generals*, 24–25.

53. Velazquez, *Woman in Battle*, 34–37.

54. Rosetta Wakeman to her father, undated, and Rosetta Wakeman to her father, 23 Dec. 1862, in Burgess, *Uncommon Soldier*, 22, 37. For discussions of why soldiers stayed in the army, see McPherson, *For Cause and Comrades*, and Hess, *The Union Soldier in Battle*, who argue that Civil War soldiers developed a strong and lasting attachment to their flag and to their comrades. Women soldiers exhibited the very same devotion.

55. "Soldier Girl, Second Minnesota," Roxbury (Massachusetts) *City Gazette,* 14 May 1863; Rowe, *Sketch of the 126th,* 37; "A Female Soldier," Cincinnati *Daily Commercial,* 4 Dec. 1863; "Romantic Story," Logansport (Indiana) *Journal,* 2 May 1863.

56. AGO, muster rolls, 6th U.S. Cavalry, Co. D, 1861–1865, RG 94, National Archives; AGO, CMSR, 6th Ohio Cavalry, Lindley, William D., RG 94, National Archives; Veterans Administration, pension application file WC 483,501, Lindley, William, RG 15, National Archives; Boldt oral history.

57. *Confederate Veteran* 15, no. 5 (1907): 230; "Women Soldiering as Men," New York *Sun,* 10 Feb. 1901; "Military," *Frank Leslie's Illustrated Newspaper,* 7 Mar. 1863; G. Wayne King, "Death Camp at Florence," *Civil War Times Illustrated* 12, no. 9 (1974): 38; Samuel Creelman, *Collections of a Coffee Cooler* (Pittsburgh: Pittsburgh Photoengraving, 1890), 40–41.

58. "Women Soldiering as Men," New York *Sun,* 10 Feb. 1901; "Gallant Female Soldier," *Fincher's Trades' Review,* 26 Mar. 1864; "Many Women Served," *National Tribune,* 17 Jan. 1935; Bureau of the Census, 1860 Census, Haney household, town of Ellenboro, Grant County, Wis.; AGO, CMSR, 7th Wisconsin Infantry, Haney, John F., RG 94, National Archives; "A Female Soldier," Chicago *Evening Journal,* 13 Feb. 1865.

59. Edmonds, *Nurse and Spy,* 20–21.

CHAPTER 3. "A Fine Looking Soldier": *Life in the Ranks*

1. Wiley, *Billy Yank,* 126–27.

2. Beatriz R. Olsen, "Exercise-Induced Amenorrhea," *American Family Physician* (Feb. 1989): 213, 215–16; "Dietary Amenorrhoea," *British Medical Journal* (Feb. 1978): 321; G. Tolis and E. Diamanti, "Distress Amenorrhea," *Annals of the New York Academy of Science* (1996): 660–61.

3. "Women in the Confederate Ranks," New Orleans *Daily Picayune,* 25 Jan. 1863.

4. Herman Weiss to his wife, 28 Mar. 1865, in "An Immigrant Goes to War: The Civil War Correspondence of Herman and Adeline Weiss," ed. Harlan B. Phillips, in *History 4: A Meridien Periodical* (New York: Word Publishing, 1961), 145.

5. Veterans Administration, pension application file C 2,573,248, RG 15, National Archives.

6. Herman Weiss to his wife, 28 Mar. 1865, in Phillips, "An Immigrant Goes to War," 145.

7. Velazquez, *Woman in Battle,* 58.

8. Wayne C. Temple, ed., *The Civil War Letters of Henry C. Bear: A Soldier in the 116th Illinois Volunteer Infantry* (Harrogate, Tenn.: Lincoln Memorial University Press, 1961), 6; Veterans Administration, pension application file C 2,573,248, RG 15, National Archives; "Woman May Have Fought," Kansas City *Star,* 24 May 1929; Meriwether, *Recollections of 92 Years,* 104; "An Amazon," (St. Louis) *Missouri Democrat,* 30 May 1861; "Eventful History," Princeton (Indiana) *Clarion,* 10 Oct. 1863.

9. William Marvel, *Burnside* (Chapel Hill: University of North Carolina Press, 1991), 241; Sheridan, *Personal Memoirs,* 1:255; Daniel Larned to his sister, 14–16 May 1863, Daniel Reed Larned Correspondence, Vol. 3, LC.

10. Maj. Joseph Darr to Col. W. Hoffman, commissary general of prisoners, 24 Dec. 1862, *OR,* Ser. 2, Vol. 5, pp. 121–22; "Romantic Incident in Camp Life," Cincinnati *Daily Commercial,* 9 Dec. 1861.

11. Griffin Frost, *Camp and Prison Journal* (Iowa City: Press of the Camp Pope Bookshop, 1994), 193, 195; "Feminine Soldier," (St. Louis) *Missouri Democrat*, 4 May 1863.

12. John Laffin, *Women in Battle* (London: Abelard-Schuman, 1967), 12; "A Pennsylvania Girl in the Army," Baltimore *American and Commercial Advertiser*, 5 May 1863; Sheridan, *Personal Memoirs*, 255.

13. Judge Advocate General (Army), court-martial case file II 704, RG 153, National Archives; Patricia L. Faust, ed., *Encyclopedia of the Civil War* (New York: HarperPerennial, 1991), 160–61; H. H. Cunningham, *Doctors in Gray: The Confederate Medical Service* (Baton Rouge: Louisiana State University Press, 1993), 165; Wiley, *Billy Yank*, 296–302; Keller, *Morgan's Raid*, 35.

14. Laura Virginia Hale, *Four Valiant Years in the Lower Shenandoah Valley, 1861–1865* (Strasburg, Va.: Shenandoah Publishing House, 1968), 180; "A Brave Bird," Washington *Daily Morning Chronicle*, 9 July 1864; Holland, *Our Army Nurses*, 463.

15. "Female Soldiers," New York *Times*, 26 Aug. 1864; Annie Wittenmyer, *Under the Guns: A Woman's Reminiscences of the Civil War* (Boston: E. B. Stillings, 1895), 20; Mast, "'Sam' Blaylock," 10.

16. "Lizzie Compton," Washington *Daily Morning Chronicle*, 24 Feb. 1864; Keller, *Morgan's Raid*, 35; "Johnny: Another Girl," *National Tribune*, 25 Sep. 1884; Massey, *Women in the Civil War*, 80; Eggleston, *Southern Soldier Stories*, 79.

17. "Another Female Soldier," St. Paul *Pioneer*, 19 Feb. 1865; "Arrival Extraordinary," 16 Feb. 1865 (Platteville, Wisconsin) *Grant County Witness*; "The Platteville *Witness* . . . ," 30 Mar. 1865 (Platteville, Wisconsin) *Grant County Witness*; Mr. Culver to Ethel Hurn, undated, Ethel A. Hurn Collection, WSHSA; Hurn, *Wisconsin Women*, 103.

18. "Adventures of a Long Island Girl," Washington *Daily Morning Chronicle*, 13 Aug. 1864; "A Female Spy," Detroit *Free Press*, 2 Aug. 1861; Albert D. Richardson, *The Secret Service, the Field, the Dungeon, and the Escape* (Hartford: American Publishing, 1865), 175.

19. Veterans Administration, pension application file C 2,573,248, RG 15, National Archives; AGO, CMSR, 95th Illinois Infantry, Cashier, Albert D. J., RG 94, National Archives.

20. AGO, EB file 3132 C 1884, RG 94, National Archives; Edmonds, *Nurse and Spy*, 99.

21. "Eventful History," *Fincher's Trades' Review*, 10 Oct. 1863; "An Amazon," St. Paul *Pioneer*, 26 May 1863; Fremantle, *Three Months*, 172; Sgt. Hiram Holt to his wife, as quoted in Daniel, *Army of Tennessee*, 153–54.

22. "Romantic Girl," (St. Louis) *Missouri Democrat*, 22 Aug. 1861; "Degradation," (St. Louis) *Missouri Democrat*, 3 Oct. 1861; "A Woman Formerly Extensively Known . . . ," Memphis *Bulletin*, 19 Dec. 1862; "Romantic Story," Logansport (Indiana) *Journal*, 2 May 1863; U.S. Army Continental Commands, part 1, entry 5812, file for Margaret Catherine Murphy, RG 393, National Archives; Velazquez, *Woman in Battle*, 70.

23. William J. Miller, *Training of an Army*, 60; *Confederate Veteran* 15, no. 5 (1907): 230; Meriwether, *Recollections of 92 Years*, 104; Velazquez, *Woman in Battle*, 58; Boldt oral history; "Mrs. Mary A. Brown," Portland (Maine) *Sunday Telegram*, 16 Mar. 1936.

24. Rosetta Wakeman to her father, 20 Jan. 1864, in Burgess, *An Uncommon Soldier*, 60–61.

25. Capt. Daniel Larned to his sister, 14–16 May 1863, Daniel Reed Larned Correspondence, Vol. 3, LC; "Women in the Confederate Ranks," New Orleans *Daily Picayune*, 25 Jan. 1863; Juanita Leisch, "The Look of the Ladies," *Military Images* 21, no. 6 (2000): 11.

26. Velazquez, *Woman in Battle*, 75; George Morey to Albert Cashier, 3 May 1863, Mr. and Mrs. Morey to Albert Cashier, 6 Sep. 1863, and Mrs. Morey to Albert Cashier, 18 June 1865, personal collection of Frank and Velma Crawford, Caledonia, Ill; "Remarkable Career," Fort Scott (Kansas) *Weekly Monitor*, 17 Jan. 1884.

27. Altus H. Jewell to his family, 10 Apr. 1863, Maness Collection.

28. Jacob Eugene Duryee, "My Three Regiments," unpublished memoir, in private possession.

29. Meriwether, *Recollections of 92 Years*, 102–5; Richardson, *Secret Service*, 175; "A Female Spy," Detroit *Free Press*, 2 Aug. 1861; Hoar, *South's Last Boys*, 10–12; Veterans Administration, pension application file C 2,573,248, RG 15, National Archives.

30. "An Amazon," St. Paul *Pioneer*, 26 May 1863; "Women Soldiering as Men," New York *Sun*, 10 Feb. 1901; Boldt oral history; Dannett, *She Rode with the Generals*, 21.

31. Velazquez, *Woman in Battle*, 70.

32. Lewis G. Schmidt, *A Civil War History of the 47th Regiment Pennsylvania Veteran Volunteers* (Allentown, Pa.: Lewis G. Schmidt, 1986), 29; "Lizzie Compton," Washington *Daily Morning Chronicle*, 24 Feb. 1864; AGO, CMSR, 95th Illinois Infantry, Cashier, Albert D. J., RG 94, National Archives; "Served as a Man," *National Tribune*, 25 Nov. 1915; Burgess, *Uncommon Soldier*, 8–10.

33. Herman Weiss to his wife, 28 Mar. 1865, in Phillips, "An Immigrant Goes to War," 145; Hurn, *Wisconsin Women*, 103; Veterans Administration, pension application file C 2,573,248, RG 15, National Archives; AGO, EB file 3132 C 1884, RG 94, National Archives; Velazquez, *Woman in Battle*, 58.

34. "A Brave Bird," Washington *Daily Morning Chronicle*, 9 July 1864; "Lizzie Compton," Washington *Daily Morning Chronicle*, 24 Feb. 1864.

35. Velazquez, *Woman in Battle*, 59.

36. Jonathan Katz, *Gay American History: Lesbians and Gay Men in the U.S.A.* (New York: Thomas Y. Crowell, 1976), 210; Herman Weiss to his wife, 28 Mar. 1865, in Phillips, "An Immigrant Goes to War," 145; Dannett, *She Rode with the Generals*, 267–69.

37. Letters of Rosetta Wakeman to her parents, 29 Mar. 1863 and 9 Oct. 1863, in Burgess, *Uncommon Soldier*, 25, 27, 48; AGO, CMSR, 153rd New York Infantry, Wakeman, Lyons, RG 94, National Archives.

38. "An Amazon," St. Paul *Pioneer*, 26 May 1863; "Eventful History," Princeton (Indiana) *Clarion*, 10 Oct. 1863; "Romantic Incident," Cincinnati *Daily Commercial*, 9 Dec. 1861; "Lizzie Compton," Washington *Daily Morning Chronicle*, 24 Feb. 1864.

39. Jane Ellen Schultz, "Women at the Front: Gender and Genre in Literature of the American Civil War" (Ph.D. diss., University of Michigan, 1988), 279; "Platteville *Witness*," (Platteville, Wisconsin) *Grant County Witness*, 30 Mar. 1865; Daniel White, 144th New York Infantry, to his wife, 9 Apr. 1865, in *Dear Wife: The Civil War Letters of a Private Soldier*, ed. Jack C. Davis (Louisville: Sulgrave, 1991), 194; Col. John Q. Wilds, 24th Iowa Infantry, to his wife, 13 Dec. 1862, Donovan Collection.

40. Capt. Alonzo D. Pratt, provost marshal, Military District of Harper's Ferry, to Lt. Col. John Wooley, provost marshal, Middle Department, 12 Sept. 1864, Mss2, P8882, al., VHS; Sheridan, *Personal Memoirs*, 1:255; Marvel, *Burnside*, 241; "Romantic Story," Logansport (Indiana) *Journal*, 2 May 1863; "Gleanings," Chicago *Evening Journal*, 18 Feb. 1865; "Women Soldiering as Men," New York *Sun*, 10 Feb. 1901; "A Romantic History," New

Orleans *Daily Picayune*, 24 May 1863; U.S. Army Continental Commands, Part 1, entry 2517 (Military Division of the Mississippi, letters sent by the Provost Marshal General, 1864–1865, Vol. 21), Capt. S. A. Stockdale, Military Division of the Mississippi, Office of the Provost Marshal General, to Capt. Hunter Brooke, provost marshal, Nashville, Tenn., 16 Nov. 1864, RG 393, National Archives.

41. Jerome Robbins diary, 11 Nov. 1861, 16 Nov. 1861, 19 Nov. 1861, 22 and 23 Dec. 1861, 20 Dec. 1862, and 4 Apr. 1863, Michigan Historical Collections, BHLUM.

42. Amos Morton to Albert D. J. Cashier, 2 Oct. 1864 and 29 Aug. 1865, John D. Caswell to "friend Albert," 11 July 1863, Cashier to Samuel Pepper, 30 Mar. 1866 and 4 Apr. 1866, and J. H. Morey to Cashier, 10 July 1864, Crawford Collection; Veterans Administration, pension application file C 2,573,248, RG 15, National Archives; Mary Catherine Lannon, "Albert D. J. Cashier and the Ninety-Fifth Illinois Infantry (1844–1915)" (master's thesis, Illinois State University, 1969), 85–87.

43. Mrs. Morey to Albert Cashier, 2 June 1863, 20 Dec. 1863, 10 July 1864, 8 Oct. 1864, 27 Dec. 1864, and 2 Apr. 1865, Michael B. Murphy to Cashier, 20 Oct. 1863 and 25 June 1863, and Lauren Hamlin to "Friend Albert," 12 July 1862, Crawford Collection.

44. Rosetta Wakeman to her parents, 13 Oct. 1863, in Burgess, *Uncommon Soldier*, 49.

45. Miller, *Training of an Army*, 60; "Women in the War," 273; AGO, EB file 3132 C 1884,RG 94, National Archives; Wheelwright, *Amazons and Military Maids*, 62, 137.

Chapter 4. "Fairly Earned Her Epaulettes": *Women Soldiers in the Military Service*

1. Hoar, *South's Last Boys*, 10–12.

2. AGO, CMSR, 153rd New York Infantry, Wakeman, Lyons, RG 94, National Archives; Burgess, *Uncommon Soldier*, 10–11; U.S. Army Continental Commands, part 4, entry 2072 (Carroll Prison guard reports, Vol. 329), RG 393, National Archives; *Confederate Veteran* 15, no. 5 (1907): 230.

3. Hurn, *Wisconsin Women*, 103; Mr. Culver to Ethel Hurn, undated, Ethel A. Hurn Collection, WSHSA; Eggleston, *Southern Soldier Stories*, 75–81.

4. "Female Soldier," Worcester (Massachusetts) *Aegis and Transcript*, 9 May 1863.

5. Herschel Gower, ed., *The Beersheba Springs Diaries of L. Virginia French, 1863–1864* (Nashville: East Tennessee Historical Society, 1986), 30; Sheridan, *Personal Memoirs*, 1:255; "Romantic Story," Logansport (Indiana) *Journal*, 2 May 1863.

6. War Department, *Revised Regulations for the Army of the United States, 1861* (Philadelphia: J. G. L. Brown, 1861), 284; Confederate War Department, *Regulations for the Army of the Confederate States, 1863* (Richmond: J. W. Randolph, 1863), 237; AGO, CMSR, 17th Ohio Infantry, Deming, Frank, RG 94, National Archives; AGO, muster rolls, 6th U.S. Cavalry, Co. D, 1861–1865, RG 94, National Archives; "Johnny: Another Girl," *National Tribune*, 25 Sep. 1884.

7. Wheelock, *Boys in White*, 114–15; Kennett, *Marching through Georgia*, 45.

8. Charlotte Palmer Seeley, comp., *American Women and the U.S. Armed Forces: A Guide to the Records of Military Agencies in the National Archives Relating to American Women*, rev. Virginia Cardwell Purdy and Robert Gruber (Washington: National Archives and Records Administration, 1992), ix; Massey, *Women in the Civil War*, 52.

9. "Female Soldier," Washington *Daily Morning Chronicle*, 16 Mar. 1864; Sheridan, *Personal Memoirs*, 1:255; Daniel Reed Larned to his sister, 14–16 May 1863, Daniel Reed Larned Correspondence, Vol. 3, LC.

10. Postwar editorial note (unnumbered page following 272), journal of Gilbert Thompson, 1861–1865, LC; "A Woman in Regimentals," Detroit *Advertiser and Tribune*, 27 Aug. 1863; Craft, *One Hundred Forty-First Regiment*, 101–2; "Hid Sex in the Army," Washington *Post*, 27 Jan. 1901.

11. "Pennsylvania Girl," Baltimore *American and Commercial Advertiser*, 5 May 1863; "Female Recruits," Detroit *Free Press*, 3 June 1864.

12. Julia Wilbur diary, 4 Apr. 1865, ALLH, microfilm.

13. AGO, EB file 3132 C 1884, RG 94, National Archives; AGO, CMSR, 2nd Michigan Infantry, Thompson, Franklin, RG 94, National Archives; Edmonds, *Nurse and Spy*, 58, 180.

14. AGO, CMSR, 2nd Michigan Infantry, Thompson, Franklin, RG 94, National Archives; AGO, EB file 3132 C 1884, RG 94, National Archives; Stephen Sears, *To the Gates of Richmond: The Peninsula Campaign* (New York: Ticknor & Fields, 1992), 103–4; Edmonds, *Nurse and Spy*, 101–311.

15. Examination of Mary Ann Pitman by Col. J. P. Sanderson, provost marshal general, Dept. of the Missouri, 20 June 1864, *OR*, Ser. 2, Vol. 7, pp. 345–55; *Papers Relating to Individual Civilians*, file for Pitman, Mary A., M345, National Archives; DeFontaine, *Marginalia*, 65–66; Velazquez, *Woman in Battle*, 70–75.

16. "Mrs. Mary De Caulp," New Orleans *Daily Picayune*, 5 Jan. 1867; Velazquez, *Woman in Battle*, 120–220.

17. Pennsylvania Broadsides: Advertisement for *The Woman in Battle*, 1876, Broadside Collection, SCLDU; Confederate Records, Chapter 9, Vol. 90, Applications for Appointments in Military Service, Confederate States, no. 1589, RG 109, National Archives; Confederate Records, Chapter 1, Vol. 56, Register of Letters Received, Adjutant and Inspector General's Office, April–July 1863, file 1145 W 1863, RG 109, National Archives; "The Female Lieutenant," Richmond *Daily Examiner*, 15 Sept. 1863.

18. "Arrest of a Female in Richmond," Louisville *Daily Journal*, 9 Oct. 1861; Velazquez, *Woman in Battle*, 95.

19. Velazquez, *Woman in Battle*, 220.

20. Examination of Mary Ann Pitman by Col. J. P. Sanderson, 20 June 1864, *OR*, Ser. 2, Vol. 7, pp. 345–55.

21. Robert Selph Henry, *Nathan Bedford Forrest: First with the Most* (New York: Konecky & Konecky, 1992), 32; examination of Mary Ann Pitman, 20 June 1864, *OR*, Ser. 2, Vol. 7, pp. 345–55; *Papers Relating to Individual Civilians*, file for Pitman, Mary A., M345, National Archives.

22. Provost Marshal General's Bureau (Civil War), entry 36 (correspondence, reports, appointments, and other records relating to individual scouts, guides, spies and detectives), file for Pitman, Mary M.[*sic*], RG 110, National Archives; examination of Mary Ann Pitman, 20 June 1864, *OR*, Ser. 2, Vol. 7, pp. 345–55; *Papers Relating to Individual Civilians*, file for Pitman, Mary A., M345, National Archives.

23. "Female Soldier," Worcester (Massachusetts) *Aegis and Transcript*, 9 May 1863; "Female Soldier," Washington *Daily Morning Chronicle*, 16 Mar. 1864; "Hid Sex in the Army," Washington *Post*, 27 Jan. 1901; Livermore, *My Story*, 119; "Another Female Soldier," St. Paul *Pioneer*, 19 Feb. 1865.

24. "Female Soldiers," New York *Times*, 26 Aug. 1864; "A Brave Bird," Washington *Daily Morning Chronicle*, 9 July 1864; "Fanny Harris," Washington *Daily Morning Chronicle*, 5 Oct. 1864; Wiley, *Billy Yank*, 296–302.

25. H. N. Hunt, 64th New York Infantry, to his wife, 27 Apr. 1863, Fredericksburg and Spotsylvania National Military Park, NPS; Smith, *Letters of Col. Elijah H. C. Cavins*, 132; "From the 75th Regiment," Logansport (Indiana) *Journal*, 9 May 1863; Scharf, *History of Baltimore*, 1:142; George Sargent diary, 6 June 1864, in *For Our Beloved Country: American War Diaries from the Revolution to the Persian Gulf*, ed. Morgan Speer and Greg Nichalson (New York: Atlantic Monthly Press, 1994), 161; "Female Soldiers," *Army and Navy Register*, 11 Feb. 1882; AGO, muster rolls, 6th U.S. Cavalry, Co. D, 1861–1865, RG 94, National Archives; AGO, CMSR, 1st Kansas Infantry, Luther, Alfred J., and CMSR, 126th Pennsylvania Infantry, Mayne, Frank, RG 94, National Archives; Rowe, *Sketch of the 126th*, 11.

26. Discharge paper of Sgt. Jennie R. Gregg, personal collection of Lee Coutts, Cedarburg, Wis.

27. "Female Soldiers," *Frank Leslie's Illustrated Newspaper*, 17 Dec. 1864.

28. "An Amazon," (St. Louis) *Missouri Democrat*, 30 May 1861; "A Romantic History," New Orleans *Daily Picayune*, 24 May 1863; Nelson Purdum diary, 33rd Ohio Infantry, 24 May 1863, Vol. 938, OHS.

29. Robert Hodges, 24th Texas Cavalry, to his father, 7 Aug. 1863, Letters of Robert Hodges, H. W. Darst Papers, G&THC; Amanda Virginia Edmonds diary, 18 June 1862, VHS.

30. *Confederate Veteran* 15, no. 5 (1907): 230; FitzGerald Ross, *Cities and Camps of the Confederate States*, ed. Richard B. Harwell (Urbana: University of Illinois Press, 1958), 116.

31. "A Female Captain," Lynchburg *Virginian*, 6 Oct. 1864; "Female Rebel Soldiers," Washington *Daily Morning Chronicle*, 30 Mar. 1865.

32. Rosetta Wakeman to her parents, undated, in Burgess, *Uncommon Soldier*, 44.

33. "Eventful History," *Fincher's Trades' Review*, 10 Oct. 1863; "Platteville *Witness*," (Platteville, Wisconsin) *Grant County Witness*, 30 Mar. 1865.

34. Wittenmyer, *Under the Guns*, 17–20; "Soldier Girl, Second Minnesota," Roxbury (Massachusetts) *City Gazette*, 14 May 1863; AGO, EB File 3132 C 1884, RG 94, National Archives.

35. Gardner, *Fourteenth Maine Volunteers*, 24; Veterans Administration, pension application file C 2,573,248, RG 15, National Archives.

36. "Romance of an Ohio Woman," Cleveland *Leader*, 7 Oct. 1896.

37. Rosetta Wakeman to her parents, 15 Jan. 1863 and 5 Aug. 1863, in Burgess, *Uncommon Soldier*, 22, 42.

38. "Pants versus Petticoats," Richmond *Daily Examiner*, 31 Oct. 1864; Louis Leon, *Diary of a Tar Heel Confederate Soldier* (Charlotte, N.C.: Stone Publishing, 1913), 66.

CHAPTER 5. "Why They Detained Her I Can't Imagine": *The Prisoner of War Experience*

1. For an extensive history of Civil War prisons, see Lonnie R. Speer, *Portals to Hell: Military Prisons of the Civil War* (Mechanicsburg, Pa.: Stackpole Books, 1997).

2. E. S., letter, 28 Aug. 1862, in Styple, *Writing and Fighting*, 119; Corp. Franklin

Twitchell to his brother, 3 Dec. 1862, in "F. S. Twitchell's Letter Describing a Female Guerrilla," ed. Chris Peña, *Louisiana History* 39 (1998): 89.

3. Edwin C. Fishel, *The Secret War for the Union: The Untold Story of Military Intelligence in the Civil War* (Boston: Houghton-Mifflin, 1996), 253–54.

4. "Hid Sex in the Army," Washington *Post*, 27 Jan. 1901; AGO document file record cards, 1,502,399, RG 94, National Archives; Wittenmyer, *Under the Guns*, 17–20; Confederate Records, Letter Sent, Commander of the Troops at Atlanta, July 1863–May 1864, Chap. 2, Vol. 186, p. 116, RG 109, National Archives; Moore, *Rebellion Record*, 8:37–38.

5. Speer, *Portals to Hell*, 92.

6. John L. Ransom, *Andersonville Diary, Escape, and List of Dead* . . . (Auburn, N.Y.: John L. Ransom, 1881), 20–21.

7. F. F. Cavada, *Libby Life: Experiences of a Prisoner of War in Richmond, Virginia, 1863–1864* (Lanham, Md.: University Press of America, 1985), 145.

8. Arch Fredric Blakey, *General John H. Winder, C.S.A.* (Gainesville: University of Florida Press, 1990), 4, 190; King, "Death Camp at Florence," 38; Creelman, *Coffee Cooler*, 40–41.

9. Blakey, *John H. Winder*, 4; King, "Death Camp at Florence," 35–38; Creelman, *Coffee Cooler*, 40–41; "Stockade History Holds Stories of Love, Sorrow," Florence (South Carolina) *Morning News*, 8 Feb. 1959.

10. "A Woman Soldier of the North," New York *Times*, 27 May 1934.

11. Heros von Borcke, *Memoirs of the Confederate War for Independence* (1865–66; reprint, Philadelphia: Lippincott, 1867), 91–92.

12. Nelson Purdum diary, 33rd Ohio Infantry, 24 Sep. 1863, Vol. 938, OHS.

13. Mary Ann Clark to Mrs. Huffman and Tucker, undated, Mary Ann Clark Collection, KHS.

14. "A Female Soldier," Augusta (Georgia) *Daily Chronicle and Sentinel*, 9 Jan. 1863; "A Female Soldier," Charleston (South Carolina) *Mercury*, 8 Jan. 1863.

15. "Women in the Confederate Ranks," New Orleans *Daily Picayune*, 25 Jan. 1863.

16. "Broken Link," Monongahela (Pennsylvania) *Republican*, 12 Jan. 1865.

17. U.S. Army Continental Commands, part 1, entry 5812, file for Mary Jane Green, RG 393, National Archives.

18. "Wants Hoops," Wheeling (West Virginia) *Daily Intelligencer*, 20 Jan. 1863; U.S. Army Continental Commands, part 1, entry 5812, file for Mary Jane Green, RG 393 National Archives.

19. Daniel White, 144th New York Infantry, to his wife, 9 Apr. 1865, in Davis, *Dear Wife*, 194.

20. David E. Cronin, ed., *The Evolution of a Life Described in the Memoirs of Major Seth Eyland* (New York: S. W. Green's Son, 1884), 253; Scharf, *History of Baltimore*, 1:142.

21. Speer, *Portals to Hell*, 75–77, 140–42; *Confederate Prisoners of War*, registers of prisoners at Gratiot & Myrtle Streets Prisons, St. Louis, Mo., and Camp Morton, Ind., M598, National Archives.

22. "Female Rebel Soldiers," Washington *Daily Morning Chronicle*, 30 Mar. 1865.

23. Frost, *Prison Journal*, 124; "Strange Birth," Sandusky (Ohio) *Commercial Register*, 12 Dec. 1864; Speer, *Portals to Hell*, 77–79, 154–55.

24. O. B. Curtis, *History of the Twenty-Fourth Michigan of the Iron Brigade* (Detroit:

Winn & Hammond, 1891), 252; Gilbert Thompson journal, 26 May 1864, LC; *Confederate Prisoners of War*, registers of prisoners at Point Lookout, Md., M598, National Archives; Abraham J. Palmer, *The History of the Forty-Eighth Regiment New York State Volunteers* (New York: Charles T. Dillingham, 1885), 151.

25. Uberto A. Burnham diary, 28 May 1864, 7542-076-NY-IN, NYSL; E. W. H. Beck, 3rd Indiana Cavalry, 30 May 1864, ISL; Capt. Thomas L. Pinckney Reminiscences, 31 May 1864, 4713-004-SC-CA, SCHS.

26. John Harrod, 132nd Ohio Infantry, to his wife, 3 June 1864, Papers of John Harrod, USAMHI.

27. Bureau of the Census, 1860 Census, Adams household, town of Danville, Pittsylvania County, Va.; Hall, *Diary of a Confederate Soldier*, 106.

28. Spencer Hitch diary, 1st Delaware Cavalry, 5 June 1864, Small Manuscripts, Hitch Papers, DSA; John Harrod to his wife, 3 June 1864, USAMHI; Holstein, *Three Years in Field Hospitals*, 72.

29. *Confederate Prisoners of War*, register of prisoners at Point Lookout, Md., M598, National Archives.

30. A. M. Keiley, *In Vinculus; or, The Prisoner of War* (New York: Blelock, 1866), 81–82; Hall, *Diary of a Confederate Soldier*, 106; Sgt. J. Jones diary, 11 July 1864, PLPOWO; report of C. T. Alexander, Acting Medical Inspector, to Col. Hoffman, Commissary General of Prisoners, 9 July 1864, *OR*, Ser. 2, Vol. 7, p. 450; *Confederate Prisoners of War*, general registers of prisoners at Point Lookout, Md., M598, National Archives; *Case Files of Investigations by Levi C. Turner and Lafayette C. Baker, 1861–1866*, file 2884 (Turner), M797, National Archives; Mary E. Terry diary, 17 Oct. 1864, VHS.

31. Bureau of the Census, 1860 Census, Adams household, town of Danville, Pittsylvania County, Va., RG 29, National Archives; Mary E. Terry diary, 3 Nov. 1864, VHS; *Case Files of Investigations*, file 2170 (Turner), M797, National Archives.

32. Examination of Mary Ann Pitman by Col. J. P. Sanderson, 20 June 1864, *OR*, Ser. 2, Vol. 7, pp. 345–55; *Papers Relating to Individual Civilians*, file for Pitman, Mary A., M345, National Archives; Provost Marshal General's Bureau (Civil War), entry 95 (Secret Service accounts), 2nd quarter 1865, file for Pitman, Mary M., RG 110, National Archives.

33. Provost Marshal General's Bureau (Civil War), entry 95, file for Pitman, Mary M., RG 110, National Archives; *Papers Relating to Individual Civilians*, file for Pitman, Mary A., M345, National Archives.

34. *Papers Relating to Individual Civilians*, file for Pitman, Mary A., M345, National Archives.

35. Provost Marshal General's Bureau (Civil War), entry 95, file for Pitman, Mary M. [*sic*], RG 110, National Archives.

36. Provost Marshal General's Bureau (Civil War), entry 36, file for Pitman, Mary M., RG 110, National Archives.

37. Michael Fellman, *Inside War: The Guerrilla Conflict in Missouri during the American Civil War* (New York: Oxford University Press, 1989), 221.

38. *Papers Relating to Individual Civilians*, file for Pitman, Mary A., M345, National Archives; Provost Marshal General's Bureau (Civil War), entry 95, file for Pitman, Mary M., RG 110, National Archives; Provost Marshal General's Bureau (Civil War), entry 36, file for Pitman, Mary M., RG 110, National Archives.

39. Frost, *Prison Journal*, 193; *Papers Relating to Individual Civilians*, file for Pitman, Mary A., M345, National Archives; Provost Marshal General's Bureau (Civil War), entry 36, file for Pitman, Mary M., RG 110, National Archives.

40. *Papers Relating to Individual Civilians*, file for Pitman, Mary A., M345, National Archives; Confederate Prisoners of War, register of civilian prisoners, Alton, Ill., M598, National Archives.

41. Provost Marshal General's Bureau (Civil War), entry 36, file for Pitman, Mary M., RG 110, National Archives; Provost Marshal General's Bureau (Civil War), entry 95, file for Pitman, Mary M., RG 110, National Archives.

CHAPTER 6. "I Would Rather Have Been Shot Dead": *Women Soldiers as Casualties of War*

1. James M. McPherson, *Battle Cry of Freedom* (New York: Oxford University Press, 1988), 854.

2. Mark Nickerson, "Recollections of the Civil War by a High Private in the Front Ranks," unpublished memoir, USAMHI.

3. Eggleston, *Southern Soldier Stories*, 75–81; "Female Soldiers," *Frank Leslie's Illustrated Newspaper*, 17 Dec. 1864; Kennett, *Marching through Georgia*, 45–46.

4. "A Romantic History," New Orleans *Daily Picayune*, 24 May 1863.

5. Edmonds, *Nurse and Spy*, 290.

6. Rowe, *Sketch of the 126th*, 10–11, 37–38, 73; William F. Fox, *Regimental Losses in the American Civil War, 1861–1865* (Albany: Albany Publishing, 1889), 60.

7. Moore, *Women of the War*, 529–31.

8. McPherson, *Battle Cry*, 486.

9. "Hid Sex in the Army," Washington *Post*, 27 Jan. 1901; Holland, *Our Army Nurses*, 341.

10. "Female Soldier," Indianapolis *Daily Sentinel*, 20 Aug. 1864; "The Brave Soldier Girl," Washington *Daily Morning Chronicle*, 30 Sep. 1864; Michael Burlingame, *The Inner World of Abraham Lincoln* (Urbana: University of Illinois Press, 1994), 182.

11. "Patriotic Woman," Washington *Daily Morning Chronicle*, 26 Aug. 1864; "Hid Sex in the Army," Washington *Post*, 27 Jan. 1901; Keller, *Morgan's Raid*, 35–36; "Johnny: Another Girl," *National Tribune*, 25 Sep. 1884.

12. Oates, *Woman of Valor*, 91–93, 97–98; Pryor, *Clara Barton*, 99.

13. "Remarkable Incident," Princeton (Indiana) *Clarion*, 14 Nov. 1863.

14. "Brave Bird," Washington *Daily Morning Chronicle*, 9 July 1864; Reardon, *Pickett's Charge*, 28.

15. Thomas Reed, 5th Michigan Infantry, to his parents, 20 Aug. 1863, Papers of Thomas Reed, BHLUM.

16. "Many Women Served," *National Tribune*, 17 Jan. 1935; "Another Female Soldier," Washington *Daily Morning Chronicle*, 1 Mar. 1864; Wittenmyer, *Under the Guns*, 17–20; AGO document file record cards, 1,502,399, RG 94, National Archives.

17. AGO document file record cards, 1,502,399, RG 94, National Archives; AGO, hospital registers (Tennessee no. 363, list of wounded, 90th Illinois Infantry, p. 290, and Tennessee no. 412, register of sick and wounded at hospital no. 2, Chattanooga, Feb. 1864), RG 94,

National Archives; "A Romantic Story of a Female Soldier," Chelsea (Massachusetts) *Telegraph and Pioneer*, 4 June 1864.

18. AGO document file record cards, 1,502,399, RG 94, National Archives; Wittenmyer, *Under the Guns*, 17–20.

19. Velazquez, *Woman in Battle*, 154–220; DeFontaine, *Marginalia*, 65–66; Pennsylvania Broadsides: Advertisement for *The Woman in Battle*, 1876, Broadside Collection, SCLDU.

20. "Another Female Soldier," St. Paul *Pioneer*, 19 Feb. 1865; "Female Soldier," Richmond *Whig*, 20 Feb. 1865; "A Female Adventurer," Charlotte *Western Democrat*, 7 Mar. 1865; Provost Marshal General's Bureau (Civil War), entry 95, file for Pitman, Mary M., RG 110, National Archives.

21. "Served by Her Lover's Side," Washington *Evening Star*, 7 July 1896; "Hid Sex in the Army," Washington *Post*, 27 Jan. 1901; "Military," *Frank Leslie's Illustrated Newspaper*, 7 Mar. 1863; "Many Women Served," *National Tribune*, 17 Jan. 1935.

22. AGO, EB file 3132 C 1884, RG 94, National Archives; Veterans Administration, pension application file SC 282,136, Seelye, S. Emma E., RG 15, National Archives; Edmonds, *Nurse and Spy*, 180–309.

23. Veterans Administration, pension application file SC 282,136, RG 15, National Archives.

24. AGO, EB file 3132 C 1884, RG 94, National Archives; Edmonds, *Nurse and Spy*, 75, 354–60; AGO, CMSR, 2nd Michigan Infantry, Thompson, Franklin, RG 94, National Archives.

25. "Female Soldiers," New York *Times*, 26 Aug. 1864; Joseph F. Shelly to his wife, 23 Feb. 1863, quoted in "The Shelly Papers," ed. Fanny J. Anderson, *Indiana Magazine of History* 64, no. 2 (1948): 186.

26. AGO, CMSR, 1st Kansas Infantry, Luther, Alfred J., RG 94, National Archives; AGO, carded medical records, 1st Kansas, cards for Luther, RG 94, National Archives; "Woman May Have Fought," Kansas City *Star*, 24 May 1929.

27. Frederick L. Haywood to his sister, 6 Apr. 1863, Manuscripts Collection 617, Correspondence of Fred. L. Haywood, KSHS.

28. McPherson, *Battle Cry*, 472, 486–88.

29. "Women in the War," 271; "Death of a Missouri Female Soldier," (St. Louis) *Missouri Democrat*, 24 Sep. 1864.

30. "The Girl Soldier," *National Tribune*, 12 Aug. 1882.

31. AGO, carded medical records, 153rd New York, cards for Wakeman, Lyons, RG 94, National Archives; AGO, CMSR, 153rd New York Infantry, Wakeman, Lyons, RG 94, National Archives; burial register, entry 6322, Chalmette National Cemetery, NPS.

32. Burgess, *Uncommon Soldier*, 81–82.

33. "Many Women Served," *National Tribune*, 17 Jan. 1935; Haviland, *Woman's Life-Work*, 262.

34. "Another Female Soldier," New York *Herald*, 12 Aug. 1864; "Long Island Girl," Washington *Daily Morning Chronicle*, 13 Aug. 1864; AGO, carded medical records, 52nd Ohio, cards for Freeman, Charles, RG 94, National Archives; AGO, hospital registers (Kentucky 121, p. 8 and Kentucky 394, p. 2), RG 94, National Archives; AGO, Administrative Precedent file ("Frech file"), 3H36, RG 94, National Archives.

35. AGO, carded medical records, 95th Illinois, cards for Cashier, Albert, RG 94, Na-

tional Archives; Veterans Administration, pension application file C 2,573,248, RG 15, National Archives.

36. Adrian Root to his mother, 5 Apr. 1863, private collection of Benedict Maryniak, Buffalo, N.Y.; Samuel Partridge, 13th New York Infantry, to his brother, 10 Apr. 1863, Fredericksburg and Spotsylvania National Military Park, NPS.

37. Thomson, *Seventh Indiana Infantry*, 150–51; "An 'Event' in Gen. Hooker's Army," New Orleans *Daily Picayune*, 3 May 1863; Solomon Newton to his mother, 12 Apr. 1863, in "Letters to a Mother from a Union Volunteer," *Yankee* (June 1961): 29; Altus Jewel, 77th New York Infantry, to his family, 10 Apr. 1863, Maness Collection; William Norris to his brother, 13 Apr. 1863, private collection of Charles Morrison, Vienna, Va.

38. Philip Cheek and Mair Pointon, *History of the Sauk County Riflemen* (Gaithersburg, Md.: Butternut, 1984), 59; John Hadley to his fiancée, 19 Apr. 1863, in "An Indiana Soldier in Love and War," ed. James I. Robertson Jr., *Indiana Magazine of History* 59, no. 3 (1963): 238.

39. Smith, *Letters of Col. Elijah H. C. Cavins*, 132; Miles H. Beatty, 149th Pennsylvania Infantry, to his father, 11 Mar. 1863, UIL; John Hadley to his fiancée, 19 Apr. 1863, in Robertson, "Indiana Soldier in Love and War," 238.

40. James Greenalch to his wife, 20 Apr. 1863, in Mellon, "Letters of James Greenalch," 205; "From the 75th Regiment," Logansport (Indiana) *Journal*, 9 May 1863.

41. U.S. Army Continental Commands, part 1, entry 916 (Department of the Cumberland and Division and Department of the Tennessee, telegrams sent, vol. 63), telegram of Frank J. Bond, aide-de-camp to General Rosecrans, to General McCook, 17 Apr. 1863, RG 393, National Archives.

42. Sgt. Joseph O. Cross to his wife, 2 Mar. 1865, CtHS.

43. George W. Ward, *History of the Second Pennsylvania Veteran Heavy Artillery* (Philadelphia: George W. Ward, 1904), 133; Herman Weiss to his wife, 16 Mar. 1865, in Phillips, "An Immigrant Goes to War," 143–44.

44. Adeline Weiss to her husband, 22 Mar. 1865, and Herman Weiss to his wife, 28 Mar. 1865, in Phillips, "An Immigrant Goes to War," 144–45.

Chapter 7. "A Congenital Peculiarity": *Women Discovered in the Ranks*

1. AGO, CMSR, 17th Ohio Infantry, Deming, Frank, RG 94, National Archives.

2. "Working Party," Austin *Southern Intelligencer*, 21 June 1866.

3. "Body of a White Female Soldier," Washington *Evening Star*, 7 Sep. 1866.

4. Craft, *One Hundred Forty-First Regiment*, 101–2.

5. "Romantic Story," Logansport (Indiana) *Journal*, 2 May 1863; Sheridan, *Personal Memoirs*, 1:254–55.

6. "Another Feminine Volunteer," Pittsburgh *Gazette*, 21 Sep. 1861; Gardner, *Fourteenth Maine Volunteers*, 24.

7. Davis, "Private Albert Cashier," 110, 112; "Who Was She?" *National Tribune*, 10 July 1902; "Women Soldiering as Men," New York *Sun*, 10 Feb. 1901; "Hid Sex in the Army," Washington *Post*, 27 Jan. 1901.

8. Caleb H. Carlton, 89th Ohio Infantry, to his wife, 27 Aug. 1863 and 15 Sep. 1863, Caleb H. Carlton Papers, LC; Schultz, "Women at the Front," 289–90; "Female Soldiers," *Army and Navy Register*, 11 Feb. 1882.

9. Richardson, *Secret Service,* 175.

10. J. R. Bowen, *Regimental History of the First New York Dragoons* (Lyons, Mich.: published by the author, 1900), 204; Marion Hill Fitzpatrick to his wife, 6 Mar.1864, in *Letters to Amanda,* ed. Raymond M. Rigdon (Nashville: Champion Resources, 1982), 115–16.

11. "The Sex of a Female Recruit . . . ," (Maysville, Kentucky) *Dollar Weekly Bulletin ,* 27 Nov. 1862; Massey, *Women in the Civil War,* 80.

12. Charles A. Cuffel, *History of Durell's Battery in the Civil War* (Philadelphia: Craig Finley, 1903), 168; "Woman in Male Attire," (St. Louis) *Missouri Democrat ,* 29 Sep. 1862.

13. "A Scotch Woman," Covington (Kentucky) *Journal,* 31 May 1862; "Female Soldiers," New York *Times,* 26 Aug. 1864.

14. C. Kay Larson, "Bonnie Yank and Ginny Reb," *Minerva: Quarterly Report on Women and the Military,* 8, no. 1 (1990): 41.

15. "A Female Volunteer," New Albany (Indiana) *Daily Ledger,* 16 Aug. 1862; Miller, *Training of an Army,* 60; Schmidt, *47th Regiment Pennsylvania,* 29; "An Amazon," (St. Louis) *Missouri Democrat,* 30 May 1861; "Feminine Soldier," (St. Louis) *Missouri Democrat* 4 May 1863.

16. "Romantic Young Ladies . . . ," New Albany (Indiana) *Daily Ledger,* 9 Apr. 1862; "A Female Volunteer," (Milledgeville, Georgia) *Southern Federal Union,* 19 Aug. 1862; "A Woman in Soldier's Clothes," Indianapolis *Daily Sentinel,* 24 July 1861.

17. AGO, CMSR, 46th Pennsylvania Infantry, Fuller, Charles, and CMSR, 17th Missouri Infantry, Williams, John, RG 94, National Archives; Fox, *Regimental Losses,* 59.

18. "Sent to Jail," Indianapolis *Daily Sentinel,* 14 Sep. 1863; "A Woman in Regimentals," Detroit *Advertiser and Tribune,* 27 Aug. 1863; "Another Female Soldier," *Fincher's Trades' Review,* 22 Aug. 1863; "A Female Corporal," Washington *Daily Morning Chronicle,* 9 Mar. 1864.

19. Joseph Wheeler to Miss E. W. Peck, 18 Feb. 1888, Wheeler Papers, SCLDU.

20. J. S. H., 12th New York State Militia, letter, 15 Aug. 1862, in Styple, *Writing and Fighting,* 116; "Fanny Harris," Washington *Daily Morning Chronicle,* 5 Oct. 1864; Pvt. Francis Beckwith, 8th Massachusetts Militia Infantry, diary, 13 and 14 Oct. 1864 and 12 Nov. 1864, CVHS.

21. "Women in the War," 274; "Female Soldier," Worcester (Massachusetts) *Aegis and Transcript,* 9 May 1863; "Pennsylvania Girl," Baltimore *American and Commercial Advertiser,* 5 May 1863; John Robertson, *Michigan in the War* (Lansing: W. S. George, 1882), 401; U.S. Army Continental Commands, part 1, entry 2517, Capt. S. A. Stockdale to Capt. Hunter Brooke, 16 and 19 Nov. 1864, RG 393, National Archives.

22. "Brave Bird," Washington *Daily Morning Chronicle,* 9 July 1864; "Female Soldier," Cincinnati *Daily Commercial,* 4 Dec. 1863; "Another Female Soldier," New York *Herald,* 12 Aug. 1864.

23. "Long Island Girl," Washington *Daily Morning Chronicle,* 13 Aug. 1864; "Woman Soldier," Washington *Daily Morning Chronicle,* 26 Aug. 1864; Kennett, *Marching through Georgia,* 45.

24. Daniel Reed Larned to his sister, 14–16 May 1863, Daniel Reed Larned Correspondence, Vol. 3, LC.

25. Massey, *Women in the Civil War,* 80; "Soldier Girl, Second Minnesota," Roxbury (Massachusetts) *City Gazette,* 14 May 1863; Senour, *Morgan,* 110; "Female Soldier" Worcester (Massachusetts) *Aegis and Transcript,* 9 Jan. 1864; "Lizzie Compton," Washington *Daily Morning Chronicle,* 24 Feb. 1864; "Johnny: Another Girl," *National Tribune,* 25 Sep. 1884.

26. Confederate Records, CMSR, Miles's Legion, Louisiana, Bradley, William, RG 109, National Archives; Arthur W. Bergeron Jr. and Lawrence L. Hewitt, *Miles' Legion: A History and Roster* (Baton Rouge: Elliott's Bookshop Press, 1983), 37, 80; John M. Stanyan, *A History of the Eighth Regiment of New Hampshire Volunteers* (Concord, N.H.: Ira C. Evans, 1892), 286.

27. Duryee, "My Three Regiments"; AGO, CMSR, 2nd Maryland Infantry, Watkins, Wesley, and Epping, Lewis, RG 94, National Archives.

28. AGO, CMSR, 81st Ohio Infantry, Finner [*sic*], Elizabeth, and Finnan [*sic*], John, RG 94, National Archives; Veterans Administration, pension application file WC 620,476, RG 15, National Archives; "Woman Served as Soldier," *National Tribune,* 25 July 1907.

29. AGO, Old Records Division reference file ("Edmondson File"), women soldiers collection, RG 94, National Archives; "Mrs. Mary A. Brown," Portland (Maine) *Herald,* 16 Mar. 1936; "Diaries and Letters of Abiel Teple LaForge," 24 Feb. 1864, unpublished transcription, USAMHI.

30. "Female Soldier," Washington *Daily Morning Chronicle,* 16 Mar. 1864; AGO, CMSR, 23rd Kentucky Infantry, Fitzallen, Henry, RG 94, National Archives; "Romantic Incident," Cincinnati *Daily Commercial,* 9 Dec. 1861.

31. "Marshal Bisbing . . . ," Indianapolis *Daily Sentinel,* 11 Apr. 1862; AGO, carded service records of hospital attendants, matrons, and nurses, cards for Brown, Harriet, RG 94, National Archives; "Female Soldiers," *Army and Navy Register,* 11 Feb. 1882.

32. Laffin, *Women in Battle,* 51; "Women in the War," 275.

33. Provost Marshal General's Bureau (Civil War), entry 36, file for Abells, Frankie, RG 110, National Archives; *Papers Relating to Individual Civilians,* file for Abel, Frank, M345, National Archives; *Union Provost Marshal's File of Papers Relating to Two or More Civilians,* file 4114, M416, National Archives; Wheelock, *Boys in White,* 114–15; Fishel, *Secret War,* 253–54.

34. DeFontaine, *Marginalia,* 65–66; "A Supposed Female Spy in Male Attire," Lynchburg *Daily Virginian,* 4 July 1863; "Female Lieutenant," Richmond *Daily Examiner,* 15 Sept. 1863; Velazquez, *Woman in Battle,* 154–300; Provost Marshal General's Bureau (Civil War), entry 36, file for Williams, Alice, RG 110, National Archives.

35. Velazquez, *Woman in Battle,* 220–300; Sanford Conover to the judge advocate general, 10 Oct. 1865, *OR,* Ser. 2, Vol. 8, p. 936.

36. Caleb H. Carlton, 89th Ohio Infantry, to his wife, 27 Aug. and 15 Sep. 1863, Caleb H. Carlton Papers, LC; "Female Adventurer," Charlotte *Western Democrat,* 7 Mar. 1865; "Female Soldier," Richmond *Whig,* 20 Feb. 1865.

37. Maj. Joseph Darr Jr., provost marshal general (Wheeling, W.Va.), to Col. W. Hoffman, commissary general of prisoners, 9 Mar. 1863, and Hoffman to Darr, 2 May 1863, *OR,* Ser. 2, Vol. 5, p. 340; "Return of Miss Prater," Wheeling (West Virginia) *Daily Intelligencer,* 19 May 1863.

38. Charles Moulton to his brother, 20 Oct. 1864, in *Fort Lyon to Harper's Ferry—On the Border of North and South with "Rambling Jour": The Civil War Letters and Newspaper Dispatches of Charles H. Moulton,* ed. Lee C. and Karen D. Drickamer (Shippensburg, Pa.: White Mane, 1987), 215; Beckwith diary, 20 and 22 Oct. 1864, CVHS.

39. U.S. Army Continental Commands, part 1, entry 5812, file for Margaret Catherine Murphy, RG 393, National Archives; "Rebel Female Prisoners," Worcester (Massachusetts) *Aegis and Transcript,* 5 Dec. 1863.

40. *Case Files of Investigations*, files 2170 (Turner) and 2884 (Turner), M797, National Archives; Schultz, "Women at the Front," 334.

41. Col. W. Hoffman, commissary general of prisoners, to Maj. Joseph Darr Jr., provost marshal general (Wheeling, W.Va.), 2 May 1863, and Darr to Hoffman, 24 Dec. 1862 and 9 Mar. 1863, *OR*, Ser. 2, Vol. 5, pp. 121–22, 340; *Papers Relating to Individual Civilians*, file for Fitzallen, Henry, M345, National Archives; AGO, CMSR, 23rd Kentucky Infantry, Fitzallen, Henry, RG 94, National Archives; "Female Soldier in Custody," Wheeling (West Virginia) *Daily Intelligencer*, 25 Dec. 1862; "Wants Hoops," Wheeling (West Virginia) *Daily Intelligencer*, 20 Jan. 1863.

42. Richardson, *Secret Service*, 175; AGO, CMSR, 1st Kentucky Infantry, Thompson, John, RG 94, National Archives; "A Female Spy," Detroit *Free Press*, 2 Aug. 1861.

43. Capt. Alonzo D. Pratt, provost marshal, Military District of Harper's Ferry, to Lt. Col. John Wooley, provost marshal, Middle Department, 12 Sep. 1864, VHS.

44. "The Romance of the War: The One Hundred Days Men of 1864," in *Rock County Wisconsin*, ed. William Fiske Brown (Chicago: C. F. Cooper, 1908), 1:392; "Another Pennsylvania Amazon," Pittsburgh *Evening Chronicle*, 9 Oct. 1861; *Papers Relating to Individual Civilians*, file for Hoffman, Lizzie, M345, National Archives.

45. "Arrest of a Female in Richmond," Louisville *Daily Journal*, 9 Oct. 1861; "Mrs. Mary De Caulp," New Orleans *Daily Picayune*, 5 Jan. 1867; Velazquez, *Woman in Battle*, 120–220.

46. "Girl in Boy's Clothes," Indianapolis *Daily Sentinel*, 6 July 1861; "Female Soldier," Indianapolis *Journal*, 22 Dec. 1863; "Another Female Soldier . . . ," Indianapolis *Daily Sentinel*, 24 Dec. 1863; Detroit *Advertiser and Tribune*, 26 Feb. 1863; "Female Soldier," Washington *Daily Morning Chronicle*, 16 Mar. 1864; "The Ruling Passion," Washington *Daily Morning Chronicle*, 5 Aug. 1864.

47. "Romantic Girl," (St. Louis) *Missouri Democrat*, 22 Aug. 1861; "The Romance All Spoiled," (St. Louis) *Missouri Democrat*, 24 Aug. 1861; "Pants versus Petticoats," Richmond *Examiner*, 31 Oct. 1864; "Sending Home the Petticoat Soldiers," Richmond *Examiner*, 25 Nov. 1864.

48. Judge Advocate General (Army), court-martial case files LL 2018 and LL 2547, RG 153, National Archives.

49. Judge Advocate General (Army), court-martial case file II 704, RG 153, National Archives.

50. Judge Advocate General (Army), court-martial case file NN 3097, RG 153, National Archives.

51. *Letters Received*, file 692 B 1864, M437, National Archives; J. M. Fain to E. Fain, 10 Dec. 1861, Huldah A. F. Briant Papers, SCLDU.

52. Eggleston, *Southern Soldier Stories*, 75–81; Hoar, *South's Last Boys*, 10–12.

53. *Confederate Veteran* 15, no. 5 (1907): 230.

54. Postwar editorial note following p. 272, Journal of Gilbert Thompson, LC; *Papers Relating to Individual Civilians*, file for Pitman, Mary A., M345, National Archives; Provost Marshal General's Bureau (Civil War), entry 95, file for Pitman, Mary M., RG 110, National Archives.

55. Jackson Crossley to his friend, 29 May 1864, Petersburg National Battlefield Park, NPS; entry for 31 May 1864, diary of Thomas L. Pinckney, MOC; John Harrod to his wife, 3 June 1864, John Harrod Papers, USAMHI.

56. Fremantle, *Three Months*, 172–73.

57. Holland, *Our Army Nurses*, 464; Paul H. Hass, ed., "A Volunteer Nurse in the Civil War: The Diary of Harriet Douglas Whetten," *Wisconsin Magazine of History* 68, no. 3 (1965): 217.

58. Temple, *Letters of Henry C. Bear*, 6.

59. Minnesota Board of Commissioners, *Minnesota in the Civil and Indian Wars, 1861–1865* (St. Paul: Pioneer Press, 1891), 1:802; Gower, *Beersheba Springs Diaries*, 30.

CHAPTER 8. "Romantic Young Ladies": *Female Soldiers in the Public Consciousness*

1. "Female Recruits," Detroit *Free Press*, 3 June 1864.

2. "Another Female Soldier," Washington *Daily Morning Chronicle*, 1 Mar. 1864; "The Ruling Passion," Washington *Daily Morning Chronicle*, 5 Aug. 1864; "Romantic Young Ladies," Indianapolis *Daily Sentinel*, 12 Apr. 1862; "Another Female Soldier," Indianapolis *Daily Sentinel*, 24 Dec. 1863.

3. "Women in the War," 270; "Wolves in Sheep's Clothing," Cincinnati *Daily Enquirer*, 21 June 1864.

4. Alfred Galpin II diary, 21–24 April, 28 April, 1 May, and 24 June 1864, Alfred Galpin Family Papers, 1861–1970, WSHSA; muster rolls, Co. D, 21st Ohio Infantry, 1861–1865, OHS; Graves Registration File, OHS.

5. "The Diary of General Marsena R. Patrick, Provost Marshal of The Army of the Potomac," 18 and 22 Jan. 1865, unpublished transcription, City Point National Historic Site, Petersburg National Battlefield Park, NPS.

6. "A Male Woman," Chicago *Evening Journal*, 16 Feb. 1865.

7. Elizabeth R. Baer, ed., *Shadows on My Heart: The Civil War Diary of Lucy Rebecca Buck of Virginia* (Athens: University of Georgia Press, 1997), 113–15.

8. "Girl in Boy's Clothes," Indianapolis *Daily Sentinel*, 6 July 1861; "Woman in Soldier's Clothes," Indianapolis *Daily Sentinel*, 24 July 1861; "A Female Volunteer," (Milledgeville, Georgia) *Southern Federal Union*, 19 Aug. 1862.

9. "Woman Soldier," Washington *Daily Morning Chronicle*, 26 Aug. 1864; "A Female Captain," Lynchburg *Virginian*, 6 Oct. 1864.

10. "Genuine Romance in Real Life," (St. Louis) *Missouri Democrat*, 1 Sep. 1863.

11. "Romantic History," Brooklyn *Daily Times*, 19 Feb. 1864; "The Romance of the War," New York *Daily Tribune*, 20 Feb. 1864; "A Sad Romance of the War," (Platteville, Wisconsin) *Grant County Witness*, 17 Mar. 1864; "Romantic History and Death of a Brooklyn Girl," Washington *Daily Morning Chronicle*, 22 Feb. 1864; "Many Women Served," *National Tribune*, 17 Jan. 1935; "Hid Sex in the Army," Washington *Post*, 27 Jan. 1901.

12. "Eventful Story of a Soldier Woman," Cincinnati *Daily Gazette*, 2 Oct. 1863; "Eventful History," *Fincher's Trades' Review*, 10 Oct. 1863; "Female Warrior," *Fincher's Trades' Review*, 21 Nov. 1863; "Eventful History," Princeton (Indiana) *Clarion*, 10 Oct. 1863; "Eventful History of a Soldier Woman," New Orleans *Daily Picayune*, 22 Nov. 1863; "An Amazon," St. Paul *Pioneer*, 26 May 1863; "Epitome," *Frank Leslie's Illustrated Newspaper*, 19 Dec. 1863.

13. "Military," *Frank Leslie's Illustrated Newspaper*, 7 Mar. 1863.

14. "The Brave Soldier Girl," Washington *Daily Morning Chronicle*, 30 Sep. 1864; "A

Dangerous Wife," *Evening Star*, 4 Feb. 1865; Veterans Administration, pension application file WC 864,342, Forehand, Lloyd, RG 15, National Archives.

15. Jackson *Mississippian*, 30 Dec. 1862, quoted in Jackson, *Southern Women*, 7–8; Robert Hodges Jr. to his father, 7 Aug. 1863, H. W. Darst Papers, G&THC; Col. John Q. Wilds, 24th Iowa Infantry, to his wife, 13 Dec. 1862, Donovan Collection.

16. "A Confederate Romance," Cairo (Illinois) *City Weekly Gazette*, 25 Dec. 1862; "A Female Soldier," Charleston *Mercury*, 8 Jan. 1863; "A Female Soldier," Augusta (Georgia) *Daily Chronicle*, 9 Jan. 1863; "Women in the Confederate Ranks," New Orleans *Daily Picayune*, 25 Jan. 1863.

17. "Broken Link," Monongahela (Pennsylvania) *Republican*, 12 Jan. 1865.

18. "Female Soldier," Chicago *Evening Journal*, 13 Feb. 1865; "A Female Soldier," *Chicago Tribune*, 14 Feb. 1865; "Another Female Soldier," St. Paul *Pioneer*, 19 Feb. 1865.

19. "The Platteville *Witness*," (Platteville, Wisconsin) *Grant County Witness*, 16 Feb. 1865; "The Platteville *Witness*, . . ." (Madison) *Wisconsin State Journal*, 3 Mar. 1865; "A Female Soldier," (Madison) *Wisconsin State Journal*, 4 Mar. 1865.

20. "The Platteville *Witness*," (Platteville, Wisconsin) *Grant County Witness*, 30 Mar. 1865.

21. "Degradation," (St. Louis) *Missouri Democrat*, 3 Oct. 1861.

22. "Supposed Female Spy," Lynchburg *Daily Virginian*, 4 July 1863, reprinted from the Richmond *Enquirer*; "Female Lieutenant," Richmond *Daily Examiner*, 15 Sept. 1863; "Adventures of a Young Lady in the Army," *Richmond Whig*, 19 June 1863.

23. "Pants versus Petticoats," Richmond *Daily Examiner*, 31 Oct. 1864; "Sending Home the Petticoat Soldiers," Richmond *Daily Examiner*, 25 Nov. 1864.

24. "Female Soldier," Richmond *Whig*, 20 Feb. 1865.

25. "Female Corporal," Washington *Daily Morning Chronicle*, 9 Mar. 1864; "Strange Birth," Sandusky (Ohio) *Commercial Register*, 12 Dec. 1864.

26. AGO document file record cards, 1,502,399, RG 94, National Archives; "A Romantic Story of a Female Soldier," Chelsea (Massachusetts) *Telegraph and Pioneer*, 4 June 1864; "Another Female Soldier," Washington *Daily Morning Chronicle*, 1 Mar. 1864; "The Brave Soldier Girl," Washington *Daily Morning Chronicle*, 30 Sep. 1864.

27. "Tragic Finale of a War Romance," New Orleans *Daily Picayune*, 8 May 1863; "Another Female Soldier," *Fincher's Trades' Review*, 22 Aug. 1863.

28. Madeline Moore, *The Lady Lieutenant* (Philadelphia: Barclay, 1862). For a complete precis of this book, see appendix.

29. Edward Edgeville, *Castine* (Raleigh: William B. Smith, 1865). For a complete precis of this book, see appendix.

30. Edmonds, *Nurse and Spy*; AGO, EB file 3132 C 1884, RG 94, National Archives; Dannett, *She Rode with the Generals*.

31. Moore, *Women of the War*, 529–31; Postmaster, Coalmont, Pa., to Frank Moore, 6 Apr. 1866, and J. R. Miller to Frank Moore, 3 Feb. 1866, Frank Moore Papers, SCLDU.

32. L. P. Brockett and Mary Vaughan, *Women's Work in the Civil War* (Philadelphia: Zeigler, McCurdy, 1867), 770.

33. David Conyngham, *Sherman's March through the South* (New York: Sheldon, 1865), 194–96.

34. F. L. Sarmiento, *Life of Pauline Cushman* (Philadelphia: John E. Potter, 1865), 368–70.

35. Benjamin F. Jackson, 33rd Alabama Infantry, to his sister, 2 Nov. 1863, in *So Mourns the Dove: Letters of a Confederate Infantryman and His Family,* ed. Alto L. Jackson (New York: Exposition, 1965), 72.

36. Daniel White, 144th New York Infantry, to his wife, 9 Apr. 1865, in Davis, *Dear Wife,* 194; J. S. H., 12th New York State Militia, 15 Aug. 1862, in Styple, *Writing and Fighting,* 116.

37. Solomon Newton, 10th Massachusetts Infantry, to his mother, 12 Apr. 1863, in "Letters to a Mother from a Union Volunteer," 29; Samuel S. Partridge to his brother, 10 Apr. 1863, Fredericksburg and Spotsylvania National Military Park, NPS; E. S., 28 Aug. 1862, in Styple, *Writing and Fighting,* 119.

38. Edmonds, *Nurse and Spy,* 75–101.

39. Mrs. E. A. W. Burbage to Mrs. Huffman and Tucker, 27 Dec. 1862, Mary Ann Clark Collection, KHS; Meriwether, *Recollections of 92 Years,* 102–5, 160–61.

40. Burgess, *An Uncommon Soldier.*

CHAPTER 9. When Jennie Came Marching Home: *Women Soldiers in the Postwar Years*

1. Ervin L. Jordan Jr., *Black Confederates and Afro-Yankees in Civil War Virginia* (Charlottesville: University Press of Virginia, 1995), 269; Julia Wilbur diary, 4 Apr. 1865, ALLH.

2. V. A. White to Mrs. Jane Trail, 6 Feb. 1866, Lowry Collection.

3. "A Female Soldier," Washington *Evening Star,* 8 Oct. 1866.

4. Veterans Administration, pension application file WC 620,476, RG 15, National Archives.

5. Boldt oral history; Veterans Administration, pension application file WC 483,501, RG 15, National Archives.

6. Veterans Administration, pension application file WC 359,526, Niles, Martin, RG 15, National Archives.

7. "Maine's Only Woman," Portland *Sunday Telegram,* 14 Sep. 1930; Veterans Administration, pension application file XC 2,651,527, RG 15 National Archives.

8. Veterans Administration, pension application file WC 620,476, RG 15, National Archives; "Last Bugle Call," Greensburg (Indiana) *News,* 19 July 1907; "Woman Served as Soldier," *National Tribune,* 25 July 1907.

9. Pension application file XC 2,651,527, RG 15, National Archives; "Maine's Only Woman," Portland *Sunday Telegram,* 14 Sep. 1930; "Mrs. Mary A. Brown," Portland *Herald,* 16 Mar. 1936.

10. Boldt oral history; "Romance of an Ohio Woman," Cleveland *Leader,* 7 Oct. 1896.

11. "Woman Who Fought," Washington *Times,* 4 Oct. 1920; Veterans Administration, pension application file WC 359,526, RG 15, National Archives.

12. AGO, reference file, Old Records Division ("Edmondson File"), women soldiers collection, RG 94, National Archives; "Woman, Civil War Enlisted 'Man,' Dies," Washington *Post,* 3 July 1928.

13. "Served by Her Lover's Side," Washington *Evening Star,* 7 July 1896; "Hid Sex in the Army," Washington *Post,* 27 Jan. 1901.

14. "Nicholls Woman Dies at Age of 113," (Douglas, Georgia) *Coffee County Progress,* 25

June 1925; "Democrat Employee's Mother," (Little Rock) *Arkansas Democrat*, 21 July 1925; Hoar, *South's Last Boys*, 10–12; Bureau of the Census, 1900 census, Pierce County, Georgia, entry for Thompson family, RG 29, National Archives.

15. AGO, EB file 3132 C 1884, RG 94, National Archives; pension application file SC 282,136, RG 15, National Archives; "Remarkable Career," Fort Scott (Kansas) *Weekly Monitor*, 17 Jan. 1884; AGO, CMSR, 2nd Michigan Infantry, Thompson, Franklin, RG 94, National Archives.

16. AGO document file record card 1,502,399, RG 94, National Archives.

17. AGO, CMSR, 95th Illinois Infantry, Cashier, Albert D. J., RG 94, National Archives; "Served as a Man," *National Tribune*, 25 Nov. 1915; Veterans Administration, pension application file C 2,573,248, RG 15, National Archives; Janice Petterchak, "A Conversation on History," *Dispatch* 4, no. 13 (1991); Gerhard P. Clausius, "The Little Soldier of the 95th: Albert D. J. Cashier," *Journal of the Illinois State Historical Society* 51, no. 4 (1958); case file of Albert D. J. Cashier, IVH; Lannon, "Albert D. J. Cashier," 88–105; Davis, "Private Albert Cashier"; Eileen Conry, great-granddaughter of Patrick Hodgers, to DeAnne Blanton, 10 Feb. 1998. The State of Illinois refuses to release the Watertown State Hospital's case file on Cashier and will not even verify whether such a file still exists (Joseph R. Buckles, Rules/Records Administrator, Illinois Department of Mental Health and Developmental Disabilities, to DeAnne Blanton, 19 Nov. 1991).

18. "The Dead Soldier Was a Woman," Washington *Evening Star*, 8 July 1896.

19. Wheelwright, *Amazons and Military Maids*, 78; Lillian Faderman, *Odd Girls and Twilight Lovers: A History of Lesbian Life in Twentieth-Century America* (New York: Columbia University Press, 1991), 42–43; Lannon, "Albert D. J. Cashier," 109.

20. Faderman, *Odd Girls*, 43; *Report of the Committee of the Senate upon the Relations between Labor and Capital, and Testimony Taken by the Committee*, vol. 2, *Testimony* (Washington: Government Printing Office, 1885), 605; Wheelwright, *Amazons and Military Maids*, 13; Jonathan Katz, *Gay American History: Lesbians and Gay Men in the U.S.A.* (New York: Thomas Y. Crowell, 1976), 209.

21. Velazquez, *Woman in Battle*; "Mrs. Mary De Caulp," New Orleans *Daily Picayune*, 5 Jan. 1867; Pennsylvania Broadsides: Advertisement for *The Woman in Battle*, 1876, Broadside Collection, SCLDU; "Arrest of a Female in Richmond," Louisville *Daily Journal*, 9 Oct. 1861; DeFontaine, *Marginalia*; Confederate Records, CMSR, 3rd Arkansas Infantry, De-Caulp, Thomas C., RG 109, National Archives; AGO, CMSR, 30th Wisconsin Infantry, Irwin, William, RG 94, National Archives; Richard Hall, *Patriots in Disguise: Women Warriors of the Civil War* (New York: Paragon House, 1993), 209; Elizabeth Young, "Confederate Counterfeit: The Case of the Cross-Dressed Civil War Soldier," in *Passing and the Fictions of Identity*, ed. Elaine K. Ginsberg (Durham: Duke University Press, 1996), 193; Loreta Velazquez to Jubal Early, 18 May 1878, Jubal Early to Congressman W. F. Slemons, 22 May 1878, and Jubal Early to J. R. Tucker, 26 May 1878, Southern Historical Collection, Tucker Papers, file 2605, LUNCCH.

22. It is quite possible that some instances of women soldiers applying for veteran's pensions have gone unreported. In order to search the various pension collections residing at the National Archives in Washington, D.C., and in state archives throughout the South, one must know the name under which a veteran filed for his or her pension. Since the names (both maiden and married) of so many Civil War women soldiers are not known, finding any extant pension files for them is nearly impossible.

23. "A Sojourn in Dixie," *National Tribune*, 29 Aug. 1895; *Confederate Veteran* 6, no. 11 (1898): 536, and 31, no. 12 (1923): 442.

24. Craft, *One Hundred Forty-First Regiment*, 101.

25. *Confederate Veteran* 3, no. 4 (1895): 109, and 4, no. 9 (1896): 312, and 6, no. 6 (1898): 263.

26. Trotter, *Bushwhackers*, 147–55; Veterans Administration, pension application file SC 58,976, Blalock, William, RG 15, National Archives; AGO, CMSR, 10th Michigan Cavalry, Blalock, William, RG 94, National Archives. For a detailed biography of the Blalocks, see Peter F. Stevens, *Rebels in Blue: The Story of Keith and Malinda Blalock* (Dallas: Taylor, 2000).

27. "Was Kate Howe in the Army?" *National Tribune*, 10 Sep. 1885; "Another Tribute to Kate Howe," *National Tribune*, 29 Oct. 1885; "Kate Raymond Howe," *National Tribune*, 26 Nov. 1885; "Kate Howe Again," *National Tribune*, 10 Dec. 1885.

28. Stanton, Anthony, and Gage, *Woman Suffrage*, 2:19–20.

29. *Confederate Veteran* 1, no. 6 (1893): 174. See also "The Hero of Pickett's Division," *Confederate War Journal*, 2, no. 3 (1894): 47.

30. "The Girl Recruit," Sturgis (South Dakota) *Weekly Record*, 20 Nov. 1885.

31. "A Woman Soldier: Strange Character Who Was a Dashing Artillerist of the 15th Ind. Battery," *National Tribune*, 25 May 1899.

32. Veterans Administration, pension application file SC 231,728, Riley, William H. C., RG 15, National Archives; AGO, CMSR, 15th Battery, Indiana Light Artillery, Riley, William H. C., RG 94, National Archives.

33. "Separated for Years," Charles Town (West Virginia) *Farmer's Advocate*, 30 July 1898.

34. "A Colorado Story of Love, Lunacy, and Revenge," (Golden) *Colorado Transcript*, 4 Feb.–11 Mar. 1885; Mountain Charley Manuscript Collection (MSS 26–40), CHS; E. J. Guerin, *Mountain Charley: An Autobiography*, ed. Fred M. Mazzulla and William Kostka (Norman: University of Oklahoma Press, 1968).

35. Capt. Thomas L. Pinckney Reminiscences, SCHS; Judge Advocate General (Army), court-martial case file LL 621, RG 153, National Archives; *Confederate Prisoners of War*, registers of prisoners at Alton, Ill., M598, National Archives.

36. "Hid Sex in the Army," Washington *Post*, 27 Jan. 1901.

37. Brooks, "Shiloh Mystery Woman," 29; Stacy Allen, Shiloh National Military Park, to DeAnne Blanton, 1 Nov. 1997.

38. Brooks, "Shiloh Mystery Woman," 29; memorandum of R. H. Bailey to the quartermaster general, 7 Feb. 1934, Shiloh National Military Park, NPS. A review of the papers of Dr. F. H. H. Roberts, including field notes, preserved at the National Anthropological Archives in Washington, D.C., reveals that Dr. Roberts routinely recorded the sex and approximate ages of the Native American remains that he and his team exhumed and examined over the course of his career with the Smithsonian Institution.

39. AGO, R&P document file record card 429572, RG 94, National Archives; AGO, "Edmondson File," RG 94, National Archives; "The Drummer Boy: Mrs. Anna Hundley Glud of Kentucky" (MSS C-D 5046 Pt. I:1), BLUCB.

40. AGO, R&P document file 158003 (filed with 184934), RG 94, National Archives.

41. "Disguised Her Sex to Go to War," Washington *Times*, 26 May 1895.

42. AGO, "Frech File," 3H36, and "Edmondson File," RG 94, National Archives.

43. "Hid Sex in the Army," Washington *Post*, 27 Jan. 1901.

CHAPTER 10. Beyond Heroes or Harlots: *The Changing Historical Perspective*

1. "Women in the War," 270.

2. Moore, *Women of the War*, iii–iv.

3. Stanton, Anthony, and Gage, *Woman Suffrage*, 2:21.

4. Richard Miller Devons, *The Pictorial Book of Anecdotes and Incidents of the War of the Rebellion* (Hartford: Hartford Publishing, 1867), 8–9.

5. Francis Butler Simkins and James Welch Patton, *The Women of the Confederacy* (Richmond: Garrett & Massie, 1936), 80–81.

6. Agatha Young, *The Women and the Crisis* (New York: McDowell, Obolensky, 1959), 98. The definitions of *demoralize* in *Webster's New World Dictionary*, include "1. to lower the morale of 2. to throw into confusion."

7. Mary Elizabeth Massey, *Bonnet Brigades* (New York: Alfred A. Knopf, 1966), 78–85.

8. Wiley, *Johnny Reb*, 334; idem, *Billy Yank*, 338; idem, *Confederate Women* (Westport, Conn.: Greenwood, 1975), 142.

9. Robertson, *Blue and Gray*, 19, 119–20.

10. Massey, *Women in the Civil War*, 195; Simkins and Patton, *Women of the Confederacy*, 80; James Longstreet to Miss Peck, 18 June 1888, James Longstreet Papers, SCLDU.

11. Young, "Confederate Counterfeit," in Ginsberg, *Fictions of Identity*, 189. For another example of the persistent conviction that Velazquez was not a real soldier, see Sylvia D. Hoffert, "Heroine or Hoaxer?" *Civil War Times Illustrated*, 38, no. 4 (1999).

12. Randy Shilts, *Conduct Unbecoming: Lesbians and Gays in the U.S. Military, Vietnam to the Persian Gulf* (New York: St. Martin's, 1993), 14.

13. Dannett, *She Rode with the Generals*; Dannett and Katherine M. Jones, *Our Women of the Sixties* (Washington: U.S. Civil War Centennial Commission, 1963), 17.

14. "Female Soldier," Richmond *Whig*, 20 Feb. 1865; "Female Adventurer," Charlotte *Western Democrat*, 7 Mar. 1865; "Romantic History," Brooklyn *Daily Times*, 19 Feb. 1864; "Female Corporal," Washington *Daily Morning Chronicle*, 9 Mar. 1864.

15. Livermore, *My Story*, 113–16; "Attempt at Suicide," New York *Herald*, 14 Oct. 1861; "Tragic Finale," New Orleans *Daily Picayune*, 8 May 1863.

16. Judge Advocate General (Army), court-martial case files LL 2547, LL 2018, and II 704, RG 153, National Archives.

17. V. A. White to Mrs. Jane Trail, 6 Feb. 1866, Lowry Collection; Maj. Joseph Darr Jr. to Col. W. Hoffman, 24 Dec. 1862, *OR*, Ser. 2, Vol. 5, pp. 121–22.

18. Henry C. Bear to his wife, 8 Dec. 1862, in Temple, *Letters of Henry C. Bear*, 6; Papers Relating to Individual Civilians, file for Able, Miss Frank, M345, National Archives.

19. "Pants versus Petticoats," Richmond *Daily Examiner*, 31 Oct. 1864; "Romantic Girl," (St. Louis) *Missouri Democrat*, 22 Aug. 1861; "Romance All Spoiled," (St. Louis) *Missouri Democrat*, 24 Aug. 1861.

20. "Strange Birth," Sandusky (Ohio) *Commercial Register*, 12 Dec. 1864; Burke Davis, *Sherman's March* (New York: Random House, 1980), 65.

21. Lowry, *Sex in the Civil War*, 68, 70–71, 79, 86.

22. Shilts, *Conduct Unbecoming*, 14; Sheridan, *Personal Memoirs*, 1:253. Blanton and Cook lecture frequently on the topic of Civil War soldier women and often find their audiences

questioning the sexuality of these women. However, both Faderman, *Odd Girls*, and Katz, *Gay American History*, reject arguments that women soldiers and other female cross-dressers were homosexual merely because of their choice of apparel.

23. "Women in the War," 275.

24. Lillian Faderman, *Surpassing the Love of Men: Romantic Friendship and Love between Women from the Renaissance to the Present* (New York: Quill William Morrow, 1981), 332, 335; see also Chapter 3, "Keeping Women Down." For a further examination of this argument, see Melissa S. Herbert, *Camouflage Isn't Only for Combat: Gender, Sexuality, and Women in the Military* (New York: New York University Press, 1998).

25. Laffin, *Women in Battle*, 11.

26. Dugaw, *Dangerous Examples;* Wheelwright, *Amazons and Military Maids;* Catherine Clinton and Nina Silber, eds., *Divided Houses: Gender and the Civil War* (New York: Oxford University Press, 1992). See also Bullough and Bullough, *Cross Dressing;* Creighton and Norling, *Iron Men, Wooden Women;* Marjorie Garber, *Vested Interests: Cross-Dressing and Cultural Anxiety* (New York: Routledge, 1992).

27. Linda Grant DePauw, *Battle Cries and Lullabies: Women in War from Prehistory to the Present* (Norman: University of Oklahoma Press, 1998); Wendy A. King, *Clad in Uniform: Women Soldiers of the Civil War* (Collingwood, N.J.: C.W. Historicals, 1992); Hall, *Patriots in Disguise;* Burgess, *Uncommon Soldier;* Elizabeth Leonard, *All the Daring of the Soldier: Women of the Civil War Armies* (New York: W. W. Norton, 1999). See also DeAnne Blanton, "Women Soldiers of the Civil War," *Prologue: Quarterly of the National Archives* (Spring 1993); C. Kay Larson, "Bonnie Yank and Ginny Reb," *Minerva: Quarterly Report on Women and the Military* 8, no. 1 (1990), "Bonnie Yank and Ginny Reb Revisited," *Minerva* 10, no. 2 (1992).

Conclusion: "I Love My Country": *A Summation of Women's Military Service*

1. In compiling statistics on the service of Civil War women soldiers, the authors used a sample group of 153 women. This sample of the approximately 240 known to have served are those women soldiers for whom enough documentation exists to fully assess their military careers.

2. For the ratio of military deaths from disease as opposed to battlefield injuries among Union troops, see Fox, *Regimental Losses.*

3. Speer, *Portals to Hell*, xiv.

4. The approximate overall casualty figure for Civil War soldiers in general is based on an average taken from battlefield reports of killed, wounded, and missing at major battles throughout the war, as reported in Livermore, *Numbers and Losses.*

5. McPherson, *For Cause and Comrades*, ix.

6. Controversies over the fitness of women for warfare, both physically and psychologically, still flare up at the dawn of the twenty-first century, and as of January 2001, legal and regulatory boundaries prohibit women's full participation in infantry combat. For numerous discussions of combat exclusions and contemporary U.S. military policy regarding women, see issues of *Minerva: Quarterly Report of Women and the Military*, published by the Minerva Center in Pasadena, Md.

7. U.S. Army Continental Commands, part 1, entry 5812, file for Margaret Catherine Murphy, RG 393, National Archives; "Genuine Romance," (St. Louis) *Missouri Democrat,* 1 Sep. 1863.

8. Nancy Isenberg, *Sex and Citizenship in Antebellum America* (Chapel Hill: University of North Carolina Press, 1998), xii.

9. For examinations of women's changing legal and social status, with particular attention to the trade-offs for women between the rights and obligations of citizenship, see Linda K. Kerber, Alice Kessler-Harris, and Kathryn Kish Sklar, eds., *U.S. History as Women's History: New Feminist Essays* (Chapel Hill: University of North Carolina Press, 1995) and Linda K. Kerber, *No Constitutional Right to Be Ladies: Women and the Obligations of Citizenship* (New York: Hill and Wang, 1998).

Index